Innovative Educational Leadership
through the Cycle of Change

Edited by

Daniel T. Cunniff
Donna Elder
Wayne Padover

Cover image © Shutterstock, Inc. Used under license.

Kendall Hunt
publishing company

www.kendallhunt.com
Send all inquiries to:
4050 Westmark Drive
Dubuque, IA 52004-1840

Contents

CHAPTER 1 INNOVATE WITH INNOVATIVE LEADERSHIP

"There's a way to do it better. Find it." –Thomas Edison

CHAPTER 2 INSPIRE WITH LEADERSHIP STYLE

"The more things change, the more they stay the same." – French Proverb

CHAPTER 3 INTERACT WITH INSTRUCTIONAL LEADERSHIP

"Leadership and learning are indispensable to each other." – John F. Kennedy

CHAPTER 4 CHANGE CONDITIONS WITH ENTREPRENEURIAL LEADERSHIP

"It is time for us to release ourselves from simplistic and ineffective prescriptions; the time to dream is upon us."—Carl Glickman

CHAPTER 5 INNOVATION THROUGH TIME

"Yesterday is gone. Tomorrow has not yet come. We only have today. Let us begin"—Mother Teresa

Foreword

Dr. Larry Powell, Fresno, CA County Superintendent of Schools
Innovative Educational Leadership Though the Cycle of Change

When theory and practice come together you can expect something good. *Innovative Educational Leadership Through the Cycle of Change* is more than expected…it is not only good, it is a real "how to" textbook for current and future administrators who really want to have an impact! It is written and edited by educational leaders who have real world experience and have taken the time necessary to include valuable theory as well.

When reading the book, I found myself in a very comfortable place. I was pleased with the personal style and also with the concrete suggestions that showed me the writers knew what was happening in the real world of educational leadership. In addition to their vast shared experience, their practical tips were supported by theory and thought.

Often textbook writers betray themselves through the widely accepted and unwritten rule that a textbook must be dominated by theory in order to meet the mark of a good scholarly textbook. It is the marriage of theory, experience and practice from successful educational leaders that gives this textbook such high marks and a unique standing. It is theoretically sound and also provides practical tips for the new and the practicing administrator.

When reading this textbook, one gets the feeling that the text is speaking to you on a personal level about real situations and circumstances. It is not just another academic exercise that will be set aside when you finish reading.

The book also offers some worthwhile cautions for future administrators. Administrative positions can be hard on marriages and family life. The reality check goes on to include such things as now being in a job with far less security than previous faculty positions and the salary difference, when considering the increased hours and responsibilities, is not a great as anticipated. It is refreshing to see these included in a textbook and gives a strong sense of credibility to the work.

This textbook is strong on the value of relationships and how the quality of a leader is enhanced by how the leader develops those relationships. At a time of increased emphasis on cold and hard statistics and test results, it is so encouraging to see a textbook that seeks to show the value and effectiveness of improving and developing relationship skills.

Administrators do not supervise the production of widgets; rather, they seek to develop creative and innovative students who become positive, contributing members of a dynamic society. The timeliness of this textbook is that it seeks to create leaders who will help keep America academically strong but without losing our creative history and advantage.

Many of the chapters are aligned with one or more of the ISLLC Standards and all use activities, role plays, discussions and examples to develop conversations around leadership. The intended purpose—I believe—is to help the administrator internalize the content and, more importantly, define who they are or who they want to become as a leader. This process is further strengthened by presenting multiple perspectives rather than the opinion and voice of a single author.

This approach blends theory with practice and creates a balanced and well written textbook on leadership and change. It is refreshing and right on target. I highly recommend it to every administrator.

Preface

The editors and authors of this publication represent a wide variety of backgrounds and experiences in the field of educational leadership, pre-K–12 as well as higher education. We have noted points of commonality related to the findings in the literature as well as our personal experience, which we believe allows for greater understanding of the leadership process on an organizational level as well as on a personal level, which sets the basis for implementation of innovative leadership.

We speak to the experienced educational leaders who, with the best of good intentions, have often been surprised to find a lack of (a) agreement of organizational direction as related to the ways to benefit students, (b) care displayed by leadership in the organization for colleagues and co-workers, and (c) sustained support for their personal and professional well-being. Often-times they experience feelings and thoughts of the proverbial "deer in the headlights." All they wanted to do as they entered the area of educational leadership was to be a positive force in the change process.

The writers ask you not to lose your sense of mission or your spirit in being a critical part of the appropriate change process for your organization and how that benefits students. It is more a matter of taking time to understand the political, economic, and organizational environment in which you find yourself. At the same time, it is critical to assess your personal perspective in marshalling the resources to effectuate the leadership you deem necessary to carry out the action plan designed to reach the organizational goals as well as foster meeting your personal goals of accomplishment.

We also speak to the current students of educational leadership and educational administration programs who are excited by the possibilities of embarking on new opportunities to bring about ways to improve what occurs in schools for students, staff, and faculty. They bring a healthy optimism in their personal confidence that they can in fact be vehicles for the organizational change that they see as needed. They have seen "the good, the bad and the ugly" as related to educational leaders they have experienced in their careers. They recognize each of the leaders with whom they have worked can be a helpful instructor of what behaviors can be utilized and those that can be discarded and those to be modified along the continuum of appropriate leadership behavior. Chapter 5 calls attention to the importance of history, presenting a historical timeline in American Educational History and stresses the importance of building on the past as we move forward in the future.

For both experienced and inexperienced educational leaders, it is important to recognize the cycle of change is a constant. The questions become (a) Will you be prepared to recognize where you and your organization are in that cycle? (b) Will you implement what you believe are the best and most appropriate strategies for the given situation, and (c) Will you evaluate the data to refine the next steps to further achieve the desired goal?

We believe this book will serve to help you identify where you and your organization are in the cycle of change. It will provide both theory and practical examples of organizations in various stages of the change process. It will also offer examples of how organizations chose to address the need for change and hopefully help generate ideas for your situation both currently and in the future. The personal aspect of innovative leadership will also be addressed to a significant extent.

If the leader cannot bring forward the wide array of attributes needed for this high level of leadership, we believe the system will wallow in mediocrity. With awareness, instruction, mentoring, determination, reflection, and commitment, we believe innovative educational leaders can be developed. Finally, the often not included aspect of an effective change process, a system of evaluation, will be presented. The inquiry model of continually utilizing data to formulate decision-making in a problem-solving format will be highlighted. It is this aspect of the change process that allows the innovative educational leader to continually lead the charge to move the organization within the cycle of change toward its agreed upon goals.

Acknowledgements

The editors would like to acknowledge the inspirational research of Howard Gardner, Kenneth Blanchard, Paul Hershey, and Tom Peters for their work on multiple intelligence, positive reinforcement, situational leadership, and management by wondering in search of excellence respectively.

A direct contributor to this textbook was Judith R. Cunniff, MPA, who tiredlessly partnered in the development, organization, and proofing of the many articles submitted by the authors. Additionally, we wish to recognize one of the authors, R. D. Nordgren, PhD, chair of the Department of Educational Administration & School Counseling/Psychology at National University, La Jolla, California for his guidance and support of this book.

Additionally, we recognize and thank the Kendall Hunt Publishing team for their professionalism and cooperation. All of these individuals demonstrated their innovative leadership and willingness to share their time and expertise.

Dedication

I dedicate this work to Dr. John W. Nicoll (1925–2005). He was recognized as one of the top 100 superintendents in the nation, and a true leader as a member of the Department of Educational Administration at National University. Additionally, I would like to dedicate this book to my brother, Herbert J. Cunniff, who was a pioneer in the early days of black and white television, working for ABC and NBC. As a Senior Director for Broadcast Operations, Herb was truly an innovative and creative leader who gave me inspiration and furthered the development of what we now see on our high definition, flat screen televisions. Daniel T. Cunniff, PhD.

I dedicate this book to my parents Bessie (1914–2001) and Milton Padover (1918–1982). Without their love, support and valuing of education for their children, this work would not have come about. In addition, I dedicate this book to my brother Steven Louis Padover (1941–   ) who paved the way to my career in education with constant encouragement and modeling behavior of caring for others. Wayne Padover, PhD.

I dedicate this book to my parents Stewart and Loretta. They provided models of how to be a courageous leader. My mother as a homemaker and my father as a member of the Navy Dental Corp retiring with 32 years of service as a Captain. They provided me with strong values and grounding to be able to be a confident leader. Donna Elder, EdD.

About the Editors

Dr. Daniel T. Cunniff is the senior editor of this textbook, and was the past interim chair of the Department of Educational Administration in the School of Education, at National University based in La Jolla, California. He holds a BS and MS from Northern Illinois University, and a PhD from Walden University in Educational Administration. Dan has been a teacher at all grade levels, a principal, an assistant superintendent in Fairbanks, Alaska, and an active superintendent of schools in the north county of San Diego. Dr. Cunniff has worked as an international business consultant and was an educational advisor to American Samoa's Educational Television System. Educational technology and leadership have been a large part of Dr. Cunniff's research agenda and he has published and presented internationally. Currently, Dr. Cunniff is working at the headquarters of National University as the lead faculty for the Department of Educational Administration. He was the State Treasurer for the California Association of Professors of Educational Administration, and has been an active member of the CAPEA Executive Board for the past nine years. He is also a recipient of National University's Professoriate Award from the Chancellor of the university.

Dr. Donna Elder is currently Associate Professor and Department Chair of Teacher Education Department at National University. She is also the Past President of the International Association of University Affiliated Schools. She brings more than 38 years of experience as a public and independent schoolteacher, coordinator, principal and superintendent of schools for three school districts in California. Additionally, she served as Director of the UCLA Laboratory School Program with specific responsibility for the fund development aspect of the program. Dr. Elder received her BS from Washington State University, MS from Texas A&M University and her EdD in Educational Leadership from the University of La Verne.

Wayne Padover, PhD is an Associate Professor at National University in La Jolla, California. He taught and served as an administrator at pre-kindergarten, elementary, middle and high school levels. His roles have been general education teacher, special education teacher, assistant principal, principal, deputy superintendent, and superintendent of schools at three school districts for a total of 20 years. He has served urban, suburban, and rural school communities. In addition, he was a consultant to the California Department of Education and Past President of the California Association of Professors of Education Administration. He currently serves on the Board of Directors of the National School Foundation Association and the California Consortium of Educational Foundations. Dr. Padover received his BS from the New York State University, College at Oneonta, MS from the University of Michigan and San Jose State University as well as his PhD in Educational Leadership from the University of Oregon.

Chapter 1
Innovate with Innovative Leadership

"There's a way to do it better. Find it."

—Thomas Edison

Innovative Educational Leadership Through the Cycle of Change: The Leader's Perspective

Wayne Padover, Ph.D., National University, La Jolla, California

ISLLC Standard 1: A school administrator is an educational leader who promotes the success of all students by facilitating the development, articulation, implementation, and stewardship of a vision of learning that is shared and supported by the school community.

ISLLC Standard 2: A school administrator is an educational leader who promotes the success of all students by advocating, nurturing, and sustaining a school culture and instructional program conducive to student learning and staff professional growth.

ISLLC Standard 3: A school administrator is an educational leader who promotes the success of all students by ensuring management of the organization, operations, and resources for a safe, efficient, and effective learning environment.

ISLLC Standard 4: A school administrator is an educational leader who promotes the success of all students by collaborating with families and community members, responding to diverse community interests and needs, and mobilizing community resources.

ISLLC Standard 5: A school administrator is an educational leader who promotes the success of all students by acting with integrity, fairness, and in an ethical manner.

ISLLC Standard 6: A school administrator is an educational leader who promotes the success of all students by understanding, responding to, and influencing the larger political, social, economic, legal, and cultural context.

▶ Abstract

The need for outstanding educational leaders in our society is obvious. What is not as obvious is how those individuals can be developed. This article identifies the qualities of innovative educational leaders. In addition, the case is made utilizing the professional literature as well as the author's experience that the pattern of change is cyclical in the field of education in the United States and having this recognition, outstanding educational leaders can use this knowledge to their advantage to provide innovative educational leadership for their institutions to directly benefit student achievement.

Key Words: innovation, leadership, personal growth, organizational change

◗ Statement of the Issue

The professional literature and educational leaders' experience, my own included, support the point that educational leadership is situational (Hersey & Blanchard, 1969; Blanchard, 1985). If it is situational and the climate in which organizational leaders find themselves is at least somewhat predictable, then the type of educational leadership they exhibit can be anticipated to be appropriate for the conditions they will encounter. With these thoughts in mind, a variety of questions arise for the aspiring and experienced educational leader as related to their prospects of becoming an *innovative educational leader*. This article explores some of the questions they would very likely have about the leadership role and the exceedingly high expectations leaders must have for themselves as well as expectations others will have for them to attain the status of an innovative educational leader. The article begins where all leadership begins and that is with the individual leader as he or she determines the kind of leader to become. The cyclical nature of the educational environment is discussed as well as the effects of the organizational change process on the individuals most closely affected. This author would prefer you take the path of becoming an innovative educational leader because students, staff, faculty, parents, and communities are in dire need of this kind of leadership in our educational institutions. At the same time, as you read the text, participate in the recommended activities, and reflect on the influence you would like to have in our society, you will know the right direction for you as a leader.

◗ What Is the Cycle of Change as Related to Educational Leadership?

It is the historical events in an educational institution or organization that have shaped its quality of performance and over time have provided a pattern of ebbs and flows of meeting prescribed goals. For the competent leader, naturally it is critical to diagnose and assess where the organization or institution is in the cycle of change (Fullan, 2006). This is accomplished in a variety of ways including (a) viewing the organization within its larger environment as education is perceived by society, possibly based on polling research and the way education is represented in the media; (b) perceiving the specific organization as it is viewed by its stakeholders, i.e., students, parents, community members, faculty, staff, and administration relative to successfully addressing its organizational mission and meeting its short-term as well as long-term goals; and (c) assessing how federal, state, and local governmental entities inclusive of the local school board view the health, vitality, and performance record of the educational organization (Goddard and Bohac-Clark, 2007).

◗ What Is Innovative Educational Leadership?

William James said when speaking of leadership, "Act as if what you do makes a difference, because it does." It does as an innovative educational leader as well. Particularly when times are difficult, the titular leader is the person whom others look to for what to do next. This individual has been described as "the keeper of the dream." Having the vision and communicating that expectation in a way that as Dr. Martin Luther King said, "a genuine leader is not a searcher for consensus but a molder of consensus." It is about creating what is needed in the organization to be successful in achieving its goals as they relate to the cultural work ethic, dedication of spirit, mutual trust among individuals, and sense that we are creating something larger than any of us bring about as individuals. It has been said that a good leader inspires confidence in the leader; an innovative leader inspires confidence in the leader and inspires confidence in themselves as well (Korach & Agans, 2011).

▶ How Does Innovation Theory Relate to Innovative Leadership?

Although there are a variety of innovation theories that are widely known (i.e., Complexity Theory, Brinnovation…breakthrough innovation, Benchmarking, the Combination Method, etc.) there doesn't appear to be agreement as to one specific leading way of thinking about innovation from an economic, business, or social perspective (Yezersky, 2008). For the most part, the following sequence appears to be common to innovation theories in one form or another (a) identification of the needs of the environment, (b) identification of the problems to be solved, (c) analysis of the problems and determination of possible solutions, (d) evaluation of the solution possibilities, and (e) proposal of the next formulation. From the perspective of educational leaders, this sounds very much like the Inquiry Model of using data to drive sound decision-making. In providing the prudent risk-taking approach, Akio Morita, co-founder and former CEO of Sony Corporation said the following, "We don't ask consumers what they want. They don't know. Instead we apply our brain power to what they need, and will want, and make sure we're there, ready."

▶ How Are Innovative Leaders Identified?

They are individuals who inspire trust among those they know. They have a track record of both serving effectively as team members and serving in leadership roles as well. They want to communicate with a wide variety of people and will "go the extra mile" to make certain that will happen. They recognize the critical nature of working in collaboration with others to achieve significant goals critical to the success of the organization. They are willing to live their lives for all to know and this includes their family and friends. They have the courage of their convictions and are willing to make their thoughts and feelings understood while recognizing the importance of being politically astute while serving as a buffer for various groups of stakeholders. This individual must be entrepreneurial in thinking creatively for the benefit of those he/she serves (Tomlinson, 2004). It is obvious by now that to be a self-starter is the same as being a bridge builder related to the development of relationships. This person also needs to recognize that not everyone will be in agreement with the educational leader all of the time. It has been said that for most decisions an innovative educational leader will make, there will be others who disagree. This is to be expected and goes back to the earlier attribute of having the courage of one's convictions and operating from a personal moral compass. Recognize, as this kind of leader, your behavior is on display beyond the time you are on the job; you are a public person. Resilience, enthusiasm, flexibility, willingness to admit when you are wrong or in error, and having a sense of humor are critical attributes as well. Finally, individuals who use data to make organizational decisions and an inquiry model to underscore the need for continuous improvement are factors that make them attractive to their constituencies as innovative leaders.

▶ What Is the Historical Perspective Relative to Being an Innovative Educational Leader?

Historically, public education has never enjoyed an over-abundance of financial resources to support the educational needs of our society. The Great Society legislation of the 1960s, with its goal of eradicating poverty in America, provided perhaps the most concerted effort. The No Child Left Behind (2002) and Race to the Top (2009) programs have offered additional support and resources to enhance public education. The end result of student achievement gains has been minimal to moderate and the majority of educational leaders would view the resources that they have available as meager. Unfortunately, this perception has not changed appreciably during the past 50 years, with few exceptions (Scott, 2011).

It is important to recognize that there will be cycles of high and low interest in the field of education, as well as periods of greater or lesser financial resources. The innovative leader needs to prepare for the hard times of the cycle and utilize the times of more resources in an effective manner. This preparation needs to happen on an organizational level as well as on a personal level. Oftentimes, authors of books such as ours will provide helpful recommendations and useful examples of best practices and theoretical points to consider. As you will note, so will we. At the same time, we would like you to recognize that the organizational pattern will be repetitious. (Olsen & Chrispeels, 2009). We view, quite naturally, the innovative leader as being the reader who very likely has all of the strengths, weaknesses, bill-paying responsibilities, distractions, and support groups that most of us experience on a daily basis. Just as we prepare the organization for its place in the cycle of change, so too do we need to prepare ourselves as innovative leaders to lead effectively in a somewhat predictable yet unpredictable environment .

The scope of this publication and the expertise of its respective authors are not to be seen as health experts. At the same time, based on our personal experience and the observations and discussions with colleagues as well as a review of the literature, we know the important role the physical and social-emotional health of the innovative leader plays in the organizational decision-making process, the effective development of relationships and the quality of representation an effective leader provides as "the face of the organization." It becomes exceedingly important for the innovative leader to utilize planning strategies to prioritize (a) good personal health, (b) effective management of stress, and (c) taking responsibility for providing a sense of personal and as seems appropriate on an individual basis, spiritual renewal. In this way innovative leaders are continually fortified to increase the likelihood they will have the personal resources to perform in the most beneficial manner for themselves as well as for the organization.

▶ What Is the Personal Price the Innovative Educational Leader Must Be Prepared to Pay?

The expectations of educational leaders are remarkably elevated. If prospective leaders have a fair amount of trepidations about what they are undertaking or about to undertake, it is a very predictable and healthy indicator. The number of administrative credentials that has been granted across the United States in comparison to those that are being utilized represent a high discrepancy. The California Postsecondary Education Commission Report (2010) indicates those participating in administrative preparation programs are often not planning to enter the field of educational leadership. This may represent a self-culling process of those that recognized (a) the difference of salary increase is not as appreciable as they might have anticipated, (b) leadership positions often provide less job security than standard faculty positions, (c) the hours on the job are generally much more than faculty positions of which they most recently served, and (d) the stresses and strains on marriage and family life can be very challenging and threatening to marriage and family stability.

▶ Is an Innovative Educational Leadership Role Right for You?

Reading this last paragraph, a very reasonable response to the previous question might be, "maybe not." In order to gain an increased perspective, it can be very helpful to establish a personal relationship with an innovative educational leader you know or work with. This should be an individual who, on a daily basis, displays the qualities of innovative educational leaders noted above. Let that individual know of your career interests in leadership. Oftentimes, those individuals are only too happy to provide mentoring and discuss their thoughts about their professional roles. You will probably want to assure them of the confidential nature of the discussions. The closer a prospective innovative educational leader comes to gain the perspective of an experienced innovative educational leader, the more rapidly the identification with the role will be (Robertson, 2008). Not many innovative educational leaders I have met over the years were immediately thrust into leadership roles without some gradual immersion. As in any educational process, we gain our confidence based on successful performance, ability to utilize constructive criticism, learning from mistakes, and maintaining a positive attitude. Putting yourself in situations of increasing responsibility, such as volunteering for committee assignments and letting supervisors know of your interest in gaining leadership experience, will assist in bringing about the "multiplier effect" for your educational leadership skills and confidence level. With an attitude of "there is always room for improvement," these kinds of experiences will facilitate your growth. Incorporating personal reflection as related to the technical skills you acquire as well as the communication skills you exhibit will also accelerate your growth and development. As you are committed to the continuous improvement of your organization as an innovative educational leader, you must also be committed to the continuous improvement of who you are personally as related to your professional talents and skills.

▶ What Is the Innovative Educational Leader's Responsibility to Manage His/Her Personal State of Mind and Heart and How Do They Foster It?

You understand that an innovative educational leader has increased responsibilities, additional time commitments with staff, faculty, parents, community members, etc. As a problem-solver, there will be time necessary for researching with individuals as well as the literature. You are the person others rely upon with your positive attitude, your consistent demeanor, your high energy, your creative thinking, your sound judgment, your sound communication skills, etc. In short, your innovative educational leadership is what others are hoping you bring to the organization on a daily basis. Your consistent, predictable behavior is what others grow to rely upon and it is what you use as the foundation for building a trusting relationship with others. It is that trust that is the essence of relationships (Lombardi, 2003).

As I have experienced, it takes only a short time to lose one's trust after taking a long time to develop the trusting relationship. It is the quality of a leader's relationships that is the basis of leadership. Generally speaking, it is not unusual for it to take several years to gain some balance in your personal life. It will be helpful for your family and friends to know that and provide the necessary support and understanding. It is part of the process and is predictable. Naturally, the expression "forewarned is forearmed" comes to mind. There needs to be comprehensive planning as you begin the leadership responsibility.

Consider "re-charging your batteries" on a regular basis as Stephen Covey might say to be critical since you are the source of motivation and inspiration of a wide variety of individuals, both personally and professionally. Suggestions for ways to address re-charging may be running, yoga, meditation, prayer, working out with weights, walking, moderate use of alcohol from time to time, reading, singing, dancing, etc. My favorites are meditation, running, reading, roller-blading, prayer, and working out with weights. Another thing you can do is express your appreciation to your spouse and children and the significant individuals in your life on a regular basis as they find themselves in roles, especially in a small community, that add complexity to their lives. Finally it is important to have ample quality time for family and friends, as well as finding time for your personal solitude to collect your thoughts and making certain you are getting enough rest each evening (Covey, 1990).

⬛ How Does the Innovative Educational Leader Motivate Others?

It is often said that "actions speak louder than words." As related to leadership, that statement could not be more evident. As an educational leader there is no place to hide on the job. Being in a fishbowl doesn't begin to describe the experience of constantly being observed, quoted, and engaged by the various stakeholders of a school or school district. For the innovative educational leader, these times are welcomed because they are opportunities to teach, generally in an informal manner, e.g., modeling the behavior you want to see prevalent in the organization. If the leader is upbeat, engaging, dedicated to the well-being of students, committed to the goals of the organization, and leads in a dynamic manner, that in itself tends to serve as a motivator for others.

If the innovative educational leader views increasing student achievement on the basis of the cycle of continuously reviewing the data available, reflecting on the instructional process in a non-threatening yet problem-solving demeanor, and making the prescribed instructional adjustments, continuous instructional improvement will take place (Marzano, 2007). The cliché "success breeds success" is true. Motivating others in a well-organized, goal-oriented, successful organization with a leader who is viewed by others as competent and caring is generally not a challenge for an innovative educational leader.

I begin with the understanding that I have never come upon an individual working in school organizations who woke up one day and said, "I want to be unsuccessful today working with students." If that is your experience as well, then the responsibility and the opportunity to provide the instruction, training, modeling. and motivation to others "is on us" as innovative educational leaders.

⬛ What Are the Neurological Effects Experiencing Change Have on an Individual?

As educational leaders, we are in a constant mode of bringing about an improved educational environment and culture for the benefit of students participating in the teaching-learning process. It is not a surprise to realize if educational institutions are functioning as they should, continuous organizational change needs to take place. The work of Rock & Schwartz (2005) reminds us, as leaders, of a basic impact our work has in very visceral terms on others.

The prevailing contemporary research confirms that, while change is personal and emotional, it is neurological as well. Here's what researchers now know about the physiological/neurological response that occurs when an individual encounters change:

A new condition (a change) is created, introduced, and transmitted. The prefrontal cortex region of the brain receives the transmission through one or more of the physical senses. The prefrontal cortex compares the new condition to the current condition by accessing another region of the brain, the basal ganglia, which stores the data we receive and contains the wiring for the habits we have. If a difference between the new condition and the existing condition is detected, an "error" signal is produced and sent throughout the brain. The "error" signal is received by the amygdala, the prehistoric part of the brain that tells us to be wary of a sabertooth tiger. The amygdala places a value to the changed condition and sounds an alarm, producing the emotion of fear. The prefrontal cortex receives the fear signal from the amygdala and creates what it believes to be a necessary response. The new condition is resisted by the prefrontal cortex and, by extension, the person (Schwartz & Rock, 2005). If the disturbance that is produced by a change isn't adequately addressed through some alignment intervention, this resistance to change is prolonged and can be damaging to the change initiative.

▶ What Are the Implications of this Neurological Research for Innovative Educational Leaders?

With the understanding that change brings about an unintended consequence of fear at the primal level, the leader needs to be an individual who is trustworthy both personally and professionally. The leader's integrity needs to be of the highest level and his or her communication skills as well. These attributes are critical for the innovative educational leader in part because change in organizations is constant and often personally threatening for faculty and staff in particular, as noted also at the neurological level. School closures and unexpected changes of teaching assignments do happen and so do administrative oversight of inappropriate faculty and staff behavior and a wide variety of other changes that might be viewed as unpleasant or unsettling experiences. In order for the innovative educational leader to serve his or her constituencies well, continuous growth and development both personally and professionally need to take place with a constant perspective of the broad effects incurred by the individuals around the leader as well as the leader. Finding the balance between leading the educational agenda in a dynamic manner as an innovative educational leader and having a sensitivity to those around you who may have adverse reactions to your role from the moment you enter the room is the exciting challenge you face.

Discussion Questions:

1. What kind of educational leader would you would like to become?

2. Are you willing to pay the price to be an innovative educational leader?

3. What kinds of mistakes have you made personally or professionally that you used as a growth experience?

4. Who are the innovative educational leaders you might use as a coach or mentor and what are you willing to commit to develop and maintain the relationship?

5. How do you view your family and friends' level of support as related to your educational leadership interests?

Leadership Activity:

The Leadership Scavenger Hunt is designed to encourage students in an online or on ground class to briefly share leadership experiences they have personally experienced with educational leaders. Each student is provided a worksheet with the following prompts:

1. Identify a classmate who personally experienced a site principal "going the extra mile" on his or her behalf as a student, faculty/staff, or as a parent and learn how that transpired.

2. Locate a classmate who knows of an educational leader who has positively impacted the culture of a school and learn what occurred to bring that about.

3. Speak to a classmate who knows an educational leader who has inspired another individual to pursue the field of education and learn the details.

4. Identify a classmate who saw a television program or film during the past two years that depicted a school site administrator or district level administrator in a complimentary manner and provide some detail about what was viewed.

5. Find a classmate who was inspired by an educational leader to pursue a leadership position in the field of education and learn how that took place.

Activity Directions:

1. Distribute the sheet of the five prompts listed above to the class members.

2. Provide a specified period of time for the students to complete the task of addressing each prompt. A minimum of 30 minutes for on ground classes and two to three days for online classes.

3. As the group comes together, provide an opportunity for them to reflect on any personal realizations they discovered as part of the activity. Oftentimes the recognition of the negative depiction of educational leaders provides an enthusiastic discussion.

Activity Critique:

1. Provide an opportunity for the class members to explore their individual experiences with educational leaders, both positive and negative.

2. Encourage the discussion to expand to the public's perceptions of educational leaders and how that influences the communication and relationship development between educational leaders and their various constituencies.

3. Finally, in small groups or as a large group, discuss what an educational leader with this realization can do with the various constituencies or stakeholders to develop sound relationships and effective communications. Role-playing can be useful here as well.

References

Blanchard, K. H. (1985). *Leadership and the one minute manager: Increasing effectiveness though situational leadership.* New York: Morrow.

California Postsecondary Education Commission. (2010). *A guide to California's degree-granting institutions and degree, certificate, and credential programs.* Commission Report 10–19. (ED516149)

Covey, S. R. (1990). *The 7 habits of highly effective people.* New York: Franklin Covey.

Fullan, M. (2006). The Future of educational change: Systems thinkers in action. *Journal of Educational Change,* 7(3), 113–122.

Goddard, T. J. & Bohac-Clarke, V. (2007). The Cycles of school change: Toward an integrated school model. *Journal of Educational Thought,* 42(2), 105–123.

Hersey, P. & Blanchard, K. H. (1969). *Management of organizational behavior: Utilizing human resources.* New York: Prentice Hall.

Korach, S. & Agans, L.J. (2011). From ground to distance: The Impact of advanced technologies on an innovative school leadership program. *Journal of Research On Leadership Education.* 6(5), 216-233.

Lombardi, Jr. V. (2003) *Lombardi rules: 26 lessons from Vince Lombardi—the world's greatest coach.* New York: McGraw Hill.

Marzano, R. (2007) The art and science of teaching: A comprehensive framework for effective instruction. Alexandria, VA: Association for Supervision and Curriculum Development.

Olsen, E. M. & Chrispeels, J. H. (2009). A pathway forward to school change: Leading together and achieving goals. *Leadership & Policy in Schools.* 8(4), 380–410.

Robertson, J. (2008). Coaching educational leadership: Building leadership capacity through partnerships. Thousand Oaks, CA: Sage Publications.

Scott, T. (2011). A nation at risk to win the future: The state of public in the U.S. *Journal for Critical Education Policy Studies.* 9(1), 267–316.

Tomlinson, H. (2004). Educational leadership: Personal growth for professional development. Thousand Oaks, CA: Sage Publications.

Yezersky, G.,(2008) An overview of the general theory of innovation. *The Triz Journal.* 31,103–118.

Chapter 2
Inspire with Leadership Style

"The more things change, the more they stay the same"
—French Proverb

Inspire with Leadership Style

▶ Introduction:

All leaders start with a vision. Leadership is the ability to translate that vision into specific goals; those goals are then translated into strategies, and the strategies become more specific tactics that are used to accomplish the goals. This is what many call an action plan. Innovative leadership is the ability to bring something new to an existing problem or make changes in something that has been established. It can be the introduction of a new thing or method that has not been previously used. Howard Gardner (1995) asserts that "leaders are those who significantly influence the thoughts, behaviors, and/or feelings of others."

Assuming that this is what innovative leadership is, the next question is how is this demonstrated as it relates to the educational or managerial leader? True innovative leadership is not manifested in the next external technological advancement; rather it is the degree in which we are able to turn self-serving interests into that of a servant leader (Blanchard, 2012). The effective leader influences others as a performance coach to help the organization complete its mission in planning, implementing, and evaluating in the mist of our changing society.

The following articles reflect on the ecology of change, the leader's role in vision development, the strategic use of data, accountability, and the need to overcome the resistors to change through involvement and focus.

Tony Wagner, in his books on *Change Management* and *The Global Achievement Gap* used the term "reinvention" rather than "innovation." Wagner, when autographing his book to this author wrote "To Dr. Dan promoting school 'reinvention'". Wagner (2006) contends that research shows that the profound changes in our society have a significant impact on teaching and learning. He asserts that "today's young people are growing up with a very different relationship to authority and self-control." Additional research reports that in our increasingly consumer-oriented culture and desire for instant gratification and results, a significant majority of parents believe that children are growing up overindulged and lacking self-control and self-discipline (Johnson, Duffett, Vine, & Moye, 2003).

The articles in this chapter touch on the many faces of leadership from business, the military, and education offering a host of methods and styles that have been exhibited in multiple organizations. The reader should read this with an open heart, keeping in mind his or her personal values as they relate to the mission of the organization he or she represents.

Educational leaders are decision makers who must react to changes both locally and internationally. They are confronted with complex issues, many similar to those who came before them. The difference is the rate and intensity of these changes.

The emerging of the Internet itself brings with it a host of both new opportunities as well as problems. An increase in the frequency and severity of homeland terrorism, decade-long sluggish economy, divisive partisan politics, a powerful China, domestic and international conflicts over oil, a struggle with racial and ethnic diversity, and tensions with international trade are but a few of the new challenges facing this generation.

Our leaders of today need only to step back and look at history and the cycle of change that occurs. Their predecessors have all been forced to deal with some of these same issues. The difference is, with our increased technology, these issues and changes are happening faster, and with greater intensity than ever before.

It is up to our leadership and our educational institutions to come to the reality that we are all a part of these changing times, and are in one way or another will be part of the solution or the confusion. In the 44th annual Phi Delta Kappa/Gallup Poll of the Public's Attitudes toward the Public Schools, almost half of the over one thousand polled, gave a mediocre grade of "C" to the nation's schools (Bushaw & Lopez, 2012).

Through strategic organizational and staff development, leaders can attain educational leadership and leadership sustainability. External and internal education of teachers and staff in collaborative decision making can pave the way for more effective decision making as well as leadership and program sustainability. Effective educational leaders of today are constantly developing the school's or district's capacity for leadership opportunities. They are becoming more aligned with community needs, personal values, and they recognize that we live in a fast-changing global society. They must make, in many cases, split-second decisions; keeping in mind the impact those decisions will have on the stakeholders.

▶ Tomorrow's Leaders Today

Leaders of today and tomorrow are working in a global society more than ever before. Their style must be flexible as they both plan and react to daily challenges. They need to use twenty-first century tools to deal with twenty-first century issues as they think critically in reacting to local issues that are impacted by global influences. Working collaboratively with individuals representing diverse cultures, religions, and lifestyles are keys to the development and sustainability of change. To do this, leaders will need, in many cases, a paradigm shift in their thinking to more innovative ways of reaching their constituency.

There are dozens of varieties of personal and leadership styles. In order to understand which leadership style will work best, alone or in combination, it is important to understand these types individually relating to their methods and what they offer.

Innovative leadership style is truly situational. We change our reactions to the situations that present themselves. Effective leadership should strengthen the performance of educational leaders with the goal of improving instruction and student achievement. There is no silver bullet in deciding the single best way to lead and inspire in education. The research on leadership styles can be narrowed to three educational leadership styles, which can be used individually or in combination.

Hierarchical: This is a top-down approach with little or no participation from those being affected. This style is manifested in the principal or superintendent carrying out all the functions of a planner, supervisor, observer, analyst, resource allocator, and reporter or directing others to do so while "micro-managing" all processes. The major emphasis is on efficiency, control, and routine. This type of leader may place a number of demands on subordinates with little or no recognition.

Transformational: This working-together style is demonstrated by collaboration in leadership activities. Subordinates are made to feel like a team working together for a common goal, thus reaping collectively the rewards of a job well done. The transformational leader promotes a sense of purpose and meaning in bringing people together for an altruistic cause.

Facilitative: This is a more democratic style than transformative. This type of administrator works with the entire management team, involving them in the preparation and implementation of the educational program. This includes staff development and curriculum design, as well as budget preparation and policy development. This leader promotes collective ideas, not by being the center of discussion, but becoming part of the group, empowering the group to make critical decisions.

What style works best depends on what the leader wants to accomplish, and how it will relate to the organizations values and mission. Leaders need an understanding that what works best, depends on physical energy, the degree of social interaction and how it is related to how education and decision making is imparted. Today's and tomorrow's educational leader's task is to adapt to the style that is most appropriate to the occasion, while serving as a resource with a clear vision of the tasks needed to be accomplished.

▶ Historical Events and Technology that Shaped America

Technology is a key factor in the cycle of change. The twentieth century saw very rapid changes in communication, transportation, and manufacturing. The early 1900s saw the San Francisco Earthquake, the development of the automobile, the Florenze Ziegfeld Follies, nickel movies, the tungsten filament lamp, the discovery of black holes in space, the 1907 Stock Market Crash, the creation of the Boy Scouts, Peary's reaching the North Pole, the first skyscraper, the invention of the toaster, the creation of income tax, the establishment of the Rose Bowl, the declaration of World War I, the first air mail, and Babe Ruth becoming a baseball great.

Most of us today have witnessed the exploration of the moon and Mars, the terrorist attack on New York's World Trade Center, more stock market upsets, new sports like snowboarding, skate boarding and sky diving. Rock concerts, reality shows, and flat screen televisions are a part of our daily lives. Buildings are getting higher and trains, planes, and automobiles are getting faster and the world is getting smaller and more diverse as a result of the Internet and other communication devices. Our educational leaders are dealing with a myriad of events and technologies on a daily basis and are on the front lines of our educational systems making decisions that impact the lives of our most precious resource, our children.

For a timeline of historical educational events, see Chapter 5.

The early twentieth century saw educators bombarded with the automobile, airplane, telephone, moving pictures, an unpredictable economy, and homeland security. The cycle has repeated itself in the twenty-first century in the same arenas, only with greater speed, but the same global impact.

The following articles on leadership delve into the various styles and aspects of this phenomenon, reported in the literature, that will have a direct impact on teaching and learning. The extent to which we identify these leadership styles, and implement the correct style for the situation, will determine our effectiveness as school administrators in motivating and inspiring those around us. In addition to recognizing what has changed in our educational system, we as educational leaders need to also recognize what has not changed: the importance of passion, integrity, keeping an open mind, and the love of children. We need to imagine and visualize how we can lead effectively, keeping the successes of the past in mind while developing a willingness to try, and even fail at new leadership approaches and styles.

References

Blanchard, K. (2012, October 10). *Lead Like Jesus*. Speech made to John Paul the Great Catholic University, San Diego, CA.

Bushaw, W. J., & Lopez, S. J. (2012). Public Education in the United States: A Nation Divided. *Phi Delta Kappen*, September 94, 9-25.

Gardner, H. (1995). *Leading minds: An anatomy of leadership*. New York: Basic.

Hersey, P., Blanchard, K., & Johnson, D. E. (2007). *Management of organizational behavior*. Upper Saddle River, NJ: Prentice Hall.

Johnson, J., Duffett, A., Vine, J., & Moye, L. (2003). *Where are we now: 12 things you need to know about public opinion and public schools*. New York Public Agenda Foundation.

Wagner, T., Kegan, R., Lahey, L., Lemons, R., Garnier, J., Heising, D., Howell, A., & Rasmussen, H. (2006). *Change leadership: A practical guide to transforming our schools*. Jossey Press: San Francisco, CA.

Effective Leadership: Research Findings vs. Practical Experience

George Beckwith, EdD, National University,
La Jolla, California

▶ Abstract

ISLLC Standard 1: Facilitating the development, articulation, implementation, and stewardship of a vision of learning that is shared and supported by the school community.

This article addressed innovative leadership practices for which general leadership recommendations and research findings in the literature were compared with the author's practical experience in a variety of roles and jobs over a period of 50 years. From athletic teams, to military organizations, and from K-12 Education to higher education, innovative personal leadership techniques vs. what was supposed to work, per the literature, were explored. The chapter concluded with recommendations of how both the findings in the literature and the author's practical experience in a variety of leadership roles may be used in an innovative and effective way in the education environment at all levels.

Key Words: leadership, management, motivation, inspiration

▶ Statement of the Issue

Leadership often made a significant difference, positive or negative, in a school, school district, university, or business—almost any entity or organization where someone in charge provides direction and exercises authority over others. The issue was that given most people recognize that good leadership can make, and bad leadership can break, the achievement and success of any group or organization, there is insufficient focus, particularly in K-12 and higher education in molding and developing techniques to promote and inculcate good leadership in those exercising authority over others. The challenge was not so much to identify good leaders, but to help mold and develop them—especially in education where school superintendents and principals play such a critical leadership role motivating teachers and students while managing vital resources in an ever increasing fiscal challenging world.

Another challenge was that, though leadership ability or prior success as a leader may be a factor in selecting a person for a position of authority, other factors often takes precedence, such as education level, subject matter, or product specialization/experience, pre-requisite positions on number of years in grade, etc. As the renowned coach Vince Lombardi observed, "Leaders aren't born; they are made" (Leadership Quotes, 2011). And they are made just like anything else, through hard work. This view was more meaningful and realistic for the current environment, especially in K-12 and higher education where when teachers and faculty were selected to be administrators, "leadership" factors were often far down the list in the selection process. If it is possible to make a leader, the author considered how it could be done, both from the consensus in the literature, as well as from the author's personal experience.

▶ Review of the Literature

Introduction

Leadership is a characteristic of human beings that may be defined differently but which most said is recognized when seen; some may even say it is recognized when it is felt. We have most likely been followers, but at some point in our lives, we have all been leaders too—however we wish to define it or describe the term. For the purpose of this paper, we defined leadership from Northhouse (2007) and used the general definition below as a starting point in exploring this characteristic that has had a profound impact on most of our lives, either as followers of leaders or as leaders ourselves.

Northhouse (2007) defined leadership "as a process whereby an individual influences a group of individuals to achieve a common goal." Northhouse (2007) clarified his definition by adding that leaders not only influenced their followers but are also influenced by their followers. The general definition, noted above, was used as a departure point from which leadership was explored as defined by those who have studied it to include those who claim, from their research, to have found the essence of leadership along with a list of leadership characteristics.

Reflections on Leadership

Many effective leaders have reflected on what leadership means. John Quincy Adams (Leadership Quotes, 2011) observed that **"if your actions inspire others to dream more, learn more, do more and become more, you are a leader."** The consumer advocate, Ralph Nader, believed that "the function of a leader is to produce more leaders, not followers" (Leadership Quotes, 2011). Sam Walton (Leadership Quotes, 2011), who built WalMart, the biggest retail business in the world, defined a leader as "one who goes out of her/his way to boost the self-esteem of people and move them toward believing in themselves, thereby enhancing their ability to achieve." The highly successful business consultant Stephen Covey (Leadership Quotes, 2011) postulated that "effective leadership was putting first things first" while George Van Valkenburg (Leadership Quotes, 2011) took the position that "leadership was doing what's right when no one is looking". Further, John C. Maxwell (Leadership Quotes, 2011) said that "a leader is one who knows the way, goes the way, and shows the way."

Military Leaders

The military was an area where notable leaders have made the difference between life and death for not only for the soldiers they lead but often for the civilians surrounding areas of conflict. Hollywood was famous for depicting the cursing, harsh and seemingly brutal leaders, but in reality, military leaders were among the first to recognize that just the opposite was what was needed in molding devoted, capable, and "die for your country soldiers." The late Lieutenant General Melvin Zais (Peters, 1985) of the US Army's blood-and-guts 101st Airborne was but one example of a successful military leader who learned and observed early in his career that **"caring" was the most important characteristic of a leader**. The following was quoted from one of his newsletters to his officers:

> *You cannot expect a soldier to be a proud soldier if you humiliate him. You cannot expect him to be brave if you abuse or cow him. You cannot expect him to be strong if you break him. You cannot ask for respect and obedience and willingness to assault hot landing zones, hump back-breaking ridges, destroy dug-in replacements if your soldier has not been treated with respect and dignity which fosters unit esprit and personal pride. The line between firmness and harshness, between strong leadership and bullying, between discipline and chicken, is a fine line. It is difficult to define, but those of us who are professionals, who have also accepted a career as a leader of men, must find that line. It is because judgment and*

*concern for people and human relations are involved in leadership that only men can lead, and not computers. In essence, be considerate, **treat your subordinates right, and they will literally die for you.***

Johann Wolfgang von Goethe (Leadership Quotations, 2011), who wrote *Faust* and had a notable influence on eighteenth and early nineteenth century Europe, believed that leaders should "treat people as if they were what they ought to be and you help them to become what they are capable of being." Goethe would have appreciated General Zais and vice versa.

Business and Industry Leaders

Tom Peters (1989) did extensive research in the 1980s on why certain companies such as GE, Marriott, Disney, WalMart, etc., were so much more successful than other companies. What was it, he asked, that these companies were doing that others were not? After interviews and visits to a number of companies, he observed the more successful companies used an employee motivation technique that he labeled as *management or leadership by wandering around.* Leaders/managers using this technique got out from behind their desks and wandered around the workplace unannounced talking to people and asking their views on how things were going and what could be done to improve the product or service they produced. Practitioners reasoned and believed that who better would have ideas and suggestions on how to improve a service or product than those who actually produced it? Peters found, however, that for this technique to be effective, the leader/manager not only had to ask for ideas and suggestions on how to improve, but had to follow-up with implementation of some of those ideas and suggestions. In those cases where the leaders took no action from the ideas received from "wandering around," the workers stopped offering ideas, drawing the conclusion that leaders did not really care about their suggestions.

Basic Leadership Theories

Most of the literature attributed the birth of leadership theory to the Hawthorne studies (Hawthorne Effect, 2011) done in the 1920s in which the Western Electric Company commissioned researchers to assess the impact of the environment on their workers. The major finding was that increased attention from their leaders/management had the greatest positive impact on their productivity. The initial study at Western Electric was continued at Harvard University by Robert Stringer and George Litwin (Hawthorne Effect, 2011) who concluded that there were basically six leadership/management styles. Those styles were: *democratic, authoritative, coercive, affiliative, coaching,* and *pacesetting.* The styles of the democratic, authoritative, and coaching were just what each label implied but *affiliative* and *pacesetting* required a little elaboration. An affiliative leader focused praise and attention of/to followers while the pacesetting leader set a high standard by example. The US Army consolidated these six styles into three basic leadership styles, which they included in the *U.S. Army Handbook.* They were authoritarian, delegative, and participative/democratic. Other important pioneers in the early research on leadership were Kurt Levin and Douglas McGregor who developed Theory X and Theory Y (Theory X and Theory Y, 2011). Each of these leadership styles is described briefly below.

Autocratic/Authoritarian

The style of the *authoritarian* leader was characterized by a minimum of consultation with followers and was more directive than consultative, which may have been appropriate in those situations where there was a shortage of time for decision making, there was adequate information available for making a decision, and employees were well motivated and understood that the leader had sufficient information to make a time-sensitive decision. Since most research showed (i.e. Hawthorne Effect) that consulting with employees/followers before making a decision brought more commitment and higher motivation to their endeavors, the authoritarian style should not often be used. Obviously, many military and other life or death situations may have required an authoritarian approach but in such cases both leader and followers recognized and usually agreed with the necessity.

Delegative

The *delegative* leader, though remaining responsible for the final decision, delegated the decision making to the employees/followers. This style of leadership was appropriate when the employees/followers were highly competent and knowledgeable in the area in which decisions needed to be made and the leader and followers had full trust and confidence in each other. It should not be used when there is any possibility that the leader may try to blame employees for decisions made on his/her behalf or when the employees are overly cautious in making the best and right decision because they were afraid they may be blamed when their decisions did not produce desired results.

Participative

The *participative* leader involved and consulted with those employees/followers who had expertise in the area where a decision was to be made before making the final decision. Tom Peters (1985) wrote a series of books on the effect of leadership in the most successful companies in which he did research to answer the question of why some companies were so successful while other companies did poorly or failed altogether. He found that, among other things, the most significant factor for the successful companies was that the leader tended to "lead/manage by wandering around." In getting out from behind his/her desk and wandering around to talk to employees and get their input on important decisions, leaders obtained the best possible information for decision making from those closest to the problem or issue while at the same time motivated employees positively by making them feel important.

Theory X and Theory Y

Theory X was opposite from Theory Y in that it was authoritarian while Theory Y could best be described as a combination of the participative and delegative. Theory X and Theory Y, in addition to assigning a leadership style to the leader, also assigned a followership style to the followers: Theory X followers were characterized as largely lazy and unmotivated thereby requiring the leader to be autocratic while the Theory Y followers are considered ambitious and driven allowing the leader to permit their participation in the decision-making.

The Best Style

As observed earlier, the general finding in the literature was that the best leaders used all leadership styles at times depending on a number of factors involved to include the interactions of the leader, situation, and followers. Other actions/forces that should be considered in determining which style to use are the type of issue or problem to be solved, existing laws, procedures, or plans, training of the employees, the information available, relationship between leader and follower, stress level, and the time available.

▶ Summary of the Literature

In summation of the literature, leaders can be identified by their leadership style based on where they fall between democratic or participative on one side and autocratic or authoritarian on the other. **The best leaders were those who use the entire range of leadership styles** as various factors dictated as opposed to poor leaders who normally settled into one style and rarely varied regardless of other factors. Most courses and workshops on leadership were usually comprised of some form of assessment that purported to determine what leadership style a person currently had and then proceeded to discuss and instruct on how that leadership style could be improved.

▶ Discussion

Discussion Approach

In this discussion, the approach and definition of leadership noted in the literature search was compared with the author's personal observation in various leadership roles such as athlete, military officer, school district IT director, university faculty senate chair, and university school dean as his experience source of information.

Route to Leadership

In the author's experience, in addition to the basic styles noted in the literature, there were basically three ways that people became leaders with various combinations of the three in-between. There was the *appointed leader*, such as a military officer, CEO, airline pilot, or school principal; a *chosen leader*, such as the captain of an athletic team, US the a senator; or finally, an *instantaneous leader*, such as any person who took charge and effectively addressed a situation or other crisis-related condition where leadership was needed. In the view of the author, **the style of the leader was often influenced by the way in which he/she became a leader**. It was observed that the leader who is appointed most often used the autocratic approach, the leader who was elected began with a facilitative approach but eventually lapsed into the being more autocratic, and the instantaneous leader most often used the autocratic method as well.

Why is it that most leaders tended to be autocratic when the literature, including leadership research, concluded that facilitative and/or varying the form of leadership to the situation or environment at hand, were more effective? The conclusion, upon further reflection and observation, was that the autocratic approach most often was used for it was the style that was easiest to use and implement *when the critical and major factor of time was considered*. Immediately upon appointment as a leader, followers were usually willing to accept direction and began taking actions as the new leader ordered, based on the hierarchical nature of most organizations. Even in the case of elected leaders, the elected leader was perceived as having a "mandate" from the electorate and, accordingly, an autocratic leader initially got away with being more *directive* than *faciliative* based on this perception. In time, however, the electorate seemed to think it was their right to question elected leaders who strayed from the perceived mandate. Finally, the *instantaneous* leader often responded to a crisis where time was critical so people were willing to follow someone who was directive because taking some kind of action quickly was perceived as necessary.

Type versus Style

As previously noted, one could lead by directing, delegating, or facilitating. As one may have anticipated, with three basic *types* of leaders—the appointed, the chosen, and the instantaneous—combined with three basic *styles* of leaders—the authoritarian, the delegator, and the facilitator—defining a leader and determining how best to lead became very problematic. How a leader was chosen (type) was often not determined by the leader, but how a leader led (style) was usually determined by the leader, though there were occasions where the type (instantaneous) may have dictated the style (autocratic).

The Appointed Leader vs. Authoritarian, Delegative, and Facilitative

An appointed leader usually was a person who was not selected by those he/she led. For example, in K-12 Education, the school board appointed the Superintendent, not the teachers, staff, school principals, or students for which the Superintendent was responsible. A coach was selected by an athletic director, not the players that he/she coached. A university dean was selected by the university president not the faculty he/she supervised. Appointed leaders may also simultaneously be considered "managers" since they may not only be responsible for people but may also be responsible for "things" such as budgets, equipment, buildings, and so forth. The same person or board/committee that had the authority and power to appoint also had the authority and power to remove, so not only did the appointed leader have to consider how to motivate people and perhaps manage diverse resources but also must satisfy the expectations of those who appointed her/him and handle those resources with efficiency. The appointed leader/manager was multitasked from day one.

An observation was that this immediate multitasking prompted many appointed leaders/managers to adopt the authoritarian versus the other two styles. This was done for expediency in addressing all of the diverse tasks while trying to keep track of what has been addressed, what has not been addressed, and what still needed to be done. When time was at a premium and there was little of it for addressing all requirements and challenges, the capability of doing things quickly was a strong point for the authoritarian style.

The tradeoff for not investing time was less involvement in decision making by subordinates, which put the leader/manager in a the position of slowing down progress when he/she was unavailable to make decisions; everything stopped until the decision-maker returned. The alternative was to move away from the authoritarian style by taking the chance of creating time by not moving as fast on a board-required or mandated action and move toward the facilitative leadership style to invest some time in bringing subordinates into the decision-making progress so that decisions could be made in the absence of the leader/manager.

The Chosen Leader vs. the Authoritarian, Delegative, and Facilitative

Whereas the appointed leader's primary objective was to be responsive to the board or group that appointed her/him, the chosen/elected leader's objective was to be responsive to the contingency/electorate that put him/her into the position. The main difference in those who appoint versus those who elect is that the first group was usually much smaller and more able to coordinate and focus their efforts in directing their appointee as opposed to the second group, which was usually much larger and less able to focus and direct their elected official. In addition, the boards/groups who appointed leaders, in most cases, were small enough to meet with the appointee to give specific direction and guidance wherein the electorate was usually too large and/or too dispersed to do so and therefore were rarely in a position to give specific direction or guidance.

Even in cases where geography was not the deterrent it once was, many electorates are too large to know one another whereas this was not usually an issue with members of a board who almost always knew each other. What this meant was that where the appointed leader immediately came under the watchful eye of the board that normally had a chair who could easily call a meeting to address any concern with the appointee's actions or inactions, an electorate rarely had someone who could act as a chair to organize such meetings which, if held at all, would have to be done electronically. This situation gave the elected leader more time to decide the priorities of the office as well as more opportunities to meet people and determine which of the three leadership styles may be most effective in delivering on the promises made to the electorate in the campaign. Though the elected leader may still have chosen the authoritarian style, there was more of an opportunity to use the delegative and facilitative styles and to get out and meet constituents and get their input and suggestions before taking action than was the case with the appointed leader.

Examples and Observations of Leadership Styles from Experience

Four examples from the author's experience were provided to include some brief observations and comments on the related success of each. The four examples were from experience as a high school football player, military officer, K-12 school district information technology director, and university faculty member.

High School Football Player

Football coaches are appointed and most often have one major mandate: win! This was particularly true at the professional and elite college levels, but high schools, had, it was believed, a second mandate, which was to teach character and sportsmanship. In the two years that the author played on a high school varsity football team, the team won the state championship one year and lost only two games in the second year. There was no question that the team had outstanding athletes, so the coaches could not be credited for all of the team's success, but they definitely had a major positive impact on the teams' success. The player consensus was that the team did have great coaches who, from the author's perspective, many, many years later, in retrospect, had a variety of leadership styles. Whether or not it was by design, the offensive coach was the foul-mouth screamer, the defensive coach was the gentle, quiet but encouraging person, and the head coach fell somewhere in between. It was difficult to determine which of the three coaches had the most influence on the team victories—the first public mandate—but there was agreement by the players, in reflection some 40 years later at a high school reunion, on which coach had had the most positive impact on their character and lives: —the second public mandate. At the referenced high school reunion, very few players mentioned neither the screaming, foul-mouthed offensive coach nor the middle of the road head coach. Nearly all, however, remembered and cited specific comments to them from the gentle encouraging coach and said they had emulated, successfully, many of his positive motivational techniques in careers and personal relationships.

Military Officer

What I Learned from General Colin Powell In 1983 I was an Air Force Lieutenant Colonel assigned to the Joint Chiefs of Staff J6 (Command, Control, Communications, and Computers—C4) Directorate in the Pentagon. As the Communications Support Officer for the National Military Command System, my duties, in addition to coordinating and supporting any C4 need of the three command centers, was to provide personal communications support of the senior Officers of the JCS. One day I received a call from Colonel George Joulwan, Executive Assistant to the Chairman, Joint Chiefs of Staff, directing me to report to the Chairman's Office immediately. The Chairman had just returned from Hawaii where he had gone golfing with CINCPAC (Commander in Chief Pacific), a four staff Admiral, who had a junior officer following them around the golf course with a small secure satellite terminal, which he carried on his back, from which the Admiral periodically received and made secure calls to his forces across the Pacific. Colonel Joulwan instructed me to find out what kind of secure communications package the Admiral had and obtain a package with similar capabilities for the Chairman since he did not have such a small transportable system.

Meeting General Powell By the way, he said, go up and see the Military Assistant to the Secretary of Defense (Casper Weinberger) and ask if he would like you to obtain a similar package for the Secretary of Defense who was the Chairman's boss. The SecDef's Military Assistant was two-star General Colin Powell whose office was located on the floor directly above the Chairman's. I went up immediately and he invited me into his office without delay. My first surprise was how cordially he received me, followed by his seemingly genuine interest in me and my job. He spent a great deal of time, unusual for an officer in the rank of general, in dealing with those below that rank. He explained that he wanted me to thoroughly research the secure communications package that I would recommend for the SecDef and make sure that not only was it secure, small, and easily transportable so that the SecDef could take it with him no matter where he traveled to including his retreat in Maine, but also that it was cost effective both to buy and maintain. This was in the day of the 200 dollar toilet seats and he wanted me to know that he did not want a system whose cost could not be justified or that could be questioned as unreasonable or too expensive—anything that could potentially embarrass his boss. By the time I left his office, I not only felt important based on all the time he spent with me, but I also felt a great sense of obligation that he seemed to trust me to do what he had asked while at the same time instilling confidence that I could do it. I spent two weeks in researching cost-effective secure transportable satellite communications packages, visiting NSA, DIA, CIA, and the

FBI. Confident that I had done my homework and was ready to make a recommendation that met all the requirements General Powell had given me, I made an appointment to go see him.

Earning his Trust When I entered his office, I was amazed and surprised to find representatives from every one of the agencies I listed above as having visited. He invited me to proceed with my description and cost of the system that I proposed for the SecDef. When I finished, he did not ask any questions of me and simply asked the various agencies' representatives if they agreed with my proposal. They all answered "yes" and he turned to me and said "Order the system you proposed." I never had to prove myself again for I had earned his trust. Whatever I recommended from that day forward, he accepted, without question. What I learned from this great leader and used successfully ever since in all my leadership roles was to take time with those you lead to insure they understand the importance and purpose of the mission you give them. Let them know you believe they can do it, and then give them the opportunity to prove they can do it. Once they have proven themselves, trust them from then on without question.

The "Hollywood" Military Officer vs. Real Officers Similar to the screaming foul-mouthed coach, noted above, too many Hollywood movies depicted the military leader in the same way whether it was someone like the drill sergeant in an *Officer and a Gentleman* (1988) or George C. Scott's version of a tank commander (George Patton) in *Patton* (1982). In fairness to both movies, the drill sergeant did, in the end, show his subordinates, in other ways, that he cared about them. Similarly, in *Patton*, four stars General Omar Bradley (Karl Maudlin) was offered, in a direct contrast to Patton, as a kind, caring leader who spoke to everyone with respect. Though once Patton's subordinate, in the end Bradley was promoted to four stars over Patton who never rose above the three-star levels. Unfortunately, it is the negative side of the military leader that moviegoers seem to remember as representative of how military leaders motivate their subordinates. In the author's 20 plus years in the military serving in some assignments with all branches of the U.S. military, he found that most really successful leaders used the Omar Bradley (participative) rather than the Patton (authoritarian) style of leadership. Obviously, an officer who led a charge up a hill, to use a familiar scenario, was going to use the authoritarian style in the charge, but remember, charging the hill took only a matter of minutes or hours out of many months and perhaps years that the officer and his team worked together. In preparing for an objective, whether it was building a command center, deploying troops to a hostile area, or troubleshooting and repairing a vital telecommunications link, the author's observation was that those military leaders who clearly explained an objective, asked for feedback and suggestions, and implemented some portion of what was suggested, were always more effective in achieving the objective most thoroughly.

K-12 School District Information Technology Director

Regarding the discussion above pertaining to the appointed versus the elected leader and how a leader/manager became so, a key point reflected on the amount of time there was to take action which in turn predisposed the leader to one style over another. The author observed an excellent example of this in California when a school district superintendent was appointed and directed by an elected board while the county office of education superintendent was elected and shared power with an elected board (note: school principals are also appointed—usually by the district superintendent but confirmed by the school board).

The author served, in separate jobs at different times, under superintendents at county and district levels and noted significant differences in leadership styles between those appointed and those elected. The elected superintendent, in interactions with his both his direct staff/advisors as well as his extended staff, appeared more relaxed and approachable and his business meetings were usually focused on his agenda and objectives with input invited from both direct and extended reporting staff. In periodic meetings of the county superintendents as a group, this same focus and approach on their agendas, versus that of the board, were apparent. This is not to say that many in the group used this "freedom," afforded to them by being elected versus appointed, to move away from the authoritarian style, but only to observe they appeared to be operating on their own time imperative and not that of their board with whom they shared power. There was, therefore, less of an imperative to be an authoritarian leader and more of an opportunity to be participative. In contrast, the appointed superintendents, in interactions with their immediate and extended staff, usually had some item related to board concerns or mandates to discuss. Meetings often contained agenda items related to board concerns and directives with the focus being on addressing these concerns and mandates immediately. As a result, input most often was limited most often to the immediate staff. As previously stated, this focus on immediate results usually pushed them toward an authoritarian or autocratic leadership style.

University Faculty Member

My observations of leadership styles at the university level is provided from two perspectives, the first as a faculty member interacting with other faculty, and the second as a faculty member interacting with the administration.

Regarding interaction with other faculty, the worldwide concept of "academic freedom" was that that those who teach should have the freedom to teach their academic subjects without interference of administrators or politicians on how they teach the subject, and, to a large extent, on what they teach in the subject. The author observed that faculty members were therefore predisposed to a participative versus an authoritarian approach in their various leadership roles within their faculty community. He found that in those instances in which one faculty member is elected or appointed to be a chair of a committee governing the actions of other faculty, anyone who tried to be authoritative as opposed to participative in their leadership of the committee was immediately called to task by the other faculty members. Any chair/leader who insisted on being authoritarian versus participative would find the other members of the committee uncooperative.

Given that almost all administrative positions in higher education are appointed, with the exception of department chairs at some universities, and are governed by a board, the time issue and the predisposition toward an authoritarian/autocratic style is similar to that noted above in most leadership positions that are appointed. The authoritarian/autocratic style is normally adopted for expediency—especially for leaders who took on such a key leadership role for the first time. Cooperation between a faculty that was predisposed to participative leadership and an administration that was predisposed to authoritarian leadership appeared to be problematic at most colleges and universities where shared governance was supposed to be practiced by all.

▶ Conclusions

When the author combined and integrated what he found in his review of the literature with what he found from experience, perhaps the best summation he could make about leadership styles was noted by the author Maya Angelou (1969) who said: "I've learned that people will forget what you said, **people will forget what you did, but people will never forget how you made them feel.**" How a leader treats people most likely determined how they felt both about the leader and the organization. The major finding of the literature review from the Hawthorne studies was that the greatest positive impact on the workers' productivity was increased attention from their leaders/management (Hawthorne Effect, 2011). This was supported by Peters (1985) who found that the leaders/managers in the more successful companies got out from behind their desks and "wandered" around engaging their staff and workers, asking for their input, and, in essence, giving them attention. General Zias (Peters, 1985) further supported this view by concluding that in order for a leader to have respect and obedience from soldiers, the leader must treat them with respect and dignity, which can only be done by spending time with them. Superintendents and principals who, in the author's experience and upon his observation, were participative and consulted their staff and teachers on major decisions, to include informing them why popular or unpopular actions were being taken, always seemed to be better supported by their staff and were more successful with their boards and constituents.

In looking back over the author's life from the advantage and perspective of experience and a study of leadership, both from the perspective of a follower and a leader, he verifies and concludes that how a leader makes his followers *feel* was probably the most important factor in the amount of success that a given leader achieved.

▶ Recommendations

One can study all the extensive literature available on the various techniques and methods of being a good leader and spend hours, days, months and perhaps, even years analyzing the best leadership style to use in a given situation, but the most effective and true leadership recommendation the author can make, based on his experience but also supported by the literature, is first to take the time and make the effort to get to know those you will attempt to lead. Treat them with dignity and respect, then move in the direction that you think will get you and them where you think it is best to go using the leadership style better suited to your personality and the environment in which you must reside. If you are skilled enough to be autocratic, delegative, facilitative, and shades in-between, to match the situation at hand, then do so. If you find, however, you are not very effective being autocratic when you are more inclined to be facilitative and cannot be facilitative when you are more inclined to be autocratic, go with what you do best, remembering that treating people with dignity and respect and spending time with them when you can manage it is the most important thing you can do to motivate followers. Even an autocratic leader, who may not consult with followers very often, can still treat them with dignity and respect and may occasionally find time to spend with them.

Remember the quote from Maya Angelou (1969) cited earlier, "I've learned that people will forget what you said, people will forget what you did, but people will never forget how you made them feel."

Discussion Questions

1. Are leaders born or made? Please explain the rationale for your choice.

2. When thinking of a leader, who is the first person who comes to mind and why?

3. What style of leadership and what type of leader do schools need today? Explain.

4. What is the best leadership style?

5. What is the best type of leader?

6. Is the quote by Maya Angelou pertinent in today's world of leadership?

Leadership Activity

Background

A new principal has been appointed to take over a low performing school. The participants in this activity may choose the school level (Elementary, Middle, or High) that best fits the experience of the group. The school is in a relatively low socioeconomic area of the county and the teachers at the school upon the arrival of the principal will be as follows:

- Half are seasoned teachers who have been at the school 5 years or more.
- Half will be new to the school: 40% are transfers and 60% new teachers for whom this will be their first teaching assignment.
- Immediately upon arrival at the school, the principal asks for a meeting with the teachers.

Activity Directions

1. Divide the activity participants into the following contingents:

   - Principal and Vice/Assistant Principal
   - Previous Teachers
   - Teacher Transfers
   - New Teachers

2. Have participants volunteer for each contingent

   - Ideally, someone who has been a principal/assistant principal will volunteer for those roles
   - Divide the remaining participants according to the background structure
     - 50% seasoned teachers previously at the school
     - 50% new to the school
       - 40% of the new are transfers (experienced teachers)
       - 60% of the new are new teachers teaching for the first time

3. Give all participants 15 minutes to discuss how they will role-play the situation

   - The Principal and Vice Principal will propose the agenda
   - The teachers' groups will consider what they expect/want
   - All will role-play the situation for 20-30 minutes

Activity Critique

1. From a leadership point of view, discuss how the role-playing captured leadership issues such as how well the Principal and/or Assistant Principal set the stage for the discussion and invited or did not invite participation and whether or not a leader emerged from the teachers' groups and what approach that leader or leaders took in response.

2. How appropriate were the leadership styles and types to the situation at hand? Were they effective?

3. In retrospect, what leadership style and type would have been more effective?

4. Was having a meeting with a teacher on the day of her/his arrival an effective strategy for the principal or would it have been better to wait for a period? If so, what period of time would be best from a leadership point of view?

5. From a leaders perspective, what actions/approaches, other than those discussed in the activity, might have been more advisable for the Principal on her/his first days on the job?

Background of the Author

Dr. E. George Beckwith is currently the Associate Dean for the School of Engineering, Technology, and Media at National University based in La Jolla, California. He has a BA in Experimental Psychology from the University of Georgia, an MA in Educational Psychology from Wayne State University, and an EdD from Alliant University. He has been chair of the Faculty Senate, the Graduate Council Assessment Committee, the Chancellor and NU Faculty Forum, and served on the NU President's Commission for Online Education. As an associate faculty member, he was responsible for teaching Educational Technology Courses both onsite and has designed, developed and implemented educational technology courses for onsite and online classes. He was previously a Director of Technology at the Inglewood and Los Angeles Unified School Districts and instructed teachers on using multimedia technology in the classroom. He also served as a Computer-Communications Officer in the United States Air Force and retired as a colonel.

References

Angelou, Maya. (1969). *BrainyQuote.com*. Retrieved (January 3, 2012) from http://www.brainyquote.com/quotes/quotes/m/mayaangelo392897.html

Elfland, M. (Producer), & Hackford, T. (Director). (1988). *An Officer and a Gentleman*. (Motion picture). USA: Lorimar Film Entertainment. Retrieved (January 4, 2012) from http://www.imdb.com/title/tt084434/

Hawthorne Effect. Retrieved (November 25, 2011) from http://psychology.about.com/od/hindex/g/def_hawthorn.htm

Leadership Quotes. Retrieved (December 16, 2011) from http://www.brainyquote.com/quotes/keywords/leadership.html.

Leadership Styles. Retrieved (December 10, 2011) from http://www.nwlink.com/~donclark/leader/leadstl.html#one.

McCarthy, F. (Producer), & Schaffner, F. (Director). (1982). *Patton*. (Motion Picture). USA: Twentieth Century Fox Film Corporation. Retrieved (January 4, 2012) from http://en.wikipedia.org/wiki/Patton-Film

Northouse, G. (2007) *Leadership theory and practice*. (4th ed.) Thousand Oak, London, New Delhe: Sage.

Peters, T., & Austin, N. (1985). *A passion for excellence: the leadership difference*. New York: Random House Inc.

Theory X and Theory Y. Retrieved (November 28, 2011) from http://www.businessballs.com/mcgregor.htm

Leadership Strategies in Facilitating Organizational Change

Glenn Sewell, EdD, National University, Stockton California

ISLLC Standard 6: A school administrator is an educational leader who promotes the success of all students by understanding, responding to, and influencing the larger political, social, economic, legal, and cultural context.

▶ Abstract

The purpose of this case study was to identify and describe effective principles used by school district leaders in dealing with the forces causing organizational change and the resulting conflict caused from change. Three main themes emerged from reviewing the literature regarding organizational change; leadership, conflict, and change. Four forces affecting organizational change, (structures, culture, people, and resources), were also revealed from the available literature. This article studied the organizational change process and compared two types of organizational changes: (1) first-order (renewal) and (2) second-order, (transformational). From the themes identified in the literature review, a model was constructed to make sense of the information and show the complex relationships between the identified themes in an organization. A case study of a school district unification provided an opportunity for these themes to be studied and analyzed in a practical transformational change. Addressing political, social, economic, legal, and cultural contexts must be considered by leaders in considering a school district unification process. From this case study, the article concluded with presenting and describing basic principles to assist leaders in facilitating a school district unification.

Key words: transformational change, structures, culture, resources, people, leadership, conflict

▶ Statement of the Issue

Due to many factors, including state and federal mandates, *high stakes testing*, and challenging financial times, educational leaders today are facing massive changes in all areas of school management and operations. The issue was that organizational changes can cause varying degrees of conflict for educational leaders. More difficult and transformative organizational changes can cause even greater conflict for leaders to manage. As a result, there is a need to provide relevant information to assist educational leaders in leading necessary transformational changes, as well as to provide strategies for managing the conflict generated from those changes.

Depending on the need, organizations may change by using first-order or second-order changes. Understanding these aspects of organizational change can help educational leaders understand the need for a school or school district to make either of these types of necessary adaptations to meet the changing needs of their communities. This chapter describes reasons why schools and school districts change, describes two types of changes that organizations make, defines and describes four internal and external forces that cause changes to occur, and provides proven strategies for educational leaders to employ in leading their organizations through necessary changes. Research and experiential information will be presented for educational leaders to consider in addressing and engaging in more complex and difficult second-order changes in their organizations. The goal of this chapter is to assist educational leaders in continuing efforts to improve student success and meet the changing educational needs of their school and communities. To begin with, two types of changes that educational leaders face will be defined and described.

▶ Review of the Literature

Introduction

Just as with all organizations, schools and school districts must make ongoing structural changes to meet the changing needs of their environment. For the growth and survival of the organization, continued adaptations, learning, and development are key characteristics of the behavior of all organizations (Capra 2002). Research reveals two types of organizational changes depending on the type of change necessary during their development process.

Organizational Change

For their growth and survival, organizations transform in order to adapt to their environment through a process of making necessary structural changes (Capra, 2002). The first type of structural change is Argyris' first-order change concept of single-loop learning (Stacey, 2003). By definition, single-loop learning organizations are incapable of getting to the root of a problem. These organizations can function, but they cannot set their own course of operation. The environment determines the organization's course of operation. In single-loop learning organizations, operational issues that can arise are solved by making changes in budgets, policies, or practices (Hatch, 1997). For educational leaders, setting annual budgetary targets is an example of a single-loop learning organizational process. If the budgetary targets are wrong, the organization must **adapt and make changes** in the budgetary targets. Making this type of adaptive or transitional change will help *right* the organization.

For educational leaders, facing a mid-year budget cut is an example of how school district leaders have to make adjustments in the previously approved budget. Educational leaders have had to adapt to changing budgetary targets for the past several years due to difficult financial times at the state level. This is a first-order change because the system renews itself while not engaging in a major change or transformation. Although the difficult decisions regarding budgetary adjustments and staff layoffs are made, school/school district operations are maintained in generally the same fashion. Single-loop learning involves sustaining group learning in a "state of stability" (Stacey, 2003, p.113).

Second-order change organizations redefine their primary behavior as they adapt to changes in their environment. Defined by Argyris as double-loop learning (Griffin 2002), this type of organizational change creates new structures or connections with its environment. In this type of structural change, the issue of widespread conflict emerges because the process of reinventing the organization opens the door for many new and diverse ideas and philosophies to emerge in developing the new organization (Hatch, 1997). An example of a second-order change is a business merger. When two businesses merge into one new business, the new business is wholly different from the two previous businesses.

For educational leaders, an example of this type of change is a school district unification. One or more school districts consolidate into one new and different unified school district. Conflict exists on many levels in this type of organizational change especially due to the affect this type of change has on the people and culture of the existing organization. Many forces emerge to cause educational leaders to engage in organizational changes. These forces are described next.

Forces Affecting Organizational Change

What are the causes of change that educational leaders need to be aware of in assessing the need for making school or school district changes? Research identifies four hidden forces, both internal and external to the organization, affecting changes that must be considered in organizations: structures, culture, people, and resources. The first force, causing change in organizations is structures. Structures are defined as the laws, policies, regulations, and rules guiding organizational practices and operations (Capra 2002).

Structures

There are two types of structures in organizations: designed and emergent. Designed structures are based on formal relationships of power including policies and rules governing operations and employee behavior. Emergent structures form the creativity and "aliveness" of the organization represented by informal relationships (Capra, 2002). In all organizations, there is tension between designed and emergent structures because, for effective organizations to exist, it is necessary to develop mechanisms of social controls. An example of the need for organizational structures is that it is necessary for organizations to have authority over people, and sanctions can be imposed when the rules or policies are not adhered to (Berger and Luckman, 1966). However, tension emerges when ideas about ways of improving operations are stifled by organizational policies and regulations instituted either locally or at the state and/or federal levels.

For educational leaders, school and school district policies, rules, and regulations are examples of designed structures of operation. Emergent structures include pathways for employees or community members to communicate potential ideas for improving organizational operations or curriculum and/or instructional practices. Designed and emergent structures define the formal and informal operations of the school or school district.

In first-order changes, such as in budget cutting due to mid-year budget cuts described above, organizational structures are designed to stabilize the organization and creativity is not important. Therefore, the designed structures prescribe the process for the type of change necessary for the organization to adapt. For example, if a school district faces a mid-year budgetary cut from state funding, administration must make necessary budgetary adjustments. School administrators may organize and mobilize site and/or district budget committees to study the issues and make recommendations for necessary budgetary adjustments for school board approval. Budgetary changes, passed on by the state after annual budgets are approved, are addressed by making necessary budgetary changes in local school districts for ongoing operations to continue.

In second-order changes, forces of change outweigh the structural forces creating organizational stability. An examples of a second-order change in school districts is a school district unification or closing schools and redistricting students to accommodate school facilities and attendance changes. Due to demographic changes in communities causing declining enrollments and ongoing state budget cuts, many educational leaders are facing these types of community changes in order to find ways to balance their budgets and become more efficient with the resources they have.

Many types of forces affect the need for these types of transformational changes in school districts to better meet the budgetary needs of the organization, as well as improve educational services for the communities they serve. In this type of change process, because of the massive cultural change that occurs for the organization, it is important to provide avenues for input and feedback for community members. Creativity should be unrestrained, fewer structures may exist, and people are encouraged to be creative in order to explore all potential ideas and options for organizational change that meet the needs of the community and the organization. Conflict can emerge in this process when suggested changes can violate the laws, policies, and regulations of the organization, state or local oversight agencies. This is an example of the conflict that can exist between emergent and designed structures. The tension that can emerge in this type of change, between emergent and designed structures, can limit the creativity of group input regarding what type of change would be best for the entire educational community.

Culture

The second type of force, affecting change in organizations, is the internal and external culture of the organization. Culture can be described as the accepted practices and patterns of organizational operations. Leadership and policy structures as well as standards and patterns of operation are all affected by cultural parameters. When necessary, cultural changes in an organization occur so the organization can adapt and remain viable. When this occurs, old cultural practices are replaced by more modern cultural practices. Examples of internal cultural changes include changes in leadership hierarchy, new organizational communication methods and patterns, combining or eliminating organizational divisions, and new personnel positions and responsibilities. External cultural changes can include housing developments and/or demographic changes. As old internal and external cultural patterns are replaced by new organizational patterns, varying degrees of conflict can emerge.

The community culture can make it difficult to make second-order changes in school district communities. The established **community culture is a large hurdle to get over**, especially if the school district has been stable for many years. Many people now living in the community attended the present local schools. As a result, changes may not be readily accepted. For example, if a large housing development is built, community changes occur including the need for more schools to house the increase in student population. As a result, school changes will have to be addressed. An example of this is in communities with elementary and a high school districts serving students K-12. Local schools for students in the new housing community will be a marketing feature of real estate agents selling homes in the new development. In this case, developer fees for building new schools will be divided up between both districts. This can cause financial problems for developers and the school districts involved. As a result, unifying the school districts may be a topic for discussion in the community. But this will change the internal and external cultures of the school district community and educational leaders will face the conflict that emerges from this process.

People

The third force affecting organizational change is people, both internal and external, to the organization. People are those individuals directly involved in the organization, such as employees or volunteers, and those indirectly involved, such as community members benefitting from organizational services. For people in the organization to grow and learn, they must interact with each other. This communicative interaction is an ongoing process of negotiation with each other to define the organization (Stacey 2001).

Interactions among internal and external organizational people are central to organizational change, especially in second-order changes. Organizational communication is both formal and informal and both are necessary and inseparable in the process of communicative interaction. In this interaction, people naturally enable and constrain each other at the same time (Straetfield, 2001). Formal and informal dialogue builds trust and connectedness among organizational people. In dialogue a group explores complex and difficult issues from many vantage points. If communication is effective, assumptions are suspended, but clearly communicated. The result is that peoples' thoughts and experiences are openly discussed, so the group can move beyond its individual viewpoints (Hatch, 1997).

Organizations know the issues and the solutions, but they may be unable to summon and focus that knowledge. Therefore, in the organizational change process, people must have the ability to **communicate honestly and openly across any boundaries** that separate them (Hurst, 1995). When avenues of communication are not readily available to organizations, organizational leaders may engage third-party facilitators to intervene and facilitate the organization in the communication and change process. Third-party intervention can have a very positive effect on the change process by breaking the constraints inhibiting open and honest communication in organizations (Hurst, 1995).

Principles of group interaction include

- open, honest and transparent discussions in which group members grow and learn from each other by sharing knowledge through communicative interactions;
- two paradoxes emerge in group interaction: communications among people in the organization are both enabled and constrained;
- principles of interaction include a commitment from group members to the group and in developing the organizational vision;
- people in the organization negotiate productive and unproductive actions and behaviors as negotiated and defined by the group;
- communication among people in organizations is both formal and informal; and
- regular feedback on group performance is sought to be sure of group effectiveness in the organizational change process.

In a second-order change, educational leaders provide a variety of avenues for members of the school district community to provide creative input and feedback on the change process. This includes the process of meeting formally with school district employee groups and informing them about the change process and its potential effect on employees.

Resources

The fourth force affecting organizational change is the effect of internal and external resources available to the organization to maintain its viability and fitness in the environment. Organizations are dependent on available resources and their ability to adapt and survive in their environment when available resources change. Resources are "raw materials, labor, capital, equipment, knowledge, outlets for products and services" (Hatch, 1997, p.78). Resource dependence theory is based on the assumption that organizations are controlled by their environment and describes the organization's fitness within its environment. Resource dependence drives organizational development toward two paths, one being improvement in an organization's effectiveness, and the other being improvement in the satisfaction of its employees (Hatch 1997).

The environment is a powerful constraint on organizational action (Hatch, 1997). Resource dependence theory suggests that **survival is the ultimate goal of the organization** and identifies two key problems that can jeopardize organizational survival: lack of autonomy and uncertainty, both of which result from interconnections among different organizations. Resource dependence theory suggests that the relationship between organizations in a community is affected by one organization's dependence on essential resources from another organization. Dependence is undesirable because the dependent organization's range of choice is minimized, which could threaten the organization's stability and even its existence (Hatch, 1997).

For schools and school districts, resources include students who generate financial resources for the educational operations. If the number of students in a school or district changes dramatically, by either increasing or decreasing, pressure will be put on educational leaders to make changes for more efficient operations. Schools today are facing these types of changes, including increasing and declining enrollments, due to demographic changes. Declining enrollments in school districts can cause school closures and redistricting of students to attend other district schools. Increasing student enrollments, due to increased housing developments and more people moving into the community, causes an increase in school housing needs. This type of community change causes community conversations about how to better meet the educational needs of the students and the changing organizational needs of the school district community.

Conflict

In any organizational change process, conflict emerges. Balancing the amount of conflict is an important factor for organizational fitness. When well managed, some conflict can be productive for the organization. However, too much conflict may not be productive and can even be destructive to the organization.

Conflict is not necessarily about a right or wrong direction for the organization to pursue. The conflict can be about which path the organization will follow. In managing conflict, some principles for leadership are (a) **change causes conflict**; therefore, conflict is a part of organizations, adaptability and innovation can be initiated through conflict, when skills and activities are commonly shared and pursued; (b) organizational change can be successful; (c) conflict can exist between the creativity of people involved in organizational change and the legal structures confining that creativity; (d) conflict can result from people in the organization having differing viewpoints, and not agreeing on a course of action to take, (e) conflict can promote higher quality decisions, and (f) when handled properly, conflict can strengthen the organization by enhancing group functioning and organizational performance.

Leadership

Leaders have influence within organizations, but their ability to mobilize this influence depends on their knowledge of, and perceived alignment with, the culture. Leadership is multifaceted and is an important cultural component in the success of leading organizational changes. Leadership is the designer, the teacher, and the steward who strives to understand the organization as a whole in making needed organizational adjustments. The leader's role is to impart and embed the organizational culture because the ability to mobilize organizational members depends on his or her knowledge of and alignment with the organizational culture.

As a symbol operating within cultural processes, leaders facilitate change when the interpretations others give them produce changes in assumptions, values, and/or artifacts. The way leaders formulate their words and deeds and display themselves will have an influence on the choices others make as they engage in the cultural processes of symbolization and interpretation. Symbolically aware leaders have a much better chance of using themselves effectively as symbols than do those who are symbolically unconscious (Hatch, 1997).

Leaders ask the evaluative questions to engage the group in an open flow of dialogue, to assist the group in resolving those questions, rather than supplying the answers. This demonstrates the participative role of leadership in the process. If the organization's leadership knows the strategy, but the colleagues do not, there may be difficulty in accomplishing anything. Organizational success is often a function of how successfully individuals can coordinate their activities (Pfeffer, 1992).

Leadership works with the organization to develop universal principles (e.g., vision), organizational change process. People are committed to the universal principles, the group interactive process, and the organization. Vision, mission, and commitment to the whole are working principles related to participation and are critical to the survival of the whole. For leaders, this means **continually seeking group harmony and consensus** with the expression of differences within the developed rules of communication and social interaction.

Based on a formal study of a transformational change, a school district unification, leadership practices for leading transformational organizational change and managing the conflict resulting from such organizational change will be presented.

▶ Summary of Literature Review

In this discussion, the four forces of change—structures, culture, people, and resources—were presented and applied to the three main themes of the study—leadership, conflict, and change. The literature review also revealed four forces having an impact on organizational change—structures, people, culture, and resources. In a transformational change, leadership is a critical theme in coordinating and guiding the change process. Since any organizational change causes conflict, having the knowledge and skill to lead a successful unification will involve navigating the white water of conflict is also important for leaders to have.

▶ Discussion

Discussion Approach

In order to make sense of the complicated interaction of these organizational change themes, presented in the literature review, the author constructed a model, representing the complex interactions of these organizational components. The application of this model will be described as it related to an actual case study of a school district unification. Leadership may employ this model in analyzing, planning, and preparing for leading a transformational change such as a school district unification.

Model for Application

In describing the model, (shown on pg. 11), three spheres are present. The outermost sphere represents the three main themes of organizational change, conflict, and leadership. The sphere also shows the effect of internal and external forces affecting the four subtheme areas of structures, culture, people, and resources. The innermost sphere represents the internal forces affecting the four subtheme areas of structures, culture, people, and resources. The two inner spheres are divided into quadrants representing the four subtheme areas. Structures and resources are non-human components of the organization and are represented as such on the right half of the construct. People and culture represent the human side of the organization and are represented separately on the left half of the construct. The arrows on the middle sphere are moving in a clockwise manner and the arrows on the innermost sphere are moving counterclockwise This represents the conflict generated by internal and external pressures on the four subtheme areas of structures, culture, people, and resources.

The arrows joining each internal and external subtheme, in the two innermost spheres, indicate the interaction between each of the subtheme areas, both internally and externally. Each subtheme is connected to the others and they are all connected to the organization as a whole. Therefore, the model shows the interconnectedness of organizational components described in the literature review.

Human Side of Model

First Quadrant - Culture First, referring to a clock, the 6:00-9:00 quadrant represents the internal and external culture of the organization. Culture represents the values, norms, and assumptions developed by people in the organization to assist in making the organizational operation more efficient, manageable, and successful. Some specific examples of culture, internally and externally, in school districts are organizational charts, ceremonies, traditions and customs, specific verbal and written communication patterns, and rewards and punishments (Hatch, 1997, p. 216). Internal culture is represented by the inner circle and external culture is the outer portion of the circle. The arrows connecting all of the human forces, both internally and externally, represent the interaction among and between these forces in the entire organization.

Second Quadrant - People People are described next. Using the clock analogy and moving in a clockwise manner, internal and external people are represented in the 9:00-12:00 quadrant. The inner circle represents the internal people and the outer circle represents the external people affiliated with the organization. In school districts, internal people are represented by board members, administration, staff, and volunteers supporting the school district in any way. Examples of external people groups are parents, community leaders, local businesses, and community organizations or clubs. The two quadrants, people and culture, (from 6:00-12:00 on a clock), represent the "human side" of the organization.

Non-Human Side of Model

Third Quadrant - Resources The right side of the model represents the *non-human* forces affecting the organization. The non-human forces are the resources and structures necessary for effective organizational operations. In continuing to look at the model as a clock, and moving in a clockwise fashion, organizational resources are found in the 12:00-3:00 quadrant. The inner circle represents internal resources and the outer circle represents external resources impacting the organization. For school districts, resources are represented by money, students, staff and local businesses, clubs and organizations, and volunteers **Money is the most important internal resource for school districts**. The largest source of internal revenue for school districts comes from student attendance. However, internal resources can also refer to staff hired to teach and work at school or in the district. Grants and other outside financial sources are external resources, as well as the availability of qualified people for filling any personnel vacancies in the school district.

Fourth Quadrant - Structures Continuing to move in a clockwise manner in the model, the 3:00-6:00 quadrant of the clock is represented by structures. The inner portion of this part of the circle represents the internal structures. These structures are the policies and procedures that guide the organization that are developed internally, based on local needs. In education, examples of internal structures are school board policies, administrative regulations, and other policies and procedures developed by local school districts or schools. The outer portion of this part of the circle represents the external structures affecting the organization. External structures are the laws and codes for school districts and schools that are developed outside of the local school district, (state and federal levels), and administered by local school districts and schools. California Education Code and No Child Left Behind, (NCLB), are examples of external structures.

Interactions among and between the internal and external forces are represented by the arrows. The arrows connecting the four forces, both internally and externally, represent the complexity of the operation of an organization. Also, notice the arrows on the circle representing the internal forces move in a counterclockwise manner. The arrows on the circle representing the external forces move in a clockwise manner. The arrows, moving in opposite directions on these two circles, represents the opposing forces, and friction/conflict, caused in the organization as change occurs. Depending on the imbalance of opposing forces, organizational change can occur.

The outermost circle contains the three aspects of leadership, change, and conflict. These aspects of the organization impact, and are impacted, during the organizational change process. When forces override the status quo of the organization, change begins. And, as we found out earlier in this inquiry, change in organizations causes conflict. Therefore, leadership is impacted as it attempts to manage the conflict due to the forces of change in the organization. This model represents the complexity of, the difficulty in, and the conflict generated by transformational changes in organizations. As organizations emerge, grow, mature, die, and regenerate or transform, these components are constantly at work causing the organization to change in order to adapt to its ever-changing environment.

Each of the forces listed changes as the organization moves through its stages of development. **As the organization grows and develops in its life cycle**, the same internal and external components have an impact on the ongoing development of the organization. The entire model attempts to simplify the

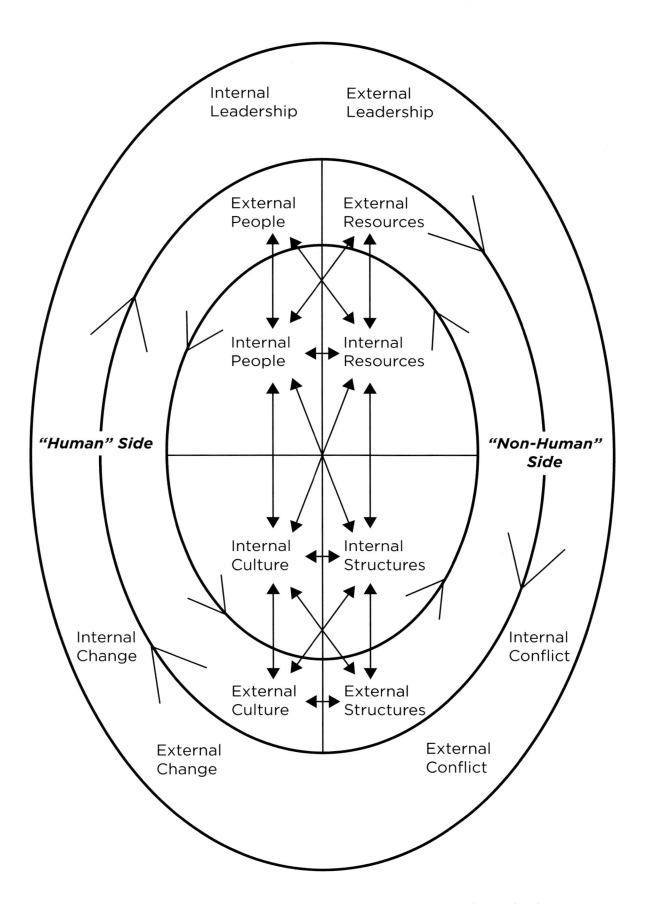

narrative representing the continual ongoing and cyclical interaction of the internal and external components that impact the development of an organization.

▶ Model for Application

School District Unification Case Study Findings

The information from the literature review and the model constructed to summarize and apply the important aspects of organizational change are now described based on data collected from a case study of school district unification.

Leadership

People

Knowledgeable and experienced leadership was involved in leading the unification process. Leaders have an important role in managing and coordinating the organizational change process. **Leadership must demonstrate a participative role** by engaging people in the open flow of dialogue and assist in resolving questions rather than supplying the answers. Through providing proper direction, as well as accurate and timely information about the unification process, trust in leadership was present in the entire school district community. It was also shown to be important for leadership to select the proper internal and external participants to be involved studying and communicating the unification process.

Culture

The unification idea must be a grassroots effort, meaning the idea comes from the community and is not generated by school district administration. In this case study, because many staff and programmatic cuts were perceived by community members as hurting students, the idea for unification came from community input at public meetings. The idea for a unification must be perceived as being good for students. Community members saw that staff and programs could be saved through the unification so the unification idea was perceived as being beneficial for the students. There must be good communication of unification information throughout the community. Various public meetings and public notifications throughout the community were used to disseminate and communicate unification information as well as seek community feedback and input into the process. Providing complete, transparent, and timely information was important in gaining support for the unification. This study also showed that having less bureaucracy was important for a more efficient educational system for their students. Therefore, having one school district in the community was economically more efficient.

Structures

A structured and organized unification study process was important in studying the impacts and effects of unification on school district operations, communicating that information to the community, and making recommendations to governing boards. Organizing a commission or committee of properly selected school district community individuals is important in developing the committee. In order to study the various school district operations that would be impacted by the unification, the commission should be broken into subcommittees so the job of gathering information can be thoroughly gathered and presented.

Resources

Outside resources are available to school district leaders to assist in providing proper school district financial and legal information as well as assistance with leading the unification process. The Department of Education and other outside educational agencies can provide assistance in supporting school district leaders with help and support in their leadership efforts.

Conflict

People

In any organizational change, various conflicts will emerge during the process because of concerns employees have with maintaining their jobs. One form of conflict to prepare for is with blending existing contracts with employee groups. Legal directions for blending the employee contracts, for certificated and classified employees, are spelled out in the *District Organization Handbook* published by the California Department of Education.

Culture

In this case study, conflict was at a minimum due to the very structured and organized unification process used by leadership. Whenever conflicts arose in the unification process, leadership properly addressed and managed the issues. Since there was a financial gain to the newly unified school district, which provided a situation that was perceived as best for students, little conflict surfaced in the unification process.

It was also interesting to note that another unification effort in this same community had been tried unsuccessfully about 10 years earlier. Community members were concerned that it would be an unsuccessful effort because of the difficulty caused in the community from the last unification attempt. Since this last attempt was still fresh in many minds of community members, leadership addressed those issues and found legal ways to avoid those same conflicts this time. By knowing the areas of conflict that existed before, leadership was able to properly address those conflicts and move the process along more smoothly.

Structures

Addressing logistical issues and meeting timelines for the unification was imperative. Involving other community and state organizations and agencies is important in a successful unification effort. Timelines for financial calculations, submitting new school district boundaries, and any bond issues or developer fees collected from the unifying school districts need to be mitigated and meet notification timelines. These are just a few of the structural issues that can cause conflicts for the unification process. If necessary, there are legal processes for granting waivers in order to address some of these necessary areas and arrive at a successful unification outcome.

Resources

There are a variety of resources available to school district leaders to address conflict situations that arise. State and county agencies can provide information and support for the unification in relation to areas of compliance and meeting those deadlines. The state department of education can provide assistance with the facilitation of granting waivers and supporting the community in various ways as needed.

Change

People

The case study revealed that as a result of the school district unification there was improved staff communication K-12. All staff was now in one organization and more formal staff meetings as well as informal gatherings of the **entire staff improved communication and staff relationships**. Staff teamwork also improved as a result of the unification and the improved staff communication. Improving staff communication, relationships and teamwork, were perceived as being good for students and the community.

Culture

Due to the unification, implementing a consistent K-12 curriculum was seen as important for improved student performance. Vertical alignment of curriculum was seen as a more coordinated curricular delivery system from one grade level to the next. Data indicated that as a unified school district, all aspects of the district, including curriculum alignment, district standards, and board policies, were important accomplishments of the unification.

Structures

Due to the unification, all district operations were **housed in one unified school district office**. As a result of the unification there were fewer school board members and school district superintendents. The school district community was adjusting to the organizational structural changes in the district operations, facilities, and governance changes. The State of California *District Organization Handbook* and California Education Code, provide the legal guidelines for the unification process to address the governance changes related to the transition of school boards. This case study established a new unified school board, appointed by the county school board, to set up the newly unified school district while the previous school districts were dissolving. This was an excellent transition strategy in this unification process.

Resources

Increased financial resources were available to the newly unified school district as a result of the unification. This was the main reason for the success of the unification in this community. As a result of the increased financial resources, the community believed that this unification would ultimately be best for the students in the community. Outside agencies, the California State Department of Education, the county school board and the county superintendent of schools, were all important resources in supporting and facilitating the successful unification process by providing and communicating accurate information in a timely manner.

▶ Leadership Practices and Strategies

The following ten leadership principles should be applied in facilitating transformational organizational changes, such as a school district unification.

- Participatory leadership seems to be the most effective style for leading transformational changes.
- Leading and organizing a structural and organized study process to determine whether there is benefit to pursuing organizational change should be considered as a prior activity that sets the feasibility of the change process.
- Selecting people to be involved in the change process should represent diverse community viewpoints and the various internal and external community groups.
- Establishing a commission to thoroughly study the various effects of the organizational change and make public recommendations on the organizational change process. For effectiveness of the commission, the commission should be divided up into subcommittees to study the various components of organizational change that could occur.
- Familiarizing leadership with the laws, policies, and procedures and have the experience to lead the organizational change process.
- Communicating the leadership vision of the organizational change so as to provide a more efficient and effective delivery of services to the community served by the organization.
- Providing thorough, public communication using a variety of avenues explaining the organizational change.
- Holding formal community meetings scheduled to provide opportunities for input and feedback on the organizational change.

- Ensuring open and honest communication regarding the effects of the organizational change is provided to the community.
- Assessing community readiness for the organizational change by providing open and transparent communication avenues, input and feedback opportunities, and a variety of formal and informal public meetings.

▶ Leadership Practices for Facilitating Conflict

To assist educational leaders further, the following practices can assist school and school district leaders in facilitating the conflict that emerges as the change process evolves.

- Manage employee conflict, which can exist due to personnel changes through negotiations approved by administration and employees.
- Familiarize leadership with the legal structures involved with employees in organizational changes.
- Identify, prepare, plan for, and manage various conflicts that can arise that were not anticipated.
- Investigate the history of the school or school district. Based on history, leadership should plan for complications to the change process and how to proactively prepare for, and address them.
- Seek the approval of procedural and policy waivers, as needed, to avoid restrictive structures and expedite the change process. Advice on this can be obtained from legal support or the State Department of Education.
- Know and prepare for meeting legal timelines. If leadership knows the legal timelines, plans can be adjusted to move the process along more efficiently and without delays that could cause legal and financial issues.
- Know the structures and timelines for obtaining the maximum financial benefit. Gain outside input to verify the figures.
- Alleviated and mitigate conflicts by outside consultants or the State Department of Education.

▶ Leadership Practices in Facilitating Constructive Change

The following practices can be employed by educational leaders to assist in facilitating constructive change.

- Concentrate on creating open and authentic communication with all stakeholders in the school or school district community.
- Continue to build teamwork. Provide opportunities for formal and informal gatherings to bring community stakeholders together and build camaraderie.
- Plan for changes in and the effect on, school or school district services. Notify stakeholders in the community of any changes and how these changes will be addressed.
- Prepare for and notify the community about any policy or governance changes in the school or the school district.
- Know about and adjust for the financial adjustments that can result from the changes.
- Provide for a period of transition for the community stakeholders to adjust to the new organizational adaptations as a result of the changes. This time allows for planning and preparations to be made for a more successful implementation of the changes.

◗ Conclusion

For a variety of reasons, educational leaders are experiencing organizational change at both the district and site levels, to better meet the educational needs of students as well as the organizational needs of the district and community. This chapter has presented research on two types of organizational change that educational administrators consider, depending on the type of organizational changes that are necessary for educational leaders to make. Specifically, this chapter provided relevant information for school district leaders considering a school district unification. The types of forces that cause organizations to change were identified and presented for educational leaders to consider and be aware of. As a result of organizational changes, educational leaders should also be aware of conflict that can and will emerge as the organization considers the type of change to make. Finally, proven strategies were presented, to assist educational leaders in leading their organizations through the change process, as well as to assist educational leaders in managing the conflict the organization will experience from second-order, transformational, organizational changes.

Discussion Questions

1. What forces of change are affecting your organization today?

2. In order to address those forces causing change, what strategies will need to be employed by leaders in developing an action plan for addressing organizational change?

3. What types of conflict might you face during the process of making needed organizational changes?

4. What leadership style and strategies will you employ in leading the change process?

5. What steps would you use in analyzing and/or determining whether a school district consolidation is needed in your community?

Leadership Activity

Background

You are the superintendent of a small elementary school district whose students move on to attend high school at a separate high school district. Both districts are experiencing declining enrollments as well as ongoing budget cuts from the state. Both districts have declining enrollments producing unused classrooms so facilities are not being used efficiently. Annually you have to lay off certificated and classified employees as well as cut programs for students to meet your budget needs. Your school district has also been in program improvement status, based on student performance, for the past three years. It is being suggested in the community that school district administrations needs to also "shoulder" some of the financial cuts. Both school districts are facing many problems that need to be addressed in a broader community way. You find out that one way both school districts can preserve staff and programs is to pursue a school district unification process.

Activity Directions

As a result of the issues facing the school districts, it is your mission to analyze the school districts in your community in order to determine whether a school district unification would benefit the students and your community.

General questions to consider are:

- Why is the unification analysis needed?
- What are the gaps between the present situation and the desired outcome?
- Who will be involved in the analysis process?
- What information is needed?
- What form of organizational structure do you need for the analysis (small group, committee, etc?)
- Where will you meet?
- When do you want to complete the analysis?
- What criteria will you use in making a final determination on whether or not to pursue the unification process?

More specific questions to address in the analysis process may include:

1. Who will you talk to and work with?

   - Key people in the community (internal and external to your organization)
   - Key staff in the school districts
   - Key people at the county level
   - Key people at the state level
   - Outside facilitators including legal and financial support

2. What type of information do you need to know?

   - Financial and other resource needs
   - Legal structures involved
   - People involved (Support both internal and external to the school district)
   - The culture of the community
   - Timelines/deadlines to meet

3. What conflicts can emerge from various constituents in the school district community?

   - How will groups of people be affected and what type of conflict will emerge from them?
   - What legal structures will hinder the unification process and how will you address them?
   - Will the financial benefits outweigh other problems?
   - What cultural conflicts exist that can cause conflict in the community?

4. What forms of communication can be used to inform the community about the need to explore the unification process?

   - Town Hall meetings
   - School District and County School Board meetings
   - Other community meetings

Activity Critique

As a result of this analysis process, you can determine whether to pursue a school district unification process or not. There may be other steps to consider other than those listed here that are unique to your specific community needs. The goal of this analysis process is to provide you with enough information and support in making the best decision for your school districts and the community.

Background of the Author

Dr. Glenn Sewell has been an associate faculty member in the School of Education, Educational Administration Department, at the National University Stockton, California Regional Center for the past six years. He is the Preliminary Administrative Services Credential Program lead and the course lead for two courses in the program. Dr. Sewell retired two years ago from service in public schools after 35 years as a high school teacher, high school assistant principal, high school principal, high school district superintendent/principal and elementary school district superintendent. He received his BA, teaching credential, and MA from California State University at Los Angeles. He received his EdD in Organizational Leadership from the University of La Verne.

References

Argyris, C. (1990) *Overcoming organizational defenses: Facilitating organizational learning.* Boston: Allyn and Bacon.

Berger, P. L., & Luckman, T. (1966). *The social construction of reality.* New York, NY: Doubleday.

Capra, F. (2002). *The hidden connections.* New York, NY: Doubleday.

Hatch, M. J. (1997) *Organization theory: Modern symbolic and postmodern perspectives.* New York, NY: Oxford Press.

Hurst, D. K. (1995). *Crisis and renewal: Meeting the challenge of organizational change.* Boston, MA: Harvard Business School.

Pfeffer, J. (1992). *Managing with power.* Boston, MA: Harvard Business School Press.

Stacey, R. D. (2001). *Complex responsive processes in organizations: Learning and knowledge.* New York, NY: Routledge.

Stacey, R. D. (2003). *Strategic management and organizational dynamics: The challenge of complexity.* London, England: Pitman.

What Are the Most Effective Leadership Styles for Improving Teaching and Learning

Clifford Tyler, Ed. D., Associate Professor, National University, San Jose, California

ISLLC Standard 1: Setting a widely shared vision for learning.

▶ Abstract

This chapter examined all sides of these issues, drawing on the latest research from leadership advocates such as Linda Darling Hammond, Mike Schmoker, Roland Barth, Dan Lortie, Grant Wiggins, and Doug Reeves. While sharing these leadership results, they offered very different approaches on achieving accountability, improving the quality of teaching and learning and the most effective leadership. This chapter concluded with a practical application case study of innovative leadership to achieve quality teaching and learning results from accurate assessment of data, setting common learning goals and strategies, arranging relevant staff development and training, and providing effective, collaborative and situational leadership to achieve these results.

Key Phrases and Words: students learn to be successful, high stakes accountability, improve the quality of teaching and learning, innovative leadership

▶ Statement of the Issue

Over the years, there seems to be universal agreement and consensus among all stakeholders to desire that **all students learn and be successful.** Nearly all local school districts, county offices of education, and many private and parochial schools include this language in their mission, vision, and/or goals in their strategic plan, and clearly communicate this to their respective parents, local community patrons, and taxpayers. Often these goals and missions are reinforced as local school districts report test score and student achievement results.

Yet there is considerable controversy among different stakeholders, i.e., school board members, administrators, teachers, community members, special interest groups, education bureaucrats, politicians, and lawmakers regarding quality student achievement and high stakes accountability. According to some sources, quality student achievement is dependent on the socioeconomic status and educational level of their parents and the non-school opportunities and environment created by their parents. Others feel that quality student achievement is related to the amount of money spent per pupil in local school districts, with the notion that there is a direct relationship between higher student achievement and more money spent, i.e., **high wealth school districts have higher quality student achievement** than low wealth school districts. Similarly, states that spend more money per student for schools have better schools and higher quality achievement than states that spend relatively less on schools.

Still others feel that the effectiveness and climate of schools, along with quality (or non-quality) school leaders, i.e., principals and effective teachers, have a profound impact on quality student achievement (Marzano, 2003) regardless of the student population or socioeconomic community make-up. Even more controversial is the belief of some social scientists that ethnicity and lower socioeconomic status are major combination components on quality student achievement. Their stereotype is that Asian and Anglo school communities have higher achieving students than African-American and Latino school communities.

Although the now-dated Coleman Report (1966) acknowledges substantial differences in student achievement due to ethnicity and socioeconomic status, other factors such as the differences of student teacher class ratio, amount of money spent on schools, education level of teachers, and the input of reformers and researchers are also significant. Based on these acknowledgements, it appears that some of the results of researchers and reformers may confirm politicians and their arguments making news headlines about failing schools and the education system, and promote reforms of their own, i.e., vouchers for private and parochial schools, restoring prayer to public schools.

Political and public pressures over the last 10 years from the perceived failure or dysfunction of public schools have fueled high stakes accountability, i.e., annual yearly progress (AYP) and standardized testing generated by No Child Left Behind federal legislation and similar legislation generated by lawmakers in most states. For example, in California, *Public Schools Accountability Act of 1999*, measures the academic performance and growth of schools on a variety of academic measures through a measure called the Academic Performance Index (API). However, the high stakes accountability emphasis has resulted in the loss of fine arts programs for students.

▶ Closing the Achievement Gap

Another controversial issue related to quality student achievement and high stakes accountability and testing is closing the achievement gap. A few years ago, there was much discussion about the achievement gap which separates low-income and minority children from other young Americans. For more than a generation, the focus was on improving the education of poor and minority students, and funding from various federal and state sources were provided. From that effort, real gains were made. Between 1970 and 1988, the achievement gap between African American and white students was cut in half, and the gap separating Latinos and whites declined by one-third. That progress came to a halt around 1988, however, and since that time, the gaps have widened again. Although everybody wanted to take credit for narrowing the gap, nobody wanted to take responsibility for widening it (Haycock, 2001).

▶ Effect of the Economy on Student Achievement

In the past several years, the Great Recession has imposed another daunting challenge on achieving or maintaining quality student achievement. These serious challenges have been created from substantial budget declines across the United StatesPerhaps the most severe losses generated by the education cuts are the **massive layoffs of teachers** spreading across the United States. According to CBS News, school districts are continuing to eliminate teaching jobs by hundreds of thousands. Teaching positions are not the only thing the school system is doing away with; various music and art programs, extracurricular activities, technology and related equipment, transportation, school hours, student counseling, and even entire schools are simply being shut down. As a result, The Christian Science Monitor reports that **classrooms are becoming more overcrowded**, repairs to school equipment remain undone, and parents have to foot the bill for classroom supplies. Those teachers managing to retain their jobs are receiving fewer funds for books, classroom activities, and field trips; they essentially have to improvise. As a result, the quality of education students are receiving is declining along with the funding (Wright, 2011).

California's high school principals report their campuses are providing less time and attention to and fewer quality programs for their students as a result of continuous deep cuts to education, according to a study that UCLA's Institute for Democracy, Education and Access recently released. California State Superintendent of Public Instruction, Tom Torlakson also recently released a report that shows two million state students—or 30% of pupils—attend a financially troubled school.

"The bottom line is that schools are suffering cuts that profoundly affect students day in and day out," Torlakson said in a recent conference, "It's making it harder for our students to do things we all once took for granted, like seeing a school counselor, getting help to make a pathway to college, getting time to ask a teacher a question in our ever-increasingly crowded classrooms and learning from an up-to-date textbook" (Tasci, 2011).

Given the above challenges that school districts are facing to maintain quality instruction and momentum for improving student academic performance and keeping pace with the No Child Left Behind requirements, there has been much research on effective leadership, but little agreement on the most effective leadership style. Some of these leadership styles will be examined in more detail.

▶ Review of Leadership Literature:

Mike Schmoker

Mike Schmoker has been a School and District Improvement, Assessment, Curriculum and Staff Development and Consultant for a number of years, offering effective instructional leadership strategies for teachers on improvements in teaching and learning. Over the years, he has strongly opposed complicated district strategic plans, which contain "a dizzying, incoherent abundance of activities and responsibilities within columns and categories like 'Goals'; 'Action Plan' (or 'Action Steps'); 'Objectives'; 'Timeline'; 'Resources needed'; 'Evaluation'; 'Target Areas' and more. Superficially, they are large, handsome documents; school boards, district offices, and accreditation agencies love them" (Schmoker, 2003).

He further states that this model is a recipe for academic bankruptcy because the length and complexity of these plans ensure that no one really knows if or how well anything is being implemented. Furthermore, teachers and administrators cannot remember what the goals are because there are too many of them. Human and financial resources are spread too thin to achieve any of them.

Schmoker instead advocates that a school site or district **settle on a maximum of two goals**, effective implementation strategies, and meaningful assessment of their results. He strongly feels that it's time to identify what we do know as educators, and to apply it to promote learning, i.e., how effective is the lesson? "Good teaching is not about charisma, it's about doing the simple things we learn will work."

Many in the business community agree with Schmoker. Kouzes and Posner, two well-known organizational thinkers, found from their research that "Strategic planning doesn't work....It's a process that detaches strategy from operations, thinking from doing." Or, as Gary Hamel of Harvard business school recently wrote, "[strategic planning] is about as effective as dancing naked around a campfire" (Schmoker, 2003).

Why does Schmoker feel that way about strategic planning? Most often, too many districts develop too many goals with too few human and financial resources to implement.

Linda Darling Hammond

Another renowned leader in improving effective learning and teaching is Linda Darling-Hammond. While at Stanford University, she founded the Stanford Educational Leadership Institute and the School Redesign Network, and served as faculty sponsor for the Stanford Teacher Education Program. From 1994-2001, she was the executive director of the National Commission on Teaching and America's Future, a blue-ribbon panel whose 1996 report, "What Matters Most: Teaching for America's Future," led to important policy changes that affected teaching and teacher education.

In her research and publications, Hammond has assembled volumes of data and stories about reform efforts in various states to explain what can really work in helping close the achievement gap and what has not. She has observed that "American education leaders seek to solve the problem of the poor by blaming the teachers and schools that seek to serve them, calling the deepening levels of poverty an 'excuse,' rewarding schools that keep out and push out the highest need students, and threatening those who work with new immigrant students still learning English and the growing number of those who are homeless, without health care and without food" (Darling-Hammond, 2011).

Hammond asserts that the typical question for school leaders today is: Are there lower scores in under-resourced schools with high-need students? She maintains that the too-often are the following: **Fire the teachers and the principals**! Close the schools! Don't look for supports for their families and communities, equitable funding for their schools, or investments in professional learning. Don't worry about the fact that the next schools are—as researchers have documented—likely to do no better. If the banks are failing, we should fire the tellers. And whatever you do, pay no attention to the "man behind the curtain" (Darling-Hammond, 2011).

Darling-Hammond maintains that the federal government has to make a financial commitment to fund education so that equality is achieved. This effort should include assurance that all students have adequate housing, health care, and food security.

She explains how three countries, Finland, **and South Korea created excellent, equitable school systems**. Although the common notion that they did it through the centralization of power is not what has happened. The key element in all three success stories was a commitment by the governments to equitably funded schools. Furthermore, these countries invest in the highest-quality preparation, mentoring, and professional development for teachers and school leaders all at government expense. Their curriculum is organized around problem-solving and critical thinking skills. And they test students rarely (in Finland, not at all)—and almost never with multiple-choice tests (Darling-Hammond, 2011).

Finland transformed from a centralized model to "a more localized system in which highly trained teachers design curriculum around very lean national standards. All assessments are school-based, designed by teachers, rather than standardized. The Finnish government put a lot of money into making sure they had a quality teaching force, raising standards for teacher preparation as well as salaries. Singapore, a country that is highly controlled by the national government, realized that regimentation in schools was counterproductive and introduced the American notion of innovation (Darling-Hammond, 2011).

Also significant is the assessment differences between the United States, i.e. standardized tests, and high performing countries such as Canada, Finland and Singapore that increasingly rely on assessments that include research projects, scientific investigation, and other intellectually challenging work—developed and scored by teachers—just as progressive educators here have been urging for years. None of these countries utilize standardized test scores to rank and compare teachers, believing that such a practice would be counterproductive. Furthermore, none of them rank and punish schools; indeed several countries forbid this practice. They empower professional educators to build schools' capacity to educate all their students (Darling-Hammond, 2011).

Darling-Hammond says another major fault of American public schools is that education leaders advocate for teachers with little training—those who come and go quickly with minimal cost, and without raising questions about an increasingly prescriptive system of testing and teaching that lines the pockets of private entrepreneurs (who provide teacher-proofed materials deemed necessary because there are so many underprepared novices who leave before they learn to teach) (Darling-Hammond, 2011).

Finally, she points out that "many education leaders seek to resolve the problem of the poor by blaming the teachers and schools that seek to serve them, calling the deepening levels of poverty an 'excuse,' rewarding schools that keep out and push out the highest need students, and threatening those who work with new immigrant students still learning English and the growing number of those who are homeless, without health care and without food. Are there lower scores in under-resourced schools with high-need students? Fire the teachers and the principals. Close the schools. Don't look for supports for their families and communities, equitable funding for their schools, or investments in professional learning. Don't worry about the fact that the next schools are—as researchers have documented—likely to do no better. If the banks are failing, we should fire the tellers (Darling-Hammond, 2011). [And whatever you do, pay no attention to the "man behind the curtain."]

Her analysis of the ups and downs of reform efforts in three states—North Carolina, Connecticut and California—lays bare how policy-makers can get things right, then get them wrong again.

Working to reduce poverty so that children have secure housing, food and health care is central; kids who go to school hungry and sick are unable to learn. But some of today's generation of reform superintendents think they can achieve their goals simply by ordering the classroom in a specific way.

How many studies must be done before policy-makers understand that supportive early learning environments are critical, that teachers and education leaders must be well-trained and well-supported, that any effort to close the achievement gap is doomed to fail if all schools are not equitably funded and properly staffed (Darling-Hammond, 2011)?

Roland Barth

Roland Barth is an author, consultant, school leader, former Harvard Graduate School of Education faculty member, but foremost he is an educator at heart. A former teacher and principal, Barth is also the founder of The Principals' Center, a professional development program based at Harvard Graduate School of Education for school principals, assistant principals, and other school leaders. Over the past four decades, Barth's work has made an impression on educators worldwide from the many books he has authored including *Open Education and the American School, Improving Schools from Within, Run School Run, Lessons Learned*, and *Learning by Heart*.

Barth (2006) offers a humane blueprint for school reform that would build on the educational staff's existing strengths, largely by improving adult relationships in the schoolhouse instead of starting with a "deficiency" model of what teachers can't do and giving them "in-service" workshops *ad infinitum*. His prescription calls for a dose of democracy, more sharing of decision making and pedagogic wisdom between teachers and principals. The principal, rather than pretending to know all the answers, would become the "head learner" in a "community of learners." The more that teachers and principals were invited to learn and take risks, the better they would serve as models for their students.

His vision is that "we need to spend more energy improving schools from within" is very helpful as far as it goes. Perhaps the within/without distinction is that schools are supremely porous institutions, and outside organizations and the community do have a valid teaching role to play. By addressing the problems of inequality in the schoolhouse only from the standpoint of management technique, without delving into the larger political and economic forces that impede democracy in the work place, the author risks a shallowly naive treatment of these crucial matters (Barth, 2006).

Dan Lortie

Dan Lortie is still another educational leader who researched the lives of teachers to conclude that they are conservative people because the flat salary schedules in the field attract socially conservative people. Lortie further notes that prior to starting their first job, they have been acclimated for 16 years in traditional patterns of thought and practice. "This degree of socialization is potent and their isolated introduction to the classroom leads teachers to fall back on this long 'apprenticeship of observation' that they undertook as school students. Conservatism is emphasized when the training experiences of beginning teachers encourage them to view teaching as an individualistic rather than a collegial enterprise. Isolated in cellular classrooms, this individualistic nature of teaching continues throughout the career. He's worth a read as his work explains why school reform is so darn difficult" (Lortie, 2002).

Grant Wiggins

Grant Wiggins is a nationally recognized assessment expert in assessment reform and president of the educational consulting firm Authentic Education. With Jay McTighe, he co-authored *Understanding by Design*, an award-winning framework for curriculum design used around the world. In addition to his publications for Edutopia, he has worked with Theodore Sizer's, Coalition of Essential Schools, and made numerous contributions to Association of Supervision and Curriculum Development (ASCD).

Wiggins argues that testing is only a small part of assessment. It's confined to an audit or snapshot as only a part of a larger picture in a family album. A test is more complex and can look for discrete knowledge and skills for an individual student, as opposed to a project being more collaborative, questioning what an individual student really knows (Wiggins, 2002).

Some state-based, performance-based assessments always have a parallel paper-and-pencil test for the individual student to gather enough data on the individual. Scientists and researchers define this as *triangulate the information*. Tests match the quiz against the project, against the PowerPoint® presentation, which may not define the whole picture. Hence, Wiggins concludes that "testing" is one piece of a portfolio (2002).

Wiggins also discusses authentic assessment, which was started 15 years ago. He states that it's realistic, as opposed to multiple choice questions in a test, which does not determine if an employee is doing his/her job. Authentic assessment parallels performance assessment in the work place. Some people misunderstand that authentic assessment is "messy and squishy because it involves many people with so many variables, making it difficult to determine the knowledge level of an individual student." Wiggins contends that there is a place for unauthentic, non–real-world assessments, and that students should not leave school without knowing what big people actually do (2002).

Why is it important that teachers consider assessment before they begin planning lessons or projects? According to Wiggins, "the challenge of teaching is not only trying to design a combination of content and instructional methods, but also assessment. There needs to evidence in the goals to be accomplished for a lesson to prevent hit or miss teaching. It is called *backward design*" (2002).

Wiggins further states, "Before a teacher decides exactly what to do with their students to achieve their lesson objectives, what does it look like? What's the evidence that they got it? What's the evidence that they can now do it, whatever the "it" is? So you have to think about how it's going to end up, what it's going to look like. And then that ripples back into your design, what activities will get you there" (2002).

Wiggins also weighs in on assessing project-based learning. It all starts with determining the goals. And asking how does this project support those goals and how are we assessing in light of those goals? He would expect to see for any project a scoring guideline, a rubric, in which there are clear links to the project, to some criteria and standards that we value that relate to some overarching objective—quite explicitly, that we're aiming for as teachers (2002).

Sometimes projects run into the problem that it is so much a creation of the student's interest that there's no question that lively learning occurs, but we sort of lose sight of the fact that now it's completely out of our control. With projects, it's difficult to determining what it's really accomplishing in terms of teacher goals other than the kid is learning a lot and doing some critical and creative work (Wiggins, 2002).

If students are given free rein to do good projects, it has to fit within the context of some objectives, standards, and criteria that we bring to it, and frame the project so that we can say by the end, "I have evidence. I can make the case that you learned something substantial and significant that relates to school objectives" (Wiggins, 2002).

Wiggins supports the role of technology to enhance assessment, because it documents that students have done more than taken quizzes and tests, but they have done something significant. This body of evidence shows that **students are actually learning something**. He contends that technology is an obvious partner, whether it's on a CD-ROM, floppies, or an old-fashioned technology like video cameras or even overheads, the student is bringing together visual, three-dimensional, and paper-and-pencil work. It has to be documented and have a trace of what the student has accomplished and how the student got there. Technology can be overused and there is not enough about the evidence for posting a student grade for putting something on the transcript, and tracking that information over time. Many educators suggest having student portfolios of the student's work K-12. While portfolios credit students for their work, few educational assessors want to spend the time wading through their portfolios (2002).

Technology actually serves as a good database system—information management, storage, and retrieval instead of forcing people to review an entire portfolio. Most educators want to review only samples, along with rubrics to get a sense of the student's current level of performance. Tracking information over time through technology is actually an important part of it as well (Wiggins, 2002).

Some educators argue that teachers don't have enough time to design and conduct authentic or performance-based assessments because they are too time intensive, and expensive. They question what the payoff and cost benefit is? This argument is valid at the state level because the state is in the audit business, looking for ways to save money, not being intrusive, and provide reliable assessment. However, the time-consuming authentic assessment arguments are not valid at a local school district level because it is not expensive, and local people make it their business to conduct assessment. Standards cannot be met at the local level without doing performance-based assessment (Wiggins, 2002).

Are standardized tests, such as the California Standardized Test, Scholastic Achievement Test, etc. used by schools as a predictor of a student's future success? Is this a valid use of these tests? Whether these tests predict future performance or success? They do not, according to Wiggins. Even with the SAT, ETS, and the College Board are quite clear about what it does and does not predict. It just predicts freshman grade point average in the first semester. That's all. There are plenty of studies to show that grades in college don't correlate with later success. Standardized testing has a role to play as an audit, but one of the things that many policymakers and parents forget, or don't know, is that these tests have a very narrow focus and purpose as audits. They're just trying to find out if you really learned the stuff you learned in school (Wiggins, 2002).

Doug Reeves

The final leadership advocate the author cites offers ideas on improving the quality of teaching and learning and the most effective leadership that will be discussed in this chapter is Dr. Douglas Reeves, founder of The Leadership and Learning Center. As part of Houghton Mifflin Harcourt, a global educational leader, The Center serves school systems around the world. The author of 30 books and many articles on leadership and organizational effectiveness, Dr. Reeves has twice been named to the Harvard University Distinguished Authors Series. Dr. Reeves was named the Brock International Laureate for his contributions to education. He also received the Distinguished Service Award from the National Association of

Secondary School Principals and the Parents Choice Award for his writing for children and parents. He is the 2010 recipient of the National Staff Development Council's Contribution to the Field Award. In writing the foreword to his most recent book, Michael Fullan wrote, "Reeves doesn't just tell us what not to do. His research is so carefully documented and so clearly argued that we see precisely what should be our focus…Reeves takes us further and deeper into the critical territory of whole system reform. He does it with such elegance and relentless insistence that we are drawn—indeed, compelled—to want to take action" (Lead and Learn.com).

Reeves poses a challenge for educators and administrators for considering profound changes essential to assess twenty-first century Skills. "Everyone talks about the need for 21st Century Skills," Reeves contends, "but too many assessments are indistinguishable from those that were administered fifty years ago—or for that matter, 100 years ago" we really want 21st Century learning, then we need 21st Century assessment (Lead and Learn.com)."

There are three needed assessment changes, Reeves suggests. The first is a shift from standardized to authentic assessment. If we expect students to perform authentic tasks, then assessment conditions must be variable, not standardized. Second, **assessments must be open, not secret**. The historic century-long tradition of secret assessments is based upon surprise and ambiguity, Reeves argues, along with distorted notions of fairness—that is, an assessment is only fair if it is secret. In fact, the global best practices in assessment include assessments where students not only know about the questions, but have contributed to the creation of test questions. Third, we must shift from assessments should be changed from exclusively for the individual student to a combination of team and individual assessments. While businesses, governments, nonprofit organizations, and educational institution extol the virtues of teamwork and collaboration, they continue to rely on assessments that are almost exclusively based on individual work. Reeves suggests that twenty-first century assessment must include a rigorous and comprehensive consideration of teamwork and collaboration (Leadandlearn.com).

Up to this point, this chapter has examined leadership results, but very different approaches on achieving accountability, improving the quality of teaching and learning and the most effective leadership. The contributors included Linda Darling Hammond, Mike Schmoker, Roland Barth, Dan Lortie, Grant Wiggins, and Doug Reeves. Their different approaches obviously reflect their respective backgrounds, careers, research, and contributions.

Is there only one correct or better approach for improving the quality of teaching learning, rendering the others invalid and without credit? The answer to that question is **there is no single correct approach**. Any of these approaches are adaptable to any single school or district setting depending on the changing needs of students. A school leader assigned to lead a school or entire school district needs to apply situational leadership to effective leadership at that particular school district or school site. This situational leadership includes a leadership vision that can be clearly communicated to the school staff and community, and establishing common learning goals and strategies in collaboration with the staff, parents, and community, arranging relevant staff development and training, and providing effective, collaborative, and situational leadership to achieve the desire academic results for students.

▶ Key Chapter Questions

What leadership approach do you feel is most effective for improving teaching and learning? Why?

Has high stakes accountability implementation improved the overall quality of education? Why or why not?

What is situational leadership? How can an educational leader provide the correct leadership to assure success of all students at his/her particular school site or district?

What is **backward design**? How is it effective in teaching and learning?

What are advantages and disadvantages of authentic assessment?

Chapter Activity

You have just been appointed as the principal of high performing school in an upper middle socioeconomic, ethnically diverse community (60% Asian, 30% Anglo, and 10% East Indian) with high expectations. Parents who live in this school community are highly educated, hold high-paying professional positions often earning over $100,000 annually, have purchased beautiful homes often worth over one million in attractive neighborhoods, and pay high annual property taxes of $10,000 or more. With this tax rate, the district is considered a basic aid district, and does not depend on state revenue limit allocations. However, for payment of these high taxes, parents expect the highest quality of education for their students to enter high quality Ivy League-caliber colleges and universities.

Your teachers are a balance of eight veteran teacher (15 years or more of experience), eight experienced teachers (5-10 years of experience), and eight young teachers with under five years of experience. For the exception of one of two older teachers, none can afford to live in the community. While the classified staff lives in the district with lower cost housing, none live in the school community due to high housing prices.

While student academic achievement scores are very high, the school's achievement level has slightly declined, and is now in some trouble with the state because the special education (handicapped population) and English Second Language (ESL) subgroups have not met expectations. Many parents are angry about this status, and demand something be done to improve the situation.

Your most immediate task as principal is to organize a strategic planning committee composed of a representation of all stakeholders, and conduct a strategic planning session that includes goals, strategies, activities, timeline, and assessments to meet the strategic plan and mission of the school. What data would you assemble for tools for this committee to utilize? What components would be included in the strategic plan that would address all student will learn and be successful, improve the quality of teaching and learning, meeting high stakes accountability, and showing innovative leadership?

Background of the Author

Dr. Clifford Tyler has been a full-time faculty member at National University in the Department of Educational Administration and School Counseling/Psychology for the past 10 years, including 18 months as the department chair. While serving at National University, Dr. Tyler has made numerous presentations at both national international conferences in Europe, the Middle East, Asia, Africa, Australia, and South America. He has written numerous professional journal and online articles on higher education/school district partnerships, online education, education leadership, and school district finance issues. Prior to his work at National University, Dr. Tyler served as both a district and county superintendent for 20 years in K-12 districts ranging in size from 200 students to 12,500 students in Oregon, Washington, California, and New Hampshire. He also served as headmaster of a private independent school for two years, has been both an elementary and high school principal for eight years, and a classroom teacher for six years, including the American School in Japan. Dr. Tyler holds an EdD from the University of the Pacific in Educational Administration, an MEd from the University of Oregon in Elementary Education, and a Bachelor of Science degree in Social Sciences from Oregon State University.

References

Barth, R. (2006). Improving relations in the schoolhouse. *Educational Leadership*, March 2006. *63*(6), 8–13.

Darling-Hammond, L. (2011). *The flat world and education: How America's commitment to equity will determine its future.* New York: Teachers College Press.

Haycock, K. (2001). Helping all student achieve: Closing the Achievement Gap. *Educational Leadership*, March 2001. 58, 6–11.

Lopate, P. (1990). *Being with children: A book about teaching.* July 1, 1990. New York: Poseidon

Reeves, D. (n.d.). Leadership and learning center. Retrieved (December 6, 2012) from http://www.leadandlearn.com

Schmoker, M. (2003). Planning for failure? Or for school success? *Education Week,* February 12, 2003 *VOLUME (), pages*

Strauss, V. (2011). The answer sheet. Darling Hammond: The mess we are in. Retrieved (February 1, 2011) from http://www.washingtonpost.com/blogs/answer-sheet

Tasci, C. (2011). Study shows effects of state budget on school districts. *Daily Bulletin.com.* Retrieved (March 23, 2011) from http://www.dailybulletin.com

Wiggins, G. (2002). Defining assessment. Edutopia Staff 2002. Retrieved (DATE) from http://www.educopia.org

University Partnerships with Teachers and Students to Enhance the Teaching/ Learning Experience

Dan Cunniff PhD, National University, La Jolla, California

(Reprinted with permission from the editors of the 23rd volume of the 2012 California Association of Professors of Educational Administration's Educational *Leadership and Administration: Teaching Program Development*.)

ISLLC Standard 4: Collaborating with families and community members, responding to diverse community interests and needs, and mobilizing community resources.

▶ Abstract

This article examined the role of partnership relationships as they related to school districts and universities. It highlighted programs and delivery modes that could be used to improve communication with the expectation of mutual benefits from achieving the goal of improved teaching and learning. The article demonstrated the cost savings opportunities and improved communication through the use of technology. The review of literature focused both on the research and the current practical applications in use today between universities and school districts. Several programs and technologies were presented to show the impact that wireless communication can have on enhancing the partnership relationship. The concept of partnership education using teams was presented as well as how partnerships can be either formal with the use of Memoranda of Agreement, or informal coaching and mentoring depending on the needs and resources of the organizations involved.

Key Words: partnership education, coaching, communication, technology

▶ Statement of the Issue

As schools and school districts find their funds being cut or eliminated, they are turning to various organizations for assistance to help in the teaching/learning process. One such organization is the university. Quite often these schools or districts not only lack the funds, but also lack the technical and resource capacities to implement the kinds of educational practices outlined in their mission statements. **The No Child Left Behind Act has exacerbated this crisis** and many schools are now embracing the help of universities in their decision making. Additionally, colleges of education work to establish partnerships with PreK-12 school systems in order to fulfill their mission and contribute to school reforms that improve the lives of teachers and students alike.

PreK-12 school partnerships can be either formal or informal. Relationships can have memoranda of agreements signed off by the local school board to one of informal individual and group meetings to address local concerns. As a result, school districts seek partnerships with key stakeholders such as universities. This paper describes several ways this process can be undertaken. Many of these partnerships are an outgrowth of teacher education programs. Often, student teachers identify areas where their university can make a contribution to school site councils and leadership teams in coaching team and administrative leaders, as well as addressing curricular and other educational issues.

▶ Review of the Literature

Developing partnerships involves the promotion of cooperation. The organization's life depends on member cooperation (Simon, 1976). The university, in coming into a school district, assumes the responsibility of creating cooperation among its members. Research has shown that reducing people's focus on their own self-interest is critical to developing a positive team (Frank, Gilovich, and Regan, 1993). The team's make up is also critical. Diversely demographic teams are less likely to develop cooperative norms than are homogeneous groups (Chatman and Flynn, 2001). The university participants must devise ways to instill cooperative norms in groups, particularly when groups are made up of diverse members. By focusing on a common issue or problems, the organizational leaders can instill a commonality of purpose among members (Chatman et al., 1998). Cooperation can also be enhanced by teaching people values, facts, and skills that promote cooperation, such as the importance of action research and applying that research in the school or district (Cialdini, 2001).

Each school has its own culture. It is up to the university to identify that culture and understand the mission statement and vision for the school selected for partnership. According to Kotter and Heskett (2002), culture is most closely related to organizational performance when three criteria are met. First, the culture should be strategically relevant in that the behaviors that are emphasized and rewarded are actually the ones necessary to accomplish pressing and relevant organizational objectives or learning outcomes. Second, the culture should be strong, and people agree what is important and care. Third, a core value needs to focus, over time, on innovation, adaptation and change if the school is to reach high levels of performance such as distinguished school status (Kotter and Heskett, 2002). Emerging partnership models could benefit from partnership literature focused on use of accreditation standards to improve program implementation and record keeping and the utilization of research on professional development, policy and practice in PreK-12 schools. Occasionally, it is possible to find similar core values in both the school district and the university. One such university is National University based in La Jolla, California, whose core values include quality, access, relevance, accelerated pace and community. The community value has not only included the university community, but has reached out into the local neighborhood school districts as well. The Faculty in this institution has embarked on several formal and informal partnerships with school districts up and down the state of California and Nevada.

Additional collaborative partnerships with school districts can be found around the United States. The University of Arizona has started "The Pathways Program" in Tucson, which partners with local school districts to offer graduate programs to bachelor's level practitioners in school and is now attempting to expand their program to include the other training programs in the state. They are considering adding graduate level slots for "grow your own" students. Arizona State University (ASU) has a partnership with the Arizona Department of Education to provide a part-time master's degree program for speech-language pathologists working in the public schools.

An interesting program has been developed by the University of Maryland and the Montgomery County Schools. This is an example of how the county schools saved money by using students to assist with other students and well as using parents in the classroom. They have partnered to produce additional master's students each year. Students are selected from applicants who commit themselves to working in a school setting. They can be selected for a scholarship covering all expenses in exchange for them working for the Montgomery County Schools. William Paterson University in Wayne, New Jersey, partners with their school district to assist with teacher shortages as does the University of Northern Colorado and the University of Colorado at Boulder. Texas Tech University and the Lubbock Independent School

District partnership employ junior and senior level students as "clerks," while they work toward a bachelor's degree (American Speech-Language Hearing Association, 2011).

The scholarship notion fostered by the Montgomery County Schools is a model that can be emulated by any school district. It demonstrates how both the students and the schools can save money and provide learning opportunities by working together in a symbiotic relationship.

Each school/university partnership is unique. Alicia Haller (2011), of the Illinois State Board of Education states "Learning to work in new ways means that the member organizations of the partnership cannot simply continue to do business as usual. Partnership work, therefore, is labor-intensive, creative, and messy. It takes time to iron out the bugs" (Haller, and Brown 2011).

▶ Adopt-A-School

One informal program that met the needs of Regan Elementary School in Clovis, California took the latter approach and met with some success. The university offered incidental consulting, mentoring and coaching to this new Central Valley school with a new principal and a new staff put together from a list of teacher volunteers in the district. This created an instant need for team building and vision development and clarification. The university helped the staff in developing these basics by becoming a member of their leadership team. In this case three faculty members representing the teacher education and educational administration departments of National University met with the principal and his leadership team in the morning before school started once each month for six months until the school was up and running. The faculty was introduced to the school through a student teacher who was assigned to this elementary school of highly diverse staff and student body. The faculty shared research on team building and the results of the Phi Delta Kappa/Gallup poll on the public's perception of public school education. Additional meetings were held via e-mails and teleconferencing. Professional memberships were suggested such as the National Teachers Association and Phil Delta Kappa. The student teacher assigned was already a member of the Association of California School Administrators Student Charter group. The student teacher was also recruited to be a member of the leadership teams giving the group a student perspective on the various education issues discussed.

The results of this initiative resulted in increased communication with the university and a cost savings for the school by not having to hire an educational consultant to help in their transition. Time was saved by teachers not having to travel to conferences to stay up-to-date on current research. The university benefited by having positive exposure to a large number of prospective master's candidates.

In the San Diego area, a private school invited the University in, also at the request of a student teacher. Here the principal was interested in offering more individualized programs. A cross-functional team of teachers from the university met to develop a strategy for the administrator and then met with the staff from the private school, introducing them to differentiated instruction and some specific computer models. This relationship has opened the door to more dialogue with the teachers and administrator and given the university an opportunity to promote their programs as well.

▶ Memoranda of Agreement

More formal partnerships have been developed with school districts and universities in the form of Memoranda of Agreement or Understanding (MOAs or MOUs). Here the university and the school district enter into an agreement of mutual support for a student or program. Most often this is used for student intern assignments or cohort classes that are formed on the school or district premises. Another type of agreement is one that is signed by the school representative, a university representative and the student. These representatives are the student's supervisors and the agreement states that the university and school will work with the student for a specific period of time on a specific program offering the student practical experience in that particular program area.

▶ E-Mentoring

With the advent of the internet, new opportunities have opened in the area of guidance and counseling. One such opportunity started by the Fresno Unified School District in the Central Valley of California, is called "E-Mentoring." Here a university professor is matched with a junior or senior high school student and meets on a regular basis over the internet to discuss any issues the student wishes. The mentor is carefully screened and finger printed by the county and the coordinator may arrange a face-to-face meeting in order to get a good match. In some cases, this meeting takes place over the Internet using SKYPE or another video conferencing platform. Mentors are available 24/7 to assist the mentee with any of their issues. This has worked well and is now in its fourth year of operation.

▶ Linking Theory and Practice

When universities partner with schools and school districts, they are bridging the gap between the schools and "the ivory tower." Sarah Pirtle, the co-editor and primary author of *Partnership Education in Action*, contends that "Partnership processes can help provide building blocks of healthy experiences of nurturing respectful human interactions." She goes on to say in her introduction of a "partnership model" that any social situation can be structured either to encourage "linking" and power *with* others, or structured to encourage "ranking" and power *over* others. As we apply this to education, our partnership can be described as the partnership becoming increasingly conscious of the entire group and the way we affect each other and in turn, help the school to be increasingly conscious of the whole community. Partnership education tends to be positive and fosters a culture of success in learning rather than the fear of failure. A partnership is a process of teaching and learning that is based on mutual respect (Pirtle, 2002).

▶ Technology in Partnerships

In any partnership experience, **timely interaction is critical in making it a success**. Technology has been and continues to be, instrumental in fostering this communication to multiple parties at lightning speed. From e-mails to video conferencing, technology has enhanced as well as facilitated the process of idea exchange.

As stated earlier, e-mail is being used in the E-mentoring program in the Central Valley of California matching university faculty to students in middle school and high school. Prior to the writing of this paper, as far as technology is concerned, this medium has been the preferred method in communicating to our adolescents. According to Dr. Ronald Berk of The Johns Hopkins University, these adolescents fall in the category of the network generation youth called "Net Geners." These students and now teachers and administrators, fall in the age group between seven and twenty-eight years of age. They were born into the computer age between 1982 and 2003. This includes students from the second grade through graduate school and our young administrators. He states that nearly ninety million or one-third of the United States population fall into this group (Berk, 2010). E-mail is being replaced by text messages sent via cell phones.

When partnering, the participants must take into consideration the backgrounds of the partner members. For the most part, university members are anywhere from ten to twenty or more years older than those in the school district. These differences, of course, will vary from school to school. With this in mind, from the university point-of-view, we need to take into consideration the best way to reach our targets, those being students, teachers, parents, and administrators in the public and private school sectors.

The Net Gener's world is focused around social media including Facebook, MySpace, and Twitter. They use iPods, iPhones, iPads, and MP3 players. To the extent that university faculty recognizes these media will determine their effectiveness in relating to this market and their success as a significant and credible partner. They need to recognize that over ninety percent of the network generation is involved in the following:

- Computers
- Smart phones
- The Internet for homework
- Search engines like Google
- News Websites
- Multitask while texting (Berk, 2010)

E-mail

Electronic mail may be the most familiar technology to all computer users. Participants can send and receive email, cut and paste, and forward email. They can search the web as a recreational or research tool. This is a widely used vehicle for district, school, and university communication. It may include:

- Communications to students, staff and community
- Requests for data, information, survey or input
- Responses to complaints
- Information to the community as to an event
- Problems to be solved.

Nu-FAST and Beyond

National University in La Jolla, California, has taken E-mail to another level. Here, faculty may open an account and have discussions in an asynchronous manner through discussion boards. These discussions can be open to faculty, students, as well as selected members of the community. It has been used with committees that involve members from across the state and nation. In some ways, it resembles a Blackboard or E-College online text chat for participants to text their opinions on various topics. Real-time video has been added with programs for classes such as Class Live Pro and Adobe Connect. Similar to SKYPE, this platform enables participants to see and talk with each other in live chat sessions. In working with schools, Nu-FAST enables participants to enter topic discussions at will, making participation convenient for classroom teachers, administrators and university faculty as well. The Adobe Connect provides a more personal interaction in that you can use webcams and have immediate responses with both voice and video in synchronous communication. An added feature is that all of these **video sessions can be recorded** and played back at a future date giving more flexibility to this communication tool.

This advanced technology is free or inexpensive for computer users with access to microphones, video cameras, and Internet. Additional uses for partnerships include:

- Conducting team collaboration across two locations
- Hosting a remote guest speaker
- Conducting personnel interviews
- Reporting current educational research

Partnering members can access web conferencing in multiple ways depending on the particular situation. SKYPE offers free web conferencing if participants use http://skype.com.

▶ Webpage or Website

Most school districts have websites describing their schools with mission and vision statements. Most sites include a calendar of events, highlights of the past year and directions on how to get in contact with the membership. It is also a place to inform the public of any partnerships that have been formed or upcoming meeting invitations. In some cases, school site councils have invited universities to present their current research and open the meetings to the public.

There are a number of Internet sites that will provide faculty and students with free electronic space for meetings and projects. Over the past few years the webpage has been replaced by other social media sites such as Facebook, MySpace, and Twitter. These media meet the Net Gener's need for instant feedback and cyber interaction.

▶ Blog

A blog is an abbreviated term for 'web log.". It is text-based, and an ongoing commentary of information. The responses are displayed in reverse chronological order with the most recent information posted first. The blog may include:

- Announcements
- Reports
- Shared reflections
- Discussion topics
- The posting of a professional challenge
- Inviting collaborative solutions to current issues.

There are free Internet sites available to faculty for setting up a blog. They are easy to use by both faculty and students. One free website is http://blogspot.com.

▶ Podcast

A podcast is "audio content" made available to the user on the Internet. Participants can use their computers, and/or other devices including iPods and MP3 players. Listeners can access the audio content at their convenience. Uses of podcasts include:

- Audio communication to students, staff and community
- Standard messages, directions or welcome announcements
- Short staff development audio trainings
- Audio summary of procedure, new laws, or new information.
- There are several free podcast websites available to faculty. One such website is http://mypodcast.com.

Electronic Portfolio

Our schools and universities rely on accreditation for their survival. Agencies such as the Western Association of Schools and Colleges (WASC) look for documentation that demonstrates collaboration, transparency, and shared governance. The electronic portfolio is one way to capture the district, school, or university activities in this area. Specifically electronic portfolios may include:

- Minutes made by partnership committees
- Advisor committee meeting minutes
- Documents
- Resumes
- Videos
- WebPages

The electronic portfolio is an easy way to capture and document the agencies activities and supports the assessment of their programs. It is one of the best options for storage, editing, retrieval, and sharing of information (Orozco, 1999).

IRIS Camera

Assuming that funding will not be available in the future to support the supervision and evaluation of interns in the San Diego and Riverside area school districts, National University's School of Education has begun to explore cost saving measures. With the help of a grant by the California Commission on Teacher Credentialing, they have purchased ten remote controlled observation cameras called IRIS Cameras. These cameras can send and receive as well as record audio and video from the classroom to any offsite location. Its purpose is to record student teacher and interns working toward a teaching credential in live classroom settings. The University Supervisor can then critique the lesson with the student intern and his or her school supervisor after the observed class lesson. It can also be used to record best practices to be shared with other students and teachers for staff development purposes. Institutional Review Board (IRB) permission was required along with school district, parent, student and supervising teacher release forms being signed (Holt & Naffziger, 2010).

Any or all of these Internet opportunities exist for partners to choose depending on the purpose for the partnership and the nature of the participants involved. They have become even more attractive with the austerity initiatives being put in place by state and local governments.

Partnership Advantages in Leadership Preparation Programs

Educational administrative programs at the university level focus on many categories in their capstone courses. One area that seems to be overlooked is that of outreach to assist school districts within their service area. If candidates were to focus on the real issues facing school district administrators and teachers, they would gain the practical experience needed when they become the instructional leaders of a school or school district. Attention to this area could provide evidence to university mission statements such as "…engaging in collaborative community service" (2011, National University Catalog).

► Cost Savings

As a result of using the resources of higher education, and the technology available, school districts can save money and time, by not hiring expensive educational consultants, as well as solving problems in real time. By using the technologies available such as podcasts and video conferencing, participants from all institutions can avoid the costs of travel and lodging. There is a good deal of money to be saved in time alone by using the internet conveying data to help with the decision making.

► Discussion and Conclusion

Inherent in a partnership is the concept of a team. Teaming provides shared governance and can reduce stress on the team leader or school administrator in charge. Andrews et al. (2007) states "The potential to share leadership functions with peers and colleagues reduces the cognitive, emotional, and effort-related strains on individual leaders are among the compelling reasons to create leadership (or partnership) teams in the first place" (Andrews, 2007).

School districts and universities have been working together for years. Today's economic pressures have made these relationships even more attractive. Partnership education will be more a part of our consciousness as we see the benefits and rewards in the growth of student achievement. As was cited in this paper, technology is helping to facilitate connecting schools and school districts with universities. Researcher Paul Murrell (1998) wrote "Joint productive work means working out the details of partnership without a blueprint or template to guide these deliberations. However, partnerships can learn from the work of others who have been doing this type of work in their communities in recent years" (Murrell, 1998). University schools of education are bringing educational research to school districts to assist in solving their curricular and financial problems. In helping PreK-12 schools, universities are fulfilling their mission as well. Technology is the vehicle that can accelerate the communication, but it is the knowledge, and caring of students by both parties in a synergistically focused manner that will make the difference in a child's education.

Discussion Questions

1. How can educational leaders increase collective learning and innovation in our public and private schools?

2. To what extent do leaders have influence on learning and innovation in organizations?

3. What is organizational culture and how does it influence the change process?

4. What are some guidelines to help leaders implement change?

5. Why do efforts in organizational change often fail?

6. What are some guidelines to help educational leaders implement and sustain change?

Activity

Develop a plan of action to reach out to a university, school, or school district to develop a relationship or partnership in research or problems solving. Include a timeline with who is responsible and when the activity is to happen. Include an assessment instrument to be administered at the end of the school year.

Additional Website Resource

www.pta.org/familyschoolpartnerships.asp

www.amazon.com/teachingpartnerships

www.answers.com/topicational

Background of the Author

See editors' biographies.

References

American Speech – Language and Hearing Association. (April 2011). *Model Collaborative University and School District Partnerships*. Retrieved from htpt://www.asha.org/advocacy/state

Andrews, K. T., Ganz, M., Baggetta, M., Han, H., & Lim, C., (2007). *Leadership, Membership, and Voice: Civic Associations That Work*. Unpublished manuscript.

Berk, R. A. (2010). How do you leverage the latest technologies, including Web 2.0 tools, in your classroom: *International Journal of Technology in Teaching and Learning*, 6(1), 1-13.

Chatman, J., & Flynn, F., J. (2001). "The Indulgence of Demographic Composition on the Emergence and Consequences of Cooperative Norms in Groups." *Academy of Management Journal* 44(5), 956-974.

Cialdini, R. B. (2001). Influence: *The Psychology of Persuasion*. 4th ed. Boston: Allyn and Bacon.

Eisler, R. (2002)." Partnership Education for the 21st Century" *Encounter Journal* 15 (3), 5-12.

Frank, R. H., Gilovich, T., & Regan, D. T. (1993). "Does Studying Economics Inhibit Cooperation?". *Journal of Economic Perspectives* 7 (2), 159-171.

Holt, S., & Naffziger, L. (2010). *A Pilot Project Using Remote Observation Equipment to View, Interact, and Evaluate Candidates in Clinical Practice Activities*. American Council on Rural Special Education Conference. Albuquerque, New Mexico.

Haller, A., & Brown, K. (2011). Creating a School/University Partnership, paper presented to the Illinois State Board of Education. Springfield, Illinois.

Kotter, J. P., & Heskett, J. L. (2002). *Corporate Culture and Performance*. New York: Free Press.

National University, (2011). Catalog, *Mission Statement*. P.20, La Jolla, California.

Murrell, P. (1998). *Like stone soup: The role of professional development schools in the renewal of urban schools*. Washington, D.C.: AACTE.

Orozco, L. (2009). "*Leadership Innovation: Preparing leaders through technology in authentic assessment*." Paper read at the California Association of Professors of Educational Administration Fall Conference. Los Angeles, California.

Managing Educational Leadership and Online Teaching in a Changing and Diverse Technological Society

Dr. Dan Cunniff, Associate Professor, National University, La Jolla, California
dcunniff@nu.edu

ISLLC Standard 3: Ensuring management of the organization, operations, and resources for a safe, efficient, and effective learning environment

▶ Abstract

Leadership is something that we know when we see it, yet when asked to define leadership we need to stop and think about leaders we have known or read about as well as our own experiences regarding this term. For the purpose of this paper, the author has narrowed this to educational leadership in the area of teaching and administration. The discussion included a description of leadership, when it occurs, where we can find it, why it happens and how does it happen. The managing and the training of leaders are the people and events that surround the leader providing support, guidance, and oversight in the form of organizational parameters. The writer showed that research indicates there is a gap in the dissemination of information technology as a leadership tool and a challenge in communicating with the various cultures inclusive in our ever-changing educational environments. The notion of additional leadership training is needed in technology for school district staff development as well as the courses we teach in our educational administration programs in order to be competitive in this rapidly changing world.

What is Leadership?

The role of a leader has had multiple definitions and connotations throughout history. The writer uses the definition "influencing others to take action, recognizing the action and reporting on the results." Although this definition can include multiple organizations, the author will direct this paper toward the educational arena including the use of technology and dealing with cultural diversity.

Leadership is power. It inflates the ego, creates perceptions, and brings about expectations. It is a dynamic for bringing about change, as well as instilling confidence and security. Moreover, it is the ability to influence people and can alter the course of history personally, locally, nationally and internationally. It is central to the success of any institution.

Philosophers have discussed the concept of leadership for centuries. Dialogues on the topic can be found in works of Plato and Caesar. According to Bass (1981), leadership is a robust concept that "occurs universally among all people regardless of culture, whether they are isolated Indian villagers, Eurasian steppe nomads, or Polynesian fisher folk" (Bass, 1981).

There are multiple theories of leadership. Included are suggestions of the "Great Man" theory. As an example, without Moses, the Jewish nation would have remained enslaved in Egypt, and without Churchill, the British would have lost to the Axis Powers in World War II. Some trait theories state that leaders are empowered with superior qualities and set them apart from followers. Environmental theories contend that leaders emerge as a result of time, place, and circumstance. No matter what theory is used to explain it, leadership is strongly linked to the effective function of complex organizations throughout the centuries as well as more simplified endeavors undertaken by individuals (Marzano, 2005).

The Great Man theory is evident in today's business world with mixed public reaction. This popular leadership notion gained its popularity in 1979 with Lee Iacocca leading Chrysler, Jack Welch heading General Electric, Microsoft's chair Bill Gates, and Berkshire Hathaway's leader Warren Buffet, all of whom became celebrities and are among the world's richest men.

On the negative side of leadership, Bernie Madoff stands out. This former broker and investment advisor developed a $50 billion Ponzi scheme causing thousands of investors to lose large sums of money. According to Greg O. McCrary, a former special agent with the FBI, who spent years working with criminal behavioral profiles, Madoff has the characteristics of a psychopath who lies, manipulates, deceives, and has feelings of grandiosity and callousness toward his victims (Creswell, 2009). Jeffrey Skilling's criminality with Enron is now a classic case of lying about the company's profits and concealing debts causing the collapse of the corporation. Maurice "Hank" Greenberg left AIG floundering in 2005 and in need of a bailout. Many of the aforementioned leaders considered themselves irreplaceable. Perhaps these leaders of industry were unaware of France's Charles de Gaulle's statement "The graveyards are full of indispensable men" (Collingwood, 2009). **In the business world, boards of directors usually manage the Chief Executive Officers. In education, it can be graduate councils, faculty senates, boards of education, school site councils, and county, state and federal agencies.**

Types of Leadership

Educators are interested in leadership that pertains to schools and the teaching/learning process. School-based or site-based leadership empowers staff to create conditions in schools that facilitate improvement, innovation and continuous improvement (David, 1989). The activities and management of these leaders are monitored by individuals and groups such as school boards, principals, superintendents, parent teacher organizations, and school-site councils.

Shared leadership distributes responsibilities, but accountability will often rest with the top administrator of the school, organization, or district. A true school-based management (SBM) empowers the principal and professional staff members with wide latitude in improving the effectiveness of the teaching/learning environment. According to Elmore (2000), teachers would be encouraged to introduce improvements that directly impact learning that in the past was the authority of upper administration. This includes budget responsibilities, personnel selection, curriculum, and program evaluations. This type of structure is a departure from the traditional leadership model and can have a positive or negative impact on the school depending on how the concept is approached (Elmore, 2000). Care must be taken to ensure that there is adequate information available to the staff and training for professional development included in order for the staff to make informed decisions. Additionally, a key part of this system is that a significant amount of time be provided to staff for planning and development, as well as a reward system set up to recognize improved performance (Odden & Wohlstetter, 1994). This does not mean that the administration can abdicate responsibility. On the contrary, it increases the need for effective leadership from those who serve in leadership roles.

The chances of success are increased when school-based management is used and the staff is given guidelines and the time to acquire new knowledge and share ideas as well and plan, implement, and report ideas on how to improve student learning. An important component of this system involves rewards such as money for professional development, materials, and reimbursements for extra time, recognition meals, plaques, reduced teaching loads, and public recognition (Cunningham & Gresso, 1993).

In the September, 2009 *Phi Delta Kappan* article "It Can Be Done, It's Being Done, and Here's How," Karin Chenoweth wrote that many schools have broken through the pattern of low achievement for poor, black, and Hispanic students by getting their teacher out of isolation and giving them time to work together in collaborative teams, and teaching what they want students to know, not assuming that parents will fill in the gaps (Chenoweth, 2009).

President Obama was quoted in a speech to the Hispanic Chamber of Commerce, "**From the moment students enter a school, the most important factor in their success in not the color of the skin or the income of their parents; it's the person standing at the front of the classroom**" (Bushaw & McNee, 2009).

The SBM system is in keeping with Thomas Friedman's contention in his book *The World is Flat*, stating "hierarchies are being challenged from below or transforming themselves from top-down structures into more horizontal and collaborative ones" (Friedman, 2005). Extending this line of thinking, universities are being challenged by students who grew up with the computer and by new delivery programs that are based in distance programs such as online classes. This knowledge and these ideas are brought into school systems as these students become teachers and administrators, thus opening the door to new forms of communication and instant messaging. Couple this with our increasing foreign populations with their diverse cultures and we have both a challenge and an opportunity to educate and communicate wide segments of our population worldwide. Friedman believes that there is an emergence of completely new business and organizational models, and new social and political models as well. With this in mind, the universities and school districts must be able to reorganize and reconnect with a world that has become smaller and flatter. He goes on to say that greater use of distance learning is one possible way to reconnect to the new world (Friedman 2005).

Online Leadership

As far as online technology leadership in education is concerned, there has been minimal research conducted on the effectiveness of complete online degree programs. Most findings have shown little or no differences in the effectiveness of the instruction be it online or face-to-face (Neuhauser, 2002).

Traditional methods of online instruction are constantly being modified with the advent of new technology. Integrating Internet video conferencing has emerged as well as the hybrid concept whereby classes are held both on site as well as online. These methods have also accelerated learning and condensed courses in what in the past was a semester course into a month long course. **The class leadership can be shared via online presentations via Skype or through traditional platforms such as Blackboard or E-College.** Learning theories, such as Howard Gardner's Multiple Intelligences (Gardner, 1993) advocate multimedia instructional approaches to enhance learning. Multimedia is the combination of the various types of media such as video, sound, text, graphics, and color to better communicate and display the characteristics of a thought, function, principle, or concept. Online lends itself to his ideas and affords a wide variety of ways to transmit learning.

Clicking on a word or phrase can now hyperlink a student to any place on earth. When teaching online, the instructional leaders must be aware of the need to translate where necessary, the time zones reached, and the technology available to the learners. Many areas of the world lower socioeconomic areas do not have internet available. In some cases, if it is available, people cannot afford the expense.

Online instruction opens the doors to a diverse population from a multitude of cultures. Limited-English speaking students often gravitate to this format where there are limited speaking opportunities and it is easier for them to text and write assignments without oral presentations. The instructional leaders must be cognizant of this as they conduct their classes.

When the instructional leader puts in place an academic program at an accelerated pace working with adults, every possible proven instructional technique that enhances learning, and reduces time required, should be used. Presenting lessons to learners from a variety of cultures, who are working, many with families, and have a finite amount of time to earn a living while taking classes, instructors have an obligation to expedite and enhance learning as much as possible (Beckwith & Cunniff, 2009).

Facing severe budget cuts have forced universities to look at more efficient ways to deliver instruction. In 2009, the University of California's 10 campuses discovered they could not educate as many students as before and proposed opening an 11th campus, online. Dean of the law school at Berkeley, Christopher Edley Jr., is very interested in hearing more about online programs and says, "In all seriousness, I feel some sense of urgency about this for fiscal reasons." (Chronicle, 2009).

Leadership Theories

Other popular theories of leadership with a focus on education include instructional leadership, situational leadership, servant leadership, transformational leadership, transactional leadership, and continuous improvement. Several of these have been a spinoff of business models used worldwide.

The instructional leadership model has been the most popular over the past two decades. It is one of the most frequently mentioned educational leadership concepts in America and yet not well defined (Leithwood, Jantzi, and Steinbach, 1999). This term is often used when defining the school principal's role and main function. Researchers have described this leadership role of one who is a resource provider, instructional resource, communicator, and is visibly present (Smith and Andrews, 1998). Some would also add availability to this list.

In 1991, Paul Hersey and Kenneth Blanchard coined the term "situational leadership." The concept focuses on the flexibility of leaders and their willingness and ability to adapt their style to the needs of the situation. Their concept included four styles involving telling, participating, selling, and delegating. They suggest that the effective leader is one who is skilled in all four styles and knows when they should be applied (Blanchard, Carew, & Parisi-Carew, 1991).

The desire to help others, or servant leadership, was the motivation for researcher Robert Greenleaf whose work became key components of other theorists such as Covey (1992); Elmore (2000); and Spillane, Halverson, & Diamond (2001). Here, the servant leader is in contact with all aspects of the organization and nurtures those within, understands personal needs, is an active listener, provides resources, and helps to develop skills within the organization (Greenleaf, 1970:1977).

Transformational leadership is a term that has its roots in the work of James Burns in 1978, who is considered the founder of modern leadership theory that was modified by Kenneth Leithwood in 1994. This concept states that the school leader must attend to the needs of individual staff members, help staff members think of old problems in new ways, communicate high expectations for students and teachers alike, and demonstrate through personal accomplishments a model for the behavior of teachers. By doing this, the leader demonstrates individual consideration, intellectual stimulation, inspirational motivation, and becomes an idealized influence in his or her organization (Leithwood, 1994).

Transactional leadership is defined by Burns as "trading one thing for another (quid pro quo), whereas transformational leadership is more focused on change" (Burns, 1978). In more detailed terms, Bass and Avolio (1994), outline three types of transactional leadership: management-by exception-passive, management-by exception-active, and constructive transactional. Other researchers have further explained the concept in that management-by exception-passive involves setting standards, then waiting for problems to arise before acting, thus keeping the status quo. Those who choose management-by-exception-active watch everything, pay attention to issues, set standards, and monitor behavior. Constructive transactional leadership sets goals, provides clarity, provides feedback, and gives rewards. A characteristic of this style is that followers are invited into the management process and followers generally focus on achieving expected organizational goals (Sosik and Dionne, 1997).

Continuous improvement and total quality management are closely related. Edward Deming (1986) is considered the founder of total quality management (TQM) because of his work after World War II in helping Japan restore its manufacturing foundation and in the United States, for working with Ford and Xerox to improve their overall product and service quality. Continuous improvement is a term that came from the Japanese word *kaizen*, meaning continual and incremental improvement in all aspects of the organization. Deming said "a leader must invite continuous improvement into the organization and keep it alive by keeping the goals of the organization up front in the minds of employees and judging the effectiveness of the organization in terms of these goals"(Deming, 1982). The Deming award is given to organizations in Japan for outstanding quality reflecting Edward Deming's beliefs. The Malcolm Baldridge award for quality products and services produced by organizations in the United States came about as a result of the work accomplished through programs of continuous improvement and total quality management.

Technology Diversity and Culture

Gutierrez and Rogoff (2003) contend that culture is dynamic, situational, and historic. **Diversity and culture include an individual's ethnicity, as well as his or her geographic location, gender, generation, age, religion, group memberships, historical context, and level of education**. A key notion in any discussion of culture issues in school settings was described by Bensman (2000) who stated "cultural interchanges within the school setting and parental consciousness outside of the classroom provide the way to facilitate student success."

There are several barriers that parents and students from diverse backgrounds must overcome to increase communications. The lack of English is one of them as is the lack of confidence. Past negative school experiences is another. Bermudez and Marques (1996) cite that work interference is another key barrier that can get in the way of good home-school partnerships.

Mark Prensky (2001) studies the students who were born into the digital age and lists a variety of digital toys and tools that have flooded the digital age student since birth. Toys, tools, and gadgets such as music players, phones, games, video cams and thousands of related applications are second nature to those born in the computer age. Many of these same devices intimidate those born prior to the digital age. Prensky coined the terms "Digital Natives" and Digital Immigrants." He also wrote **about the biggest problem in education today is that our immigrant instructors fail to engage the digital natives in their classes**. Many bring this mentality to the creation of classes and programs that bore the natives. Prensky goes on to say that we need to confront this diversity issue of the native-immigrant gap or we should just forget about educating digital natives who in essence, will educate themselves (Prensky, 2001).

The digital natives are considered leaders as Internet experts, and in the early days of the dotcom boom, showed a bias toward the young over those with long experience in the organization. That bias for youth angered many mature adult leaders who thought that it was unfair that these young people were getting so rich so fast. Older administrators and instructors must get younger in spirit to fit in and in today's fast-paced era of technology, must be willing to take direction by those who are their juniors and adjust their leadership style (Kanter, 2001).

It is time for universities and educators at all levels to address this issue in our programs and staff development training. Educators need to work with students and parents in this process so that we can learn to talk to the digital age youth in their language. Timothy Van Slyke (2007) believes it is not necessary to change completely our traditional approach to teaching and administration, but we definitely need to incorporate digital age applications into our methods of teaching and communicating to our public (Van Slyke, 2007).

Technology Available to Leaders

It is not possible to list all the technology that is available to today's educational leaders. By the time this is read, a new application and device will be on the market. Some common technologies are already embedded within our daily routines such as cell phones, computers, and electronic calendars. **What seems common to the educator may be a mystery to a parent or student from another culture**. It will be up to the educator to educate his or her student and the public, in order to obtain the communication needed for a successful program. The following is a list of common technologies available to our educational leaders, those that manage them and their students, faculty and community:

- E-mail
- Laptops
- Storage Clouds
- Pads
- Pods
- iPhones
- Blogs
- Search Engines
- News Websites
- Podcasts
- Tweets
- Video Conferencing
- Community Networks

Educational administration credential courses have been taught online for years. What has not been taught effectively is how to use technology for administrative use. Brooks-Young states that "In essence, the focus of educational technology preparation programs has long been on instructional technology and teacher education rather than technology for administrative use" (Brooks-Young, 2002). **There has not been enough focus on the development of pre-service and in-service administration programs**. Many colleges and university schools of education have not been keeping up-to-date with the new technology available to our future administrative leaders and the challenges they will face, not the least of which is the digital divide. In many ways, the digital divide separates the haves and have not's when it comes to being educated and having the tools of technology. Our university administrative programs and school district staff development training can go a long way in closing this gap.

Overcoming Barriers when Working with Students and Parents of Diverse Backgrounds

Apart from the tradition methods of potlucks and international fair days, researchers have concluded that administrators must have a plan for communication with parents and students and should use both soft and hard skills in their approach. Technology is not enough. Diverse students and family members need to be made welcome and encouraged through positive interactions. Boethel (2003) suggests meeting families away from the physical school campus and using the multiple forms of communication described in this paper in the multiple languages of the school. He goes on to say that administrators should use a variety of volunteers to talk with students and parents about what they believe about education and specifically, what they believe about their school and their particular teaching/learning environment.

Navigating New Waters

In many ways, history does repeat itself, in that we are all influenced by our environment, upbringing, our religion, our politics, heroes, media, and customs. The fact is **the change cycle has become much different and more intense**. Society is changing, and these changes are having a significant impact on teaching and learning. Children of today and tomorrow are and will grow up with a very different relationship to authority and self-control. Our children are overindulged and lack discipline. Young people today show less deference toward authority and more than nine out of ten Americans surveyed agreed that young people's lack of respect for adults is a problem: more than half see it as a significant problem (Johnson, 2003).

During and after World War II, there were a significant number of "latch key" kids who would come home after school to an empty house because both parents were working for the war effort. Today, more and more children are growing up "home alone" for other reasons. **The two-parent, single-wage earner family is fast becoming a thing of the past**. The downturn of the economy and the high rates of divorce have curtailed the two-parent family. Large numbers of mothers now have full-time jobs outside the home. A landmark study of American adolescence by Mihaly Csikszentmihalyi and Reed Larson, found that teenagers spent only about 5% of their free time with their parents, and most of that time was spent with their mother (1984, Csikszentmihalyi & Larson).

Yesterday's children grew up with the radio and comic books. Today's and tomorrow's children are and will be growing up in an age of instant access to information, knowing more at an earlier age than their counterparts of a few decades ago, and they are more adept at and motivated to learn new technologies than most adults. Additionally, **they will be working at jobs that do not exist today** and will have global competition for those positions.

Freidman stated, "Clearly, it is now possible for more people than ever before to collaborate and compete in real time with more other people on more different kinds of work from more different corners of the planet and on a more equal footing than at any previous tie in the history of the world" (Friedman, 2005). Computers, iPhones, iPads, e-mail, networks, clouds, teleconferencing, and new software are all connecting the knowledge centers of the world together, opening the doors for new forms of leadership in the teaching/learning arena.

▶ Conclusion

Increasing training in technology per se is not enough for an existing or future school administrator seeking to increase effective communication within his or her community. **There needs to be a greater understanding of state standards** and the opportunities in school leadership preparation programs, as well as staff development in school districts, to discuss diversity in general, and race, poverty, language, and class specifically. Students and staff need to be made more aware of the challenges currently being faced by school administrators and how they can be an advocate for the needs of diverse groups in our changing demographics, including an understanding of students' and parents' values, beliefs, and practices in each individual culture. The advent of iPhones and iPads have revolutionized the communications market. As they become more affordable and user friendly, they will become commonplace in our society. Using technology is one way to communicate, gaining the community trust through a shared vision, professional growth, and collaboration within each cultural context is the avenue to lasting and meaningful relationships. Managing educational leaders traditionally has been the responsibility of school boards.

Today's and tomorrow's leaders will have many more stakeholders observing and becoming involved in decision making. Technology has provided us with instant global communication, observations, and evaluations. In the end, it will be the educational leader who will be managing him or her-self, being held accountable for decisions made as they respond to the changing cycles that are and will impact the field of educational management.

Discussion Questions

1. Using your school or a school in which you are familiar, how do you see the educational leadership being managed?

2. How does an educational leader go about identifying the stakeholders necessary for collaboration?

3. How can the educational leader use technology in sharing the school's vision?

4. Integrating technology into the curriculum is proving to be a major problem in many school districts. How do you see this problem being resolved? What role does online instruction play in education?

5. When working with non-English speaking parents, what is the best way to gain their support and involvement?

6. Schools can be described and analyzed as social systems. How do you define a social system? Who are the major participants in this system? What are their roles, if any in planning and implementing programs?

Leadership Activity

Develop an Action Plan to bring a diverse parent population into the planning of an educational program. Consider the cultural population, their past experience with the system and those who are influential in the target community.

Background of the Author

References

Bass, B. M., & Avolio, B. J. (1994). *Improving organizational effectiveness through transformational leadership.* Thousand Oaks, CA: Sage.

Bass, B. M. (1981). *Stoydilli Handbook of Leadership: A survey of theory and record.* New York: Free Press.

Beckwith, E., & Cunniff, D. (2009). Integrating internet video conferencing. Techniques and online delivery systems with hybrid classes to enhance student interactive and learning in accelerated programs. *The Journal of College Teaching and Learning.* 6 (4), 25. July/August.

Beju, M. (2009, August 7). Online Campus could solve problems at University of California, a dean says, *The Chronicle of Higher Education.* LV (43).

Blanchard, K. H., Carero, J., & Parisi-Carew, E. (1991). *The one minute manager builds high performing teams.* New York: William Morrow.

Bensman, D. (2000). *Building school-family partnerships in a South Bronx classroom.* New York: NCREST.

Bermudez. A., & Marquez, J. (1996). An examination of a four-way collaborative to increase parental involvement in schools. *The Journal of Educational Issues of Language Minority Students*, 16 (6), 1-16.

Brooks-Young, S. (2002). *Making technology standards work for you: a guide for school administrators.* Eugene, OR: ISTE.

Burns, J. M. (1978). *Leadership.* New York: Harper & Row.

Bushaw, W.J., & McNee, J.A. (2009). Americans speak out: Are educators and policy makers listening. *Phi Delta Kappan*, September, 2009, 14.

Csikszentmihalyi, M., & Larson, R. (1984). *Being Adolescent.* New York: Basic Books.

Chenoweth, K. (2009). It can be done, it's being done, and here's how. *Phi Delta Kappan*, September, 2009, 41.

Collingwood, H. (2009, June). Do CEO's matter. *The Atlantic.* New York, NY., 54-60.

Creswell, (2009, January 24), The talented Mr. Madoff. New York: *The New York Times.* NY.

Cunningham, W. G., & Gresso, D. W. (1993). *Cultural leadership: the culture of excellence in education.* Boston: Allyn and Bacon.

Deming, W. E. (1982). *Out of crisis.* Cambridge, MA: MIT Center for Advanced Engineering.

Friedman, T. L. (2005). *The world is flat.* New York: Farrar, Strauss, and Giroux.

Gardner, H. (2003). *Multiple intelligence: the theory in practice.* New York, NY: Harper Collins Publishers.

Greenleaf, R. (1970). *The servant as leader.* Indianapolis, IN: Robert K. Greenleaf Center for Servant Leadership.

Greenleaf, R. (1977). *Servant leadership: a journey into the nature of legitimate power and greatness.* New York: Paulist Press.

Gutierrez, K., & Rogoff, B. (2003). Cultural ways of learning: Individual traits or repertoires of practice. *Educational Researcher*, 32(5),19-25.

Johnson, J., & Duffett, A. (2003). *Where we are now: 12 things you need to know about public opinion and public schools*. New York: Public Agenda Foundation.

Kanter, R. M. (2001). *Evolve!: Succeeding in the digital culture of tomorrow*. Boston, MA: Harvard Business School Press.

Leithwood, K. (1994). Leadership for school restructuring. *Educational Administration Quarterly*, 30(4), 498-518.

Leithwood, K., Jantzi, D., & Steinbeck, R. (1999), *Changing leadership for changing times*. Philadelphia, PA: Open University Press.

Marzano, R., Waters, T., & McNulty, B. (2005). *School Leadership that Works: From research to results.*

Neuhauser, C. (2002). Learning style and effectiveness of online and face-to-face instruction. *The American Journal of Distance Education*. Alexandria, VA. 16 (2), 99-113.

Prensky, M. (2001, October). Digital natives, digital immigrants. *On the Horizon*. NCB University Press. 9.

Sosik, J. J., & Dionne, S. D. (1997). Leadership styles and Deming's behavior factors. *Journal of Business and Psychology*. 11 (4). 447-462.

Van Slyke, T. (2007, May/June). Digital natives, digital immigrants: some thoughts from the generation gap. Commentary in *Interact Magazine*.

The Higher Education Leadership Personal Skill Set for the Twenty-first Century

Joseph M. Marron, EdD, National University, La Jolla, California

ISLLC Standard 1: Facilitating the development, articulation, implementation, and stewardship of a vision of learning that is shared and supported by the school community

ISLLC Standard 6: Understanding, responding to, and influencing the larger political, social, economic, legal, and cultural context.

▶ Abstract

This article examined the ever-increasing complexity in higher education administration and identified a set of beneficial leadership skills for today's higher education administrator. Noting the ever-changing landscapes in technology, social media, instructional delivery methods, public and private support, and assessment and accountability, this article presented leadership traits necessary for administrators to successfully navigate the hierarchal ladder of higher education administration from entry level personnel to board of trustee members. The author recommends today's higher education administrator need not focus on developing one individualized leadership style, but rather demonstrate the ability and flexibility to draw on any number of the higher education leadership personal skill set items in order to maximize effectiveness.

Key Words: leadership, higher education, administration, leadership skill set, education, assessment, accountability

▶ Review of Literature

The study of leadership style began to emerge in the early twentieth century. The first research centered on leadership traits that were being exhibited by the commonly accepted "great leaders" of the time. The general belief was that people were born with leadership characteristics or traits. Furthermore, only "great" people possessed these traits (Northouse, 2012). Most of the research of that time focused on determining what those traits were and were they universal (Bass, 1990). It took until the late 1940s for Stogdill (1948) to surmise that no specific set of leadership traits had been found that identified leaders versus non-leaders. Stogdill did use one-word characteristics, much like the higher education leadership personal skill set, but was not able to prove that traits such as insight, responsibility, and initiative were indeed universal characteristics of great leaders. By the time Stogdill (1974) had published his second work, he was openly speaking about situational leadership and how that relates or interacts with the leadership traits or characteristics one possesses.

Dungy and Whitaker (2010) outlined the leadership attributes that "A Mentor Leader" must possess. They identified character, courage, leading by example, faith, and the willingness to examine and change paradigms as key characteristics of a leader. They clearly put forth the notion that **character is the foundation on which all leadership is built** (Dungy and Whitaker, 2010). Trustworthy traits, integrity, confidence, accountability, loyalty. and approachability are other "marks" of a leader espoused by Dungy and Whitaker (2010).

Key elements that leaders must exhibit to create a strong sense of confidence within an organization were identified by Ritscher (1985). He speaks of leaders needing to create a shared vision, maintaining a high level of integrity and creating a culture that values service, dedication, and excellence. Jackson, Moneta and Nelson (2009) also tell us that Ritscher wrote of creating cooperation, communication, and community while creating an environment that is supportive of the individual. Kirkpatrick and Locke (1991) asked if traits mattered in leadership, then answered their own question by identifying six traits leaders have in common. Task knowledge, cognitive ability, integrity, drive, confidence, and motivation were judged to be critical characteristics for a leader to possess.

"Skills" leadership hasn't been around quite as long as "trait" leadership. It was not until the 1950s that Katz (1955) first wrote about the skill set an administrator needed to possess to be effective. His work centered on identifying three levels of management (top, middle and supervisory) that needed to exhibit proficiency in three skill areas (technical, human and conceptual) in order to be considered a successful administrator. A more recent skills model was developed by Mumford, Zaccaro, Harding, Jacobs, and Fleishman (2000) that introduced individual attributes, competency, and outcomes to the skills discussion. Northouse (2012) gives us very recent work, identifying both the strengths and the negative aspects of conceptualizing leadership from a skills perspective.

Dungy and Whitaker (2010) give us seven "methods" of a mentor leader that they believe will enhance the potential of all leaders. They suggest that leaders engage, educate, equip, encourage, empower, energize, and elevate to achieve maximum success.

Hersey and Blanchard (1969) introduced us to situational leadership over 40 years ago. Over the years Blanchard (1983) continued to define and refine the situational leadership approach. It remains today as one of the most widely recognized and most respected approaches to leadership training, employed throughout both the public and private sectors.

Anatonakis (2012) has given us recent work in the area of transformational and charismatic leadership that is worth examining. Greenleaf (1970) gave us the first work of servant leadership and many have continued to add to the field of knowledge including prolific leadership authors, Bennis, Covey, Senge (2002) and Blanchard and Hodges (2003).

■▶ Statement of Issue

Higher education in the twenty-first century is changing more rapidly than most experts would have ever imagined. Technology seems to advance almost on a daily basis. Social media touches every part of the academy. Academic instruction and student service delivery methods that did not exist a decade ago are now commonplace. Public support to higher education has eroded to alarming levels. For-profit institutions have seen unprecedented growth and now face intensified scrutiny from the accrediting bodies. Assessment and accountability, which many in higher education community hoped would be quick moving fads that would fade away, instead became a permanent part of the landscape.

Today's higher education administration is dealing with complex issues on a daily basis. Leadership is required at all levels of the Institution. Senior administrators should exhibit leadership traits with trustees, senior colleagues, deans, and directors. Middle managers must demonstrate leadership to an incredibly large number of constituencies in the various departments and programs, including senior supervisors, fellow middle managers, entry-level professional staff, and support staff to ensure that the needs of the students are being adequately serviced. For entry-level staff, there is a role modeling type of leadership that is needed for most interactions that occur with students. Leadership with fellow entry-level staff, supervisors, and senior management should be viewed as a growing and maturing work in progress. It is important that the leadership growth and maturation be observable by the various constituencies through daily interactions.

In today's society there is a great deal of leadership that must be delivered on college and university campuses on a daily basis. It doesn't matter that the college is complex. It doesn't matter that the university is rapidly changing. The leadership that is provided to a program, a department, a division, or the college itself should be strong and consistent throughout the institution's organizational chart. Higher education administrators are often asked to identify a personal individual leadership style. Perhaps the best answer to that question in the modern college or university is to be a proponent of higher education administration leadership. A very dogmatic style of leadership, no matter how inclusive it might be will not be as effective as understanding that each situation that requires leadership attention is unique.

Leadership does not stay the same for each individual interaction, administrative decision, or crisis situation. People and policies change in higher education every day. The exceptional leader understands this and has the ability and flexibility to shift leadership style to maximize effectiveness.

For any leadership style to be effective, there still needs to be a higher **education Personal Leadership Skill Set that serves as the foundation for an individual's leadership style. The skill set that I feel will serve all** higher education **administrators from** assistant student activities directors to vice presidents, or even **presidents is a bit more personal than those that appear on most leadership characteristics lists**.

Strategy

Strategy would be the first leadership characteristic that I would identify for the administrator: How well do you plan? Are your planning, organizing and implementation skills readily apparent to all of the college constituency groups that you interact with? What is your working knowledge of your institution's strategic plans? Do you understand how to move or maneuver projects to successful completion? Do both your subordinates and your supervisors readily understand your strategy for resource allocation within your program, department, or division? Are the strategies you employ always viewed as having integrity and not self-serving? **Do your colleagues express faith in the strategies you put forth**, particularly if they impact their program or department? Are the strategies developed in a transparent manner, with great inclusiveness from appropriate constituencies? Is maximum communication utilized up and down the organizational ladder as strategies are developed and implemented? Finally, are your strategies viewed as successful and most importantly seen as improving or bettering your program, department, division, or institution? If you have answered yes to most of the questions above, then strategy is an important leadership tool you have as part of your higher education skill set.

Passion

Passion is an extremely critical skill that cannot be overlooked in higher education administration. Remembering that we are discussing all higher education administrators from entry-level to senior management. There **is no substitute for passion for the profession**. Even as one rises further and further up the administrative ladder and daily contact with students diminishes, a passion for working with students should not be lost. Senior administrators will have to create intentional opportunities to maintain interaction with students. It will not be the easiest thing in the world to carve out time for students, but it will be worth it. Colleagues, subordinates, and students will note which administrators have retained a passion for working with students.

Another difficult aspect of higher education administration is maintaining your passion for all the responsibilities within your department or division. As human beings, it is only natural that there would be parts of our jobs that we would lose our passion for. What is critical for the higher education administrator is to not show that lack of passion to the various constituencies. Try to find ways to revitalize your interest in whatever aspect of our job you no longer care for. Never delegate tasks or assignments because you have lost your passion for the responsibility. Never publicly acknowledge that you don't enjoy budgeting, personnel matters, strategic planning, technology, assessment, or any other areas that you can grow weary of and lose the passion you once possessed. Passion fuels motivational drive, so it is an incredibly important leadership skill to possess throughout your career.

Talent

Is talent a leadership skill? This author answers that question with a resounding yes! People respect talent. **People will follow leaders whom they believe have the talent to lead them**. Did you enter higher education administration because you thought you had the ability or the talent to be a good at it? Somewhere along the line did you discover your had a talent for dealing with people? With students? Did you improve your talent by preparing yourself professionally with your graduate degree in higher education, student personnel or educational administration? Do colleagues or supervisors respect you for your knowledge base in various aspects of higher education administration? Do you attend conferences, workshops, seminars and stay up on the latest technological advances in the field? If you increase your knowledge base, you increase your talent. Are you the go-to person on your campus for any aspect of higher education administration? Do you remain humble about your talent, so others see it as a positive part of your leadership skill set? Your talent and others' respect for it can be a powerful leadership tool that can be used effectively with all of the institution's constituencies, including the president and the board of trustees.

Discipline

Discipline is a multifaceted leadership skill that is critically important to either possess or develop very quickly upon entering the higher education administration profession. Self-discipline is what I am referring to. First and foremost it is vital that all administrators have a great sense of civility. There is a saying that I have used extensively throughout my higher education career when I have observed interactions that are not appropriate: "This is NOT how we act in higher education." In other words, our behavioral culture in higher education demands civility from our practitioners. We have a culture on our college and university campuses that promotes discipline from the students to the board of trustees. Demonstrating self-discipline openly spills out into the institution by promoting organization and efficiency. Budgets are adhered to, institutional policies are followed, and personal issues are resolved because discipline is practiced as a leadership skill on a daily basis on campuses across this country.

Heart

Heart is a necessary leadership skill central to everything we do in higher education. It gives the leader a sense of compassion that comes into play every day on our campuses. This skill gives us pause to think for a few moments about individual situations and not lump everything together for the ease of dealing with it only via institutional policies.

Heart as a leadership skill allows us to give great meaning to the work that we do. It lets us enjoy a sense of celebration within the institutions. Heart lets us legitimately develop relationships and a caring attitude toward our fellow employees. Staff and faculty morale has a direct connection to our institutional heart. I have observed great differences in attitude, work ethic, and morale between two divisions at the same university based on the heart leadership skill demonstrated by the vice presidents who were overseeing those divisions.

Trust

Trust cannot be overstated as a leadership skill. **Once trust is broken between colleagues or a supervisor or supervisee, it has been my observation that it is virtually impossible to repair**. Though I wouldn't list honesty as a separate leadership skill, it goes hand in hand with trust. The slightest dishonest act can immediately cause a loss of trust between two individuals, especially in higher education where honesty is held as a very high standard. Trust is particularly important in establishing the direct reporting relationship between supervisor and supervisee. The critical point to make here is that the trust must go both . Often it appears that the trust is reciprocal, but ultimately in times of crisis or stress one of the administrators reveals that he/she does not trust the other administrator to perform in an admirable way or even to handle the situation at all. Another unique situation within higher education that requires trust is the use of shared governance committees. Throughout the institution, committees are formed from strangers within the college or university, who are then asked to tackle major issues facing the institution. Trust must be developed very quickly among the committees and in most cases the trust leadership skill does emerge from the members of the committee and the work is successfully completed.

Perseverance

Perseverance has emerged in the last five years as one of the most critical leadership skills a higher education **administrator can possess**. The condition of the economy, the drop in state public support for higher education, and the increased call for assessment and accountability have required administrators to make detailed plans on just how to persevere through the hard times. Leaders at all levels of administration are working with their teams on how to survive the crisis, while still moving forward. Higher education leaders in this climate realize that growth is stalled and is not likely to return until the economy and public support rebound. Perseverance is seen in administrators just trying to hold onto resource levels for their program or department. Trying to replace retiring or departing staff members now requires long, drawn out search processes, persistent and often argumentative discussions, and perseverance unheard of a decade ago. Budgets must be checked and rechecked on almost a daily basis. Perseverance is a relevant leadership skill when expectations are to improve and grow a program, when resources are being cut to the bone at the same time.

Speed

Speed is a leadership skill that elicits applause from fellow administrators. How do some administrators seem to move at the speed of sound and accomplish tasks and projects in the shortest time possible? There is a sense that they just "get it done." Leaders who possess this skill excel at putting together and leading committees through their charge. As a leadership skill, speed is only relevant if quality work accompanies the speed. Many of us have had employees who have passed the speed test, but failed the quality control examination. There can sometimes be very distinct advantages to speedy leaders. Often items that are finished first are viewed in a superior manner. This may lead to some improved resource allocation for their department. Speedy leaders are perceived as very accomplished because whatever they submit to the institution is on time and complete while others are still working on their committees, projects, and tasks.

Confidence

There really is no substitute for **confidence** as a leadership skill. You gain your level of leadership confidence by developing your own skill set and then developing total trust in these skills that you possess. When you are appropriately confident, it gives confidence to your colleagues and to your team. People are assured at all levels of the administration that tasks will be accomplished with your leadership. A reliance on your ability to succeed soon develops within others. Your belief in yourself can become inspiring for your employees, especially those looking to develop their own leadership skill set. Your other higher education leadership skills will all be enhanced by your confidence. Confident leaders wish and want to take on more responsibility and usually the college or the university comes to rely on them. **Confident leaders attack problems head on** and are not really satisfied until they are solved. Finally, confident leaders will try to fill in all of their checklists to make sure that they have developed an outstanding leadership skill set that they can call on throughout the rest of their higher education careers.

Strength

Strength is the last leadership skill in the higher education skill set. The leader who possesses strength is viewed as a powerful force to be reckoned with. This skill also gives fellow administrators pause and they will be less likely to challenge you, especially in a one-on-one situation. The administrative leader who possesses this skill is often spoken of as having a greater "will" than others to succeed. **Subordinates like to have their leader perceived as strong and confident.** In many cases they develop a sense that their career is going in the right direction and that they are part of the best department or division within the institution. Strength is also the hardest skill to maintain on a constant basis. People within the institution will seldom question strategy, passion, heart, or discipline, but will quickly pounce on an opportunity to question your leadership strength.

▶ Conclusion

Development of all ten higher education personal leadership skills is highly recommended for all levels of higher education administration. Outstanding leadership in higher education administration creates success for students both inside the classroom and outside the curriculum. Development is facilitated for both graduates and undergraduate students when administrators examine their own personal leadership skill set and expand their vision of how to best serve the multiple populations on today's college and university campuses.

Discussion Questions

1. As an educational administrator which of the higher education leadership personal skill set items have you developed and put into use on a regular basis in your educational administrative work?

2. What traits of the higher education leadership personal skill set could you improve on in order to maximize your workplace effectiveness?

3. What specific steps could you take to improve in the higher education leadership skill areas that you are not using on a regular basis?

4. Which of the higher education leadership personal skill set traits has proven to be the most effective in performing your daily educational administrative responsibilities?

5. How does the higher education leadership personal skill set compare with other leadership approaches such as trait leadership, situational leadership, leadership-followership and servant leadership? What are the similarities and what are the differences that you notice when you compare the other leadership styles to the higher education leadership personal skill set?

6. Think of the individuals that you have felt were outstanding education or higher education leaders. What higher education leadership personal skill set traits could you easily indentify in the leadership approach? Which of the skills did you note as being particularly effective in their daily administrative workload? Were there any of the higher education leadership personal skill set traits that they exhibited that you felt did not maximize their leadership talent level?

Leadership Activity

- Develop a "Personal Checklist System" for maximizing the use of the higher education leadership personal skill set in your educational administrative setting.
- Examine all ten of the higher education leadership personal skill set traits and objectively rate yourself on a 1 to 5 scale (with 5 being the highest) on your successful use of the individual scale on a daily basis in your workplace setting.
- Examine how you use each of the higher education leadership personal skill set items in dealing with the administrative responsibility connected with technology. Social media? Internal and external communication?
- Examine where the higher education leadership personal skill set comes into play when dealing with instructional or student service delivery methods.
- Ask yourself how you could better use the higher education leadership personal skill set to deal with the assessment and accountability associated with and required of your educational position.
- Break down and examine each of the higher education leadership personal skill set traits as they relate to your educational constituency groups. Board of trustees? Senior administrators? Middle managers? Entry-level personnel? Faculty? Administrative staff? Students? General public? Are you stronger when using certain higher education leadership personal skill set items with one constituency group over another group? Do certain skills seem to work better with one group versus another?
- Write out your detailed plan to develop, use and then maximize each of the higher education leadership personal skill set traits, first as it relates to your administrative duties and responsibilities and then as it relates to each of the constituency groups which you interact with in your educational setting.
- Do a six month re-assessment of how you have improved your use of the higher education leadership personal skill set skills and whether you met your goals for maximizing the benefit of the higher education leadership personal skill set.

Activity Direction

This activity may be completed by an individual attempting to assess their own higher education leadership personal skill set level of proficiency or by a department or administrative unit as a professional development activity within an educational or higher education setting.

Background of the Author

Dr. Joseph M. Marron is currently Professor and Program Lead Faculty for the Master of Science Degree Program in Higher Education Administration at National University in La Jolla, California. Dr. Marron received his Doctorate in Higher Education Administration from Vanderbilt University and his Post-Doctoral work was completed at the Institute for Educational Management at Harvard University. Dr. Marron served as Vice President for Student Services and Enrollment Management at a number of public and private colleges and universities for more than two decades. He also previously held academic positions as Professor, Program Director and System-wide Director for Educational Leadership developing and overseeing a Higher Education Administration Doctoral Program and administrating a K-12 Master of Educational Administration Degree and an Administrative Credential Program. Dr. Marron has presented over 100 juried professional presentations at National and Regional Higher Education Conferences, Institutes and Symposiums and held numerous leadership positions in various Higher Education Professional Associations.

References

Antonakis, J. (2012). Transformational and charismatic leadership. In D.V. Day & J. Antonakis (Eds.), *The nature of leadership*, Thousand Oaks, CA: Sage.

Bass, B. M. (1990). *Bass and Stogdill's handbook of leadership: A survey of theory and research.* New York: Free Press.

Bennis, W. (2002). Become a tomorrow leader. In L.C. Spears & M. Lawrence (Eds.), *Focus on leadership: Servant-leadership for the twenty-first century.* New York: John Wiley & Sons.

Blanchard, K. H. (1985). *SLII: A situational approach to managing people.* Escondido, CA: Blanchard Training and Development.

Covey, S. R. (2002). In R. K. Greenleaf (Ed.), *Servant leadership: A journey into the nature of legitimate power and greatness.* New York: Paulist Press.

Dungy, T., & Whitaker, N. (2010). *The mentor leader: Secrets to building people and teams that win consistently.* Carol Stream, Illinois: Tyndale House Publishers.

Greenleaf, R. K. (1970) *The servant as leader.* Westfield, IN: The Greenleaf Center for Servant Leadership.

Hersey, P., & Blanchard, K. H. (1969). *Management of organizational behavior: Utilizing human resources.* Englewood Cliffs, NJ: Prentice Hall.

Jackson, M. L., Moneta, L., & Nelson, K. A. (2009). *Effective management of human capital in student affairs.* In McClellen, G.S., Springer, J. *The handbook of student affairs administration.* San Francisco: John Wiley and Sons.

Kirkpatrick, S. A., & Locke, E. A. (1991). Leadership: Do traits matter? *The Executive, 5.*

McClellen, G. S., & Stringer, J. (2009). *The handbook of student affairs administration.* San Francisco: John Wiley & Sons.

Mumford, M. D., Zaccaro, S. J., Harding E. D., Jacobs, T. O., & Fleishman, E. A. (2000). Leadership skills for a changing world: Solving complex social problems *Leadership Quarterly, 11*(1).

Northouse, P. G., (2012). *Leadership: Theory and Practice.* Thousand Oaks, CA: Sage.

Ritscher, J. A. "Spirituality in Business." *IN CONTEXT: Living Business.* Retrieved (DATE) from www.context.org/ICLIB/IC11/Tirscher.htm

Senge, P. M. (2002). In R. K. Greenleaf (Ed.), *Servant leadership: journey into the nature of legitimate power and greatness.* New York: Paulist Press.

Stodgill, R. M. (1948). Personal factors associated with leadership: A survey of the literature. *Journal of Psychology, 25.*

Stodgill, R. M. (1974). *Handbook of leadership: A survey of theory and research.* New York: Free Press.

Chapter 3
Interact with Instructional Leadership

"Leadership and learning are indispensable to each other."
—John F. Kennedy

Introduction Chapter 3

*Donna Elder, EdD, Associate Professor, National University,
La Jolla, California*

Instructional leadership has become more and more important in schools with higher accountability for student achievement. With the passage of No Child Left Behind Legislation (2001), accountability is at the forefront of all discussions in schools and districts. School administrators have to take a proactive role in leading their schools to foster student achievement. School administrators need to have a good understanding of how to facilitate teachers in improving their practice so that every student has the opportunity for a productive learning environment. **Principals do make a difference in improving student achievement.**

Educational Leadership Policy Standards (ISLLC) leaves no doubt that anyone who serves as an administrator in a district must place student success first. Each standard begins with the statement, "**An education leader promotes the success of every student.**" Standards 2 and 3 speak directly to the role of the instructional leader promoting a school culture and environment that promotes student achievement as well as providing a strong instructional programs and professional development for staff.

The importance of **understanding the pedagogy of instruction helps ground the leader in knowing the direction of the school instructional program**. The first article by Dr. Weegar goes into depth on the behaviorist and constructivist models of instruction and how each looks in a classroom setting. Her article ends with discussing where the emphasis of instruction will be as we move forward in the twenty-first century.

Dr. Kurth shares a very practical approach of how to implement a school wide management plan. He shares very interesting research on how the management of student behavior increases student achievement. This article may challenge some of your current thinking on how to manage student behavior.

Dr. Cunniff and Dr. Naffziger share how technology can be used as part of an evaluation program for student teachers, but also the potential this technology could have in schools to assist teachers in improving their instructional practice.

The final article in this chapter is by Dr. Nordgren who discusses what we need to do to provide students with the twenty-first century skills they will need to succeed in the workplace. He suggests that this country may be missing crucial ideas that if implemented would improve our overall success. He compares our system to Sweden's system of education.

To be an innovative instructional leader, it is important to be a continual learner and always question the status quo. Are we doing this the best way or can we improve? Continuous improvement should be the hallmark of an innovative instructional leader. From the Japanese comes the system of continuous improvement known as kaizen. **Kaizen is the process of continuous improvement in an organization that involves everyone and costs little money** (*Masaaki Imai*). As an innovative leader it is important to remember this concept as we lead our schools.

Applied Learning Theories: Behaviorist vs. Constructivist

Mary Anne Weegar, EdD, National University, La Jolla, California

ISLLC Standard 2: Promoting the success of all students by advocating, nurturing, and sustaining a school culture and instructional program conducive to student learning and staff professional growth.

▶ Abstract

The two theories of learning discussed are behaviorist and constructivist. Skinner and Watson, the two major developers of the behaviorist school of thought, sought to prove that behavior could be predicted and controlled (Skinner, 1974). They studied how learning is affected by changes in the environment. The constructivists viewed learning as a search for meaning. Piaget and Vygotsky described elements that helped predict what children understand at different stages (Rummel, 2008). Details of both theories illuminate the differences and connections between the behaviorist and constructivist theories in relationship to how children learn and how their behavior is affected. Also reviewed are how curriculum and instruction work with these theories to promote learning and how educators view learning with respect to both theories.

Key Words: instructional design, cognitive development, behaviorism, constructivism

▶ Introduction

The two theories of learning discussed in this paper are behaviorist and constructivist. Behaviorists believed that "only observable, measurable, outward behavior is worthy of scientific inquiry" (Bush, 2006). Hence, their focus was on learning as affected by changes in behavior. They concluded that given the right environmental influences, all learners acquire identical understanding and that all students can learn. In contrast to the beliefs of behaviorists, the constructivists viewed learning as a search for meaning. They believed that knowledge is constructed by the learner and that the learner develops her/his own understanding through experience. Whereas a behaviorist would continue to look at the content to be learned and the influence of the environment upon that learning, a constructivist would be more interested in knowing how the learner is attempting to construct meaning (Bush, 2006). Given the different points of view expressed by psychologists and educators who advocate for selected theories of learning to increase student achievement, educators have the daunting task of determining from the research how to design instruction and develop curriculum that will promote student learning in a culturally and linguistically diverse society.

Learning Theory A: Behaviorist Learning Theory

Psychology became an accepted science in the latter part of the nineteenth-century and was defined as the science of consciousness. "Behaviorism was, and is, a moment primarily in American psychology that rejected consciousness as psychology's subject matter and replaced it with behavior" (Leahey, 2000, p. 686). Behaviorism was rooted in the 1880s and continues to evolve in the twentieth-century and beyond. Although behaviorism has been intensely studied, behaviorists continue to have difficulty agreeing on a definition for behaviorism and identifying who were the true behaviorists (Mills, 1998).

The publication of Theory A by Watson (1913) was responsible for the movement towards behaviorism and away from functionalism, the study of the relationship between organisms and their environment (Overskeid, 2008). Watson used Pavlov's findings on animal responses to stimuli as a basis for his work. For example, Pavlov rang a bell when his dog was going to be fed. The ringing of the bell caused Pavlov's dog to salivate because the dog had been conditioned to feed at this time. This behavior resulted in Pavlov asserting that canines had been "conditioned" to respond to external stimuli. Hence, Pavlov believed that humans could also be "conditioned" to respond to similar stimuli. In support of his beliefs, Pavlov demonstrated how a different musical tone, which has never been paired with receiving food, could elicit similar behavior in humans (Thomas, 1997). Watson mirrored Pavlov's research findings in his conditioning experiment with a young child who he conditioned to fear a white rabbit by repeatedly pairing it with the loud "clang" of a metal bar. The child's "conditioned" fear of a white rabbit was so ingrained in his behavior that he became fearful of other white furry objects such as a Santa mask and Watson's white hair (Watson & Rayner, 1920). Although most psychologists have agreed that psychology is the study of human behavior, the only scientists that consider themselves behaviorists today are those who are followers of Skinner (Leahey, 2000).

Skinner based much of his work on the study of Watson's former research. Skinner did extensive research with animals, notably rats and pigeons, and invented the famous Skinner box, in which a rat learns to press a lever in order to receive food. Consequently, every time the rat pushed the lever, the rat obtained food, which reinforced the behavior. "The behaviorism of Watson and Skinner is based on a positivistic approach to science, that is, a reductionist view in which all that can be addressed is the relation between sensory stimuli and the unique corresponding response" (Webb, 2007, p. 1086). However, Skinner eventually came to the realization that human beings go beyond just responding to the environment. He found that they also react to the environment based on prior experiences (Skinner, 1974).

Rotfeld (2007) suggested that "psychologists 'invented' behaviorism itself as a basis for theoretical explanations, prediction, and testing." (p. 376). From its inception, the term behaviorism provided a "direction for social science research that would allow control and measurement of all relevant variables by ignoring human thought or cognition." (p. 376). Therefore, behaviorists were not interested in what might occur in people's minds; they were only interested in behavior responses. As a result, these responses were measured in relation to test stimuli. In other words, behaviorists saw this as a way for them to be viewed as scientific in the same way as the hard sciences of chemistry or physics are viewed. By narrowing their focus, the **behaviorists provided for greater use of statistical analysis of experimental results**. Their goal was to achieve a greater use of scientific methods for developing stronger theories.

Skinner (as cited by Gregory, 1987) stated that the mind and mental processes are "metaphors and fictions," and that "behavior" is a function of the "biology" of the organism. Skinner expressed no interest in understanding how the human mind functioned. He was a behaviorist in the strictest sense as was John Watson. Both Skinner and Watson were only concerned with how behavior is affected by external forces. Skinner believed that everything human beings do is controlled by their experience. Therefore, the "mind" (not the brain) had nothing to do with how people behaved. Furthermore, thoughts, feelings, intentions, mental processes, and so forth have no bearing on what humans do. Skinner was known for making audacious statements in keeping with Watson's tradition of being provocative and controversial to gain people's attention (WGHB, 1998).

Learning Theory B: Constructivist Learning Theory

Theory B evolved from the extensive study of cognitive development (i.e., how thinking and knowledge develop with age) by Swiss psychologist Jean Piaget and the Russian psychologist Lev Vygotsky. Their study of cognitive development provided the foundation for the psychological theory of constructivism. Constructivists believed children develop knowledge through active participation in their learning. Piaget believed that cognitive development was a product of the mind "achieved through observation and experimentation whereas Vygotsky viewed it as a social process, achieved through interaction with more knowledgeable members of the culture" (Rummel, 2008). Piaget referred to his work as "cognitive" constructivism (Chambliss, 1996). Piaget's theory was comprised of two major elements "ages" and "stages." According to Piaget, "these elements help to predict what children can and cannot understand at different ages" (Rummel, 2008, p. 80). It is the theory of development that is the major foundation for cognitive constructivist approaches to teaching and learning.

Piaget's theory of cognitive development suggested that humans are unable to automatically understand and use information that they have been given, because they need to construct their own knowledge through prior personal experiences to enable them to create mental images. Therefore, the primary role of the teacher should be to motivate the children to create their own knowledge through their personal experiences (Rummel, 2008). Vygotsky referred to his work as social constructivism. Vygotsky's theory was very similar to Piaget's assumptions about how children learn, but Vygotsky placed more importance on the social context of learning. In Piaget's theory, the teacher played a limited role whereas in Vygotsky's theory, the teacher played an important role in learning. Learning activities in constructivist settings are characterized by active engagement, inquiry, problem solving, and collaboration with others. Rather than a dispenser of knowledge, the teacher is a guide, facilitator, and co-explorer who encourages learners to question, challenge, and formulate their own ideas, opinions, and conclusions. "How constructivism is interrupted and whether the learning strategies account for individual and social diversity are issues that gain limited attention during curriculum development" (Gulati, 2008, p. 184).

McBrien and Brandt (1997), described constructivism as an approach to teaching based on research about how students learn. Constructive learning is based on the principle that students learn best when they gain knowledge through exploration and active learning. Hands-on materials are used instead of textbooks, and students are encouraged to think and explain their reasoning instead of memorizing and reciting facts. Students' education is centered on themes and concepts and the connections between them. According to Glasserfield (as cited in Gulati, 2008), a constructivist approach to teaching and learning requires professional educators to change their ways of thinking and doing things. Brooks and Brooks (1995) assert that constructivism emphasized the importance of the knowledge, beliefs, and skills an individual brings to the learning environment. Constructivists recognized the construction of new understanding as a combination of prior learning, new information, and readiness to learn.

Epistemological Comparison

Relationship of Epistemology to Education

Epistemology is an area of philosophy that examines questions about how we know what we know. Four well-known philosophical schools of thought are idealism, realism, pragmatism, and existentialism. Each of the aforementioned philosophies has implications for education. The idealist is idea centered rather than subject or child centered. The idealist believes that the teacher is central to learning. Therefore, the idealist tends to emphasize lecture, discussion, and imitation. The realist sees the role of the teacher as a person who presents content in a systematic and organized way. Contemporary realists are behind standardized tests, serialized textbooks, and specialized curriculum for each discipline. The pragmatist stresses applying knowledge—using ideas for problem solving. Realists and idealists are most closely associated with the behaviorist's theory of learning, because they believe in a standardized curriculum centered on academic disciplines. Pragmatists prefer a curriculum that is interdisciplinary, and they are, therefore, most closely associated with the constructivists' beliefs about how students learn best (Johnson, Musial, Hall, Gollnick, & Dupuis, 2008).

Epistemological Comparison of Theory A with Theory B

Theory A focuses mainly on objectively observable behaviors and, consequently, discounts mental activities. This approach emphasizes the "acquisition of new behavior" (Bednar, Cunningham, Duffy, & Perry, 1992). Behaviorists believe all behavior is the result of an individual's responses to external stimuli (operant conditioning). In other words, behaviorists believe that the external environment contributes to the shaping of an individual's behavior. Behaviorists also believe that the environment triggers a particular behavior, and whether the behavior occurs again is dependent upon how an individual is affected by the behavior. According to Morrison, Ross, and Kemp (2004), Theory A places emphasis on the effects of external conditions such as rewards and punishments in determining future behaviors of students.

In a school setting, teachers use positive and negative reinforcements to either reward or punish a student's behavior. Theory A relies on extrinsic motivators such as grades, prizes, and privileges, as well as recognitions and praises, as a means to ensure the replication of the learned activity or behavior. Teachers who follow Theory A present lesson objectives in a linear fashion. In so doing, the teacher provides hints or cues to guide students to a desired behavior, and then uses consequences to reinforce the desired behavior. Behaviorists begin with first introducing lower-level cognitive skills. This is followed by the building of higher-level cognitive skills. The problem with this type of instruction is that lessons are focused on learning skills in isolation (Gonzalez, n.d.). Those who disagree with Theory A believe that this theory fails to take into consideration the influence the mind has over behavior. Therefore, instead of involving students in solving problems, behaviorists use methods of direct instruction (i.e., lecturing and teaching skills in isolation) and assess their learning based on their responses to questions on oral or written tests.

Constructivism "is the philosophy, or belief, that learners create their own knowledge based on interactions with their environment including their interactions with other people" (Draper, 2002, p. 522). Theory B understands learning as an interpretive, recursive, building process by active learners interrelating with the physical and social world (Fosnot, 1996). Theory B has been proven effective in assisting teachers in meeting the challenge of improving student achievement. "Assuming the role as 'guide on the side' requires teachers to step off the stage, relinquish some of their power, and release the textbooks to allow their students to be actively engaged and take some responsibility of their own learning" (White-Clark, DiCarlo, & Gilchriest, 2008, p. 44). Furthermore, constructivism involves developing the student as a learner through cooperative learning, experimentation, and open-ended problems in which students learn on their own through active participation with concepts and principles (Kearsley, 1994).

Teachers who use Theory B concentrate on showing students relevance and meaningfulness in what they are learning. For example, in the constructivist classroom teachers would pose realistically complex and personally meaningful problems for students to solve. Students would then work in cooperative groups to explore possible answers, develop a product, and present findings to a selected audience (Carbonell, 2004). "Cooperative learning, hands-on activities, discovery learning, differentiated instruction, technology, distributed practice, critical thinking, and manipulatives are elements that embrace the constructivist educational philosophy" (White-Clark, et al., 2008, p. 41).

Theory A and Theory B provide two examples of how individuals acquire knowledge. According to Panasuk and Todd (2005), Theory A focuses on changes in behavioral patterns being repeated until they become automatic. Theory B supports the belief that the learners construct their own perspective of the world through individual experiences and schema. In other words, Theory B proponents suggest that learning is an ongoing search for creating meaning. The author believes that both Theory A and Theory B should be used "to draw instructional strategies from, and suggest correlating different theories with the needs of the learners, the content to be learned, and the environment to be created" (Panasuk & Todd,

2005, p. 223). The teaching strategies based on Theory A would help facilitate mastery of curriculum content through identification of course objectives and student outcomes. The teaching methods based on Theory B encourage students' active engagement and facilitation of knowledge development. Furthermore, Panasuk and Todd believe that instructional approaches go beyond one particular theory and must be based on the integration of different theories and models. Various strategies allow the teacher to make the best use of all available practical applications of the different learning and instructional theories. With this approach, the teacher is able to draw from a large number of strategies to meet a variety of learning situations (p. 223).

Impact on Curriculum Development

Historically, the application of psychological theories to education was not consistent. John Dewey (1938) was credited for beginning the constructivist movement. In fact, the whole thinking-skills movement began for the most part with Dewey's work (Sternberg, 2008). "The three fundamental learning theories that were found to be most important in the formulation of the learning design model were those based upon behaviorism, cognition and constructivism (including both socio-constructivism and communal constructivism)" (Barker, 2008, p. 130). Theory A has influenced curriculum development for many years. Behaviorists view learning as a process that results from the connections created from a stimuli-response relationship, and the desire to learn is assumed to be driven by these relationships (Kim & Hatton, n.d.). Furthermore, Theory A focuses primarily on objectively observable behaviors.

Curriculum for the constructivist learning model is designed to actively engage the students in their learning. The learning that occurs for students is considered an internal cognitive activity where students are allowed to construct knowledge (models) from their classroom experience. The teacher's role is to facilitate and negotiate meaning, rather than to dictate an interpretation (Driscoll, 2005). Kumar (2006) developed a constructivism oriented instructional framework to bridge the gap between theory and practice. This framework suggested a repertoire of heuristic instructional strategies that facilitated students' independent construction of various classes of scientific knowledge. Theory B promotes learning to be an active process in which learners construct new concepts based upon prior knowledge. Learners select and process information through constructing hypotheses, decision making, and giving meaning and organization to experiences. Appropriate instructional strategies need to be framed to facilitate student learning of declarative and procedural knowledge through constructivist pedagogy.

Impact on Instructional Design

Theory A subscribers believed that meaning exists in the world separate from personal experience. All instructional goals are framed in specific, behavioral, and observable terms. In this approach, the instructor is the focus of the presentation and interaction. Teachers work with the individual students when they need extra help. The student's role is to absorb instructional presentations and material, and use them to create performances that indicate attainment of correct mental models. Structured assignments are directly linked to the learning objectives. There is minimal or no cohort discussion in this model of direct instruction. Assessment and evaluation are based upon individual tests and performances to demonstrate mastery of entities, activities, and processes.

Gagne (1985) identified five categories of learning reflecting the behaviorist thought process. These categories were verbal information, intellectual skills, cognitive strategies, attitudes, and motor skills. According to Gagne, different internal and external conditions are necessary for each type of learning. For example, for Theory B strategies to be learned, there must be a chance to practice developing new solutions to problems; to learn attitudes, the learner must be exposed to a credible role model or persuasive arguments (Driscoll, 2005). Furthermore, Gagne suggested that learning tasks for intellectual skills can be organized in a hierarchy according to complexity: stimulus recognition, response generation, procedure following, use of terminology, discriminations, concept formation, rule application, and problem solving. The primary significance of the hierarchy is to identify prerequisites that should be completed to facilitate learning at each level. Prerequisites are identified by doing a task analysis of a learning/training task. Learning hierarchies provide a basis for the sequencing of instruction. Gagne's design was tied to Skinner's design of sequenced learning events as displayed in Gagne's "Nine Events of Instruction Associated with the Internal Learning Theory" (as cited in Driscoll, 2005; Gagne, Briggs, & Wager, 1992). Gagne's instructional events are: (a) gaining attention, (b) informing the learner of the objective, (c) stimulating recall of prior learning, (d) presenting the stimulus, (e) providing learner guidance, (f) eliciting performance, (g) giving feedback, (h) assessing performance, and (i) enhancing retention and transfer. These events should satisfy or provide the necessary conditions for learning and serve as the basis for designing instruction and selecting appropriate media.

When reviewing the impact of Theory B on instructional design, much of the research was attributed to the work of Dewey, Piaget, and Vygotsky. The overall philosophy of these constructivists holds that learners impose meaning on the world, and so "construct" their own understanding based on their unique experiences. All instructional goals are framed in experiential terms specifying the kinds of learner problems addressed; the kinds of control learner's exercise over the learning environment; the activities in which they engage and the ways those activities could be shaped by leaders or instructors; and the ways in which learners reflect on the results of their activity together.

The learning outcomes emphasized three characteristics of how learners should be able to think or solve problems differently when they are finished, and what settings, activities or interactions instructors predict will lead to these new abilities. First, learners need some opportunity to define for themselves the goals and objectives for the class. Second, focus is more on process and interaction, and less on what is specifically to be accomplished as a result of the lesson. Third, outcomes are defined more in terms of a new common perspective rather than particular tasks or actions that individuals will be able to carry out, which assumes learners are motivated by a common interest in some problem or issue.

Principals' and Teachers' Roles in Improving Student Achievement

Principals and teachers have defining roles in improving student achievement. Principals, who assume the role of instructional leaders, establish clear goals, allocate resources for instruction, manage the curriculum, monitor lesson plans, and assess teachers' instructional practices. The principal may chose to delegate to teacher leaders instructional activities for promoting ongoing growth in student achievement (Flath, 1989). In the twenty-first century, the role of the principal has shifted from teaching to learning (DuFour, 2002). The National Association of Elementary School Principals (2001) defined instructional leaders as leaders of learning communities. Learning communities are composed of members of the principal's staff who assist the principal in solving problems and improving the educational system within their school.

The teacher's role is to construct a learning environment and to assist students as they explore in designed experiences. Thus, the curriculum is based on the foundation that lasting learning comes as a result of activities that are both meaningful to the learner and anchored in some social context (i.e., other learners, colleagues, instructors, and clients). Teachers should be prepared to teach their students to take an active role in the learning process, which has shown to have a positive effect on student understanding and transferring of knowledge (Kruse, 1998). The teacher is the facilitator and architect of learning. The student's role is to explore the learning environment in concert with others and construct meaning from learning experiences.

The activities for learning provided by the teacher emphasize discussion and collaboration among the class of students. There is an application of principles of the material being taught to case studies and projects. Open-ended assignments are linked to changing learning objectives. Assignments are constructed to reflect "real world" conditions and requirements. Assessment or evaluation of learning is based on reporting on active, authentic experiences, activities, and projects. Emphasis is placed on interaction, reflection, and collaboration among a group of learners. Assessment is integrated throughout the curriculum rather than in final products. There are nine principles to consider when developing instruction for the Theory B classroom (Arts in Education Institute of Western New York, 2002). First, learning is an active process in which the learner uses sensory input and constructs meaning out of it. Second, people learn to learn as they learn. Learning consists both of constructing meaning and constructing systems of meaning. Third, physical actions and hands on experience may be necessary for student learning, but teachers also need to provide activities that engage the mind as well as the hand. Dewey called this "reflective activity. Fourth, learning involves language; the language that is used influences learning. Lev Vygotsky, a psychologist that helped in Theory B, argued that language and learning are inextricably intertwined. Fifth, learning is a social activity; learning is intimately associated with the connection with other human beings, teachers, peers, family, as well as casual acquaintances. Dewey advocated that most of traditional learning is directed toward isolating the learner from social interaction, and towards seeing education as a one-on-one relationship between the learner and the objective material being learned. Sixth, learning is contextual, people learn in relationship to what else they know, what they believe, their prejudices, and their fears. Seventh, one needs knowledge to learn; it is not possible to absorb new knowledge without having some structure developed from previous knowledge to build on. The more people know, the more they learn. Eighth, learning is not instantaneous; it takes time to learn. For significant learning, it is important to revisit ideas, ponder them, try them out, play with them, and use them. Ninth and last of all, the key component to learning is motivation.

Examples of Theory B can be found in a number of instructional designs. In an attempt to formulate a comprehensive adult learning theory, Knowles developed a theory to address the needs of the adult learner. Knowles labeled the instructional design "andragogy." Knowles' theory of andragogy is an attempt to develop a theory specifically for adult learning. Knowles emphasized that adults are self-directed and expect to take responsibility for decisions.

Andragogy makes the following assumptions about the design of learning: (a) Adults need to know why they need to learn something; (b) Adults need to learn experientially; (c) Adults approach learning as problem-solving; and (d) Adults learn best when the topic is of immediate value (Knowles, 1973).

Conclusion

"After being the dominant paradigm in American psychology for some decades, behaviorism was overtaken by a variety of research results that yielded anomalies revealing its limitations as an overall account of psychological functioning" (Wakefield, 2007, p. 170). As the field of psychology continued to evolve, researchers began to reject behaviorism and seek ways to identify cognitive processes in learned behaviors (Fisher, 2008). This led to the development of the field of cognitive science, which "includes the study of thinking, perception, emotion, creativity, language, consciousness and learning" (Harman, 2008, p. 76).

Overskeid (2008) discussed how psychology was redefined in the late 1950s and the 1960s when many psychologists began practicing cognitive psychology, which examined how people problem solve, memorize information, and use language. Others believed that science would gain little from studying mental phenomena instead of behavior, its antecedents, and consequences. This latter group, who were guided by Skinner, continued to attack those who subscribed to Theory B. Those who wished to return to Theory A viewed cognitive psychology as having a fundamental weakness in thinking that mental processes could be measured.

In education today, there continues to be considerable debate as to whether teachers follow Theory A practice of dispensing information through direct instruction or through Theory B practice of being facilitators of learning. Theory B point of view is presently considered the more popular of the two theories in "education policies, education models and education practices focus on constructivism" (Brown, 2006, p. 109). Undoubtedly, most educators would agree that neither the Theory A nor the Theory B view of learning is flawless in its perception of how students learn and how teachers should instruct. There are two significant differences between Theory A and Theory B in defining the role of the classroom teacher. In a teacher-centered classroom, the teacher assumes the responsibility for instruction. In a learner-centered classroom, the learner accepts the responsibility for his/her learning. The traditional view of education is rooted in the research performed by Piaget (as cited in Moore, 2001) who believed "students develop according to a maturational unfolding of their abilities. Therefore, the set of cognitive structures possessed at each stage of development defines what they (students) can and cannot do." (p. 49). On the other hand, Fosnot (1996) suggested that Theory B views learning as an interpretive, recursive, and building process by which active learners interrelate with the physical and social world. Kruse (1998) supported Fosnot's views on Theory B, because he also indicated that this approach has shown to have a positive effect on students' ability to increase their knowledge. Although theorists and educators will continue to debate the strengths and weaknesses of Theory A and Theory B, it is important to remember that there are ongoing shifts in the promotion of educational theories.

▶ The Key to Success for Improving Future Education in the United States

The problems the United States is facing in educating students today for future employment go far beyond choosing which learning theory is essential for educating our nation's children to succeed in school. Educators play an important role in preparing students for the workplace and lifestyle in today's world. This preparation requires students to balance cognitive, personal, and interpersonal abilities. A group of experts from the National Academies' Division of Behavioral and Sciences and Education collaborated with researchers, educators, and policy makers for more than a year to define deep learning and twenty-first century skills. According to Sparks (July, 2012), the National Research Council of the National Academies of Science in Washington concluded in their report that current education policy has not been successful in defining these abilities. Pellegrino (2012), a co-editor of the report and co-director of the Interdisciplinary Learning Science Research Institute at the University of Illinois in Chicago, suggested that schooling is a place where students learn a cluster of skills. The committee divided these skill areas into cognitive, interpersonal, and intrapersonal. Linda Darling-Hammond, a Stanford University professor of education, suggested that developing common definitions for these three skill areas is critical to having meaningful discussions on education policy such as the Common Core State Standards.

The economic future of the United States rests with encouraging more students to become proficient in science, technology, engineering, and mathematics, which are collectively referred to as STEM. In 2012, a time of high unemployment in the United States, many jobs are not being filled, because they require STEM-related skills. As Raytheon Company Chairman and CEO William Swanson said at a Massachusetts' STEM Summit in the fall of 2012, "Too many students and adults are training for jobs in which labor surpluses exist and demand is low, while high-demand jobs, particularly in STEM fields, go unfilled" (Massachusetts' STEM Summit, 2011). A report from Georgetown University Center on Education found that forty-seven percent of Bachelor's degrees in STEM occupations exceed the earnings of individuals with a Doctor of Philosophy Degree working in occupations unrelated to STEM. In a recent study by the Lemselson-MIT Intervention Index, 60% of young adults ranging in age from 16-25 listed at least one factor that kept them from pursuing STEM education such as they were not well-prepared in school (Engler, 2012). The solution to this problem rests with being able to identify ways to better educate students in STEM-related subjects. For the United States to maintain its standing as a world leader, we have a responsibility to offer students an education that has the potential to increase our nation's STEM talent to compete in the world marketplace.

Discussion Questions

1. Discuss the differences between the behaviorist learning theory and the constructivist learning theory.

2. What is the principal's role in improving student achievement?

3. What is the teacher's role in improving student achievement?

4. What is the value of establishing learning communities?

5. What is the relationship of epistemology to education?

6. Describe STEM education and what it means to the future economy of the United States?

Leadership Activity

You have recently been selected by the board of trustees in a large urban school district to become the principal of a middle school in a lower socioeconomic area. The school has been identified for the past three years as a low performing school and is in danger of being taken over by the state. You have been tasked with improving the teaching and learning of the students who attend this school. After reading the article on *Applied Learning Theories*, how would you go about improving the teaching and learning at the school were you are now the principal?

Background of the Author

Dr. Mary Anne Weegar is currently an Assistant Professor in the School of Education at National University in La Jolla, California. She has a BA in Education from Bucknell University, an MA in Education from San Diego State University, and an EdD in Organizational Leadership from Nova Southeastern University. She has been the coordinator for the student teaching program, faculty credential advisor for the Bachelor of Arts in Interdisciplinary Studies with a CA Preliminary Multiple Subject Teaching Credential, faculty credential advisor for the BA in English with a CA Preliminary Single Subject Teaching Credential, and the developer of numerous educational technology courses for both face-to-face and online delivery. She was previously a secondary school teacher, Director of Curriculum and Instruction, Director of State and Federal Education Programs, Coordinator of a Regional Occupation Program, and Assistant Principal at a Continuation High School. She has also presented scholarly papers at numerous local, state, and international educational conferences.

References

Arts in Education Institute of Western New York (2002). *Constructivist Learning Theory*. Retrieved (January 21, 2008) from http://www.artsined.com/teachingarts/Pedag/Dewey.html

Barker, P. (2008). Re-evaluating a model of learning design. *Innovations in Education and Teaching International*, 45(2), 127–142.

Bednar, A. K., Cunningham, D., Duffy, T. M.& Perry, J. D. (1992). Theory into practice: How do we link? In T. M. Duffy & D. H. Jonassen (Eds.), *Constructivism and the technology of instruction* (pp 17-34), Hillsdale, NJ: Lawrence Erlbaum Associates.

Brooks, J. G., & Brooks, M. G. (1995). *Constructing Knowledge in the Classroom*. Retrieved (January 21, 2008) from http://www.sedl.org/scimath/compass/v01n03/1.html

Brown, T. H. (2006). Beyond constructivism: Navigation in the knowledge era. *On the Horizon*, 14(3), pp.108–120

Bush, G. (2006). Learning about learning: from theories to trends. *Teacher Librarian*, 34(2), 14–19.

Carbonell, L. (2004) *Instructional Development Timeline*. Retrieved (January 21, 2008) from http://www.my-ecoach.com/idtimeline/learningtheory.html.

Chambliss, J. J. (1996). *Philosophy of education: An encyclopedia*. New York & London: Garland Publishing Company.

DuFour, R. (2002). The learning centered principal. *Educational Leadership* 59(8), 12-15.

Dewey, J. (1938). *Experience and Education*. New York, NY: The Macmillan Company.

Draper, R. J. (2002). School mathematics reform, constructivism, and literacy: A case for literacy instruction in the reform-oriented math classroom. *Journal of Adolescent & Adult Literacy*, 45(6), 520-529.

Driscoll, M. (2005). *Psychology of learning for instruction*, (3rd ed.). Boston, MA: Pearson Education Inc.

Engler, J. (2012, June 15). STEM education is the key to the U.S.'s economic future. *US News and World Report*. Retrieved August 12, 2012 from http://www.usnews.com/topics/author/john_engler

Fisher, P. (2008). Learning about literacy: From theories to trends. *Teacher Librarian*, 35(3), 8–13.

Flath, B. (1989). The principal as instructional leader. *ATA Magazines*, (69)3m 19–22, 47–49.

Fosnot, C. T. (1996). *Constructivism: Theory, perspectives, and practice*. New York: Teachers College Press.

Gagne, R. (1985). *The conditions of learning* (4th ed.). New York: Holt, Rinehart & Winston.

Gagne, R., Briggs, L., & Wager, W. (1992). *Principles of Instructional Design* (4th Ed.). Fort Worth, TX: HBJ College Publishers.

Gonzalez, J. C. (n.d.). *Constructivism vs. direct instruction.* Retrieved (January 21, 2008)

Gregory, R. L. (1987). *The Oxford Companion to the Mind.* Oxford: Oxford University Press.

Gulati, S. (2008). Compulsory participation in online discussions: Is this constructivism Innovations in Education and Teaching International. *Journal of the Association for Programmed Learning ETTI,* 45(2), 183–193.

Harman, G. (2008). Mechanical mind. *American Scientist,* 96(1), 76-79.

Johnson, J. A., Musial, D., Hall, G. E., Gollnick, D. M., & Dupuis, V. L. (2008). *Foundations of American education: Perspectives on education in a changing world* (14th ed.). Boston, MA: Pearson Education Inc.

Kearsley, G. (1994). *Constructivist Theory.* Retrieved (January 21, 2008) from http://tip.psychology.org/bruner.html

Kim, C., & Hatton, N. (n.d.). *Cognitive theory and curriculum application.* Retrieved (January 21, 2008) from http://www.umm.maine.edu:300/education/students/curriculumDesign/Hatton.htm.

Knowles, M. S. (1973). *The Adult Learner: A Neglected Species.* Houston: Gulf Publishing Company.

Kruse, G. D. (1998). Cognitive science and its implications for education. *NASSP Bulletin, 82* (598), 73–79.

Kumar, M. (2006). Constructivist epistemology in action. *The Journal of Educational Thought,* 40(3), 247–262.

Leahey, T. H. (2000). Control: A history of behavioral psychology. *The Journal of American History,* 87(2), 686–687.

McBrien J. L., & R. S. Brandt (1997). *The language of learning: A guide to education terms.* Alexandria, VA: Association for Supervision and Curriculum Development.

Mills, J. A. (1998). Control. *A history of behavioral psychology!* New York, NY: New York University Press.

Moore, J. (2001). On certain assumptions underlying contemporary education practices. *Behavior and Social Issues,* 11, 49-64.

Morrison, G. R., Ross, S. M., & Kemp, J. E. (2004). *Design effective instruction.* Hoboken, NJ: Wiley Jossey-Bass.

National Association of Elementary School Principals (2001). *Leading learning communities: Standards for what principals should know and be able to do.* Alexandria, VA.

Overskeid, G. (2008). They should have thought about the consequences: The crisis of cognitivism and a second chance for behavior analysis. *The Psychological Record,* 58(1), 131–152.

Panasuk, R. M., & Todd, J. (2005). Effectiveness of lesson planning: Factor analysis. *Journal of Instructional Psychology,* 32(3), 215–233.

Rotfeld, H. H. (2007). Theory, data, interpretations, and more theory. *The Journal of Consumer Affairs,* 41(2), 376–380.

Rummel, Ethan. (2008). Constructing cognition. *American Scientist,* 96(1), 80–82.

Sparks, S. D. (2012). Study: '21st-century learning' demands mix of abilities. *Edweek.org.*

Swanson, W. H. (2011). *Executive speech reprint.* Massachusetts' STEM Summit in Newton, Massachusetts.

Skinner, B. F. (1974). *About behaviorism.* New York: Vintage.

Sternberg, R. Applying psychological theories to educational practice. *American Education Research Journal,* 45(1), 150–166).

Thomas, R. K. (1997). Correcting some Pavlovian regarding "Pavlov's bell" and Pavlov's "mugging." *American Journal of Psychology*, 110, 115–125.

Wakefield, J. C. (2007). Is behaviorism becoming a pseudoscience? Replies to Drs. Wyatt, Midkiff, and Wong. *Behavior and Social Issues*, 16(2), 170–190.

Watson, J. B., & Rayner, R. (1920). Conditioned emotional responses. Journal of *Experimental Psychology*, 3, 1–14.

Webb, J. L. (2007). Pragmatisms (Plural) part I: Classical pragmatism and some implications for empirical inquiry. *Journal of Economic Issues*, 41(4), 1063-1087.

WGHB (1998). *A science odyssey: People & discoveries*. Retrieved (May 20, 2008) from http://www.pbs.org/wgbh/aso/databank/entries/bhskin.html

White-lark, R., Diarlo, M., & Gilchriest, N. (2008). "Guide on the side": An instructional approach to meet mathematics standards. *The High School Journal*, 91(4), 40–45.

Collaborative School Management: An Innovative Model for Administrators

David Harrison Kurth, EdD, Associate Professor, School of Education, National University, San Bernadino, California

ISLLC Standard 3: An education leader promotes the success of every student by ensuring management of the organization, operation, and resources for a safe, efficient, and effective learning environment.

ISLLC Standard 4: Collaborating with families and community members, responding to diverse community interest and need, and mobilizing community resources

▶ Abstract

This paper identified basic building educational climate percepts and integrated them into a systematic collaborative school management model. The model is characterized by a series of postulates that, when applied, guide administrators to consistent issue resolution in the context of acceptable organizational outcomes.

Key Words: classroom management, collaboration, and discipline

This article presents a model that leads to a school wide blueprint for a positive school climate. The model's postulates, when consistently applied, help building leaders develop a collaborative management system that all stakeholders will understand and support.

▶ Statement of the Problem

School districts have recognized that the principal has a major influence on the school building's educational climate. However, few districts have emphasized the importance of that educational climates, helped principals to identify the central issues connected to positive educational climate, nor allowed principals to prioritize time use as a function of addressing those issues.

▶ Research Methods

*The ideas presented here are derived from the conclusions of many building climate research studies conducted over the past thirty years (Cotton, 1996; Emmer, Evertson, & Anderson, 1980; Evertson & Emmer, 1982; Marzano, 2003; Rosas & West, 2009; Wong, 2009). These researched concepts were tempered by 20 years of building application. Practicing building administrators and faculty refined various sections of the Collaborative School Management model, which has seen more than six iterations. When the mature model was implemented, a year-end poll showed all faculty either agreed or strongly agreed the model's use improved the school climate.

Discussion

The Principal's role in setting positive school climate

It is unproductive to ask whether a principal can have a positive impact on student achievement if there is doubt about whether a school's characteristic qualities are linked to student achievement. "One of the fundamental tenets of research and practice in the school improvement community concerns the apparently powerful impact of principals on processes related to school effectiveness and improvement. The international chorus of support for this belief has, however, occasionally been broken by discordant voices questioning the empirical validity of this claim" (Hallinger & Heck, 1998, p. 185). There are several studies that find it difficult to demonstrate the principal's impact on student achievement (Bridges, 1982; Rowan & Denk, 1984). "It is the complexity of the relationship between school outcomes and principal leadership that makes it extremely difficult to determine whether a relationship exists" (Hallinger & Heck, 1998). However, the methodology and focus changed after 1995 to allow more definitive conclusions. It became increasing more sophisticated, moving from direct effects to mediate-effects conceptualizations of the principal's role. Researchers have extended the bounds of inquiry. They have sought to understand not only if principals have effects on school outcomes, but more particularly the paths through which such effects area achieved" (Hallinger & Heck, 1998, p. 187). This new approach led later studies to more useful lines of inquiry and research. These studies provided evidence to support the contention that principals exercise a measurable effect on school effectiveness and on student achievement. In particular, the principal's role in shaping the school's direction through vision, mission, and goals came through in these studies as a primary avenue of influence. While the state of this research is still evolving, the variables represent both a reasonable focus for principal practice and also for future research into school effectiveness and improvement (Hallinger & Heck 1998, p. 187).

Thus, newer studies are less tepid in proposing a link between instructional leadership and student achievement. Samuel Krugwhen (1992), summarizing a study involving more than 72 principals, 1523 teachers and 9415 students concluded, "the findings provide empirical evidence for a strong relationship between instructional leadership and student learning outcomes"(1992, p. 3). Even more convincing are Waters, Marzano, and McNulty (2003), who examined more than 5000 studies to select 70 that met their criteria for design, control, data analysis, and rigor (2003). They found there was a substantial relationship between leadership and student achievement.

> *We found average effect size (expressed as a correlation) between leadership and student achievement is .25. A one standard deviation improvement in leadership practices is associated with an increase in average student achievement from the 50th to the 60th percentile. To interpret this correlation, consider two schools school A and school B with a similar student and teacher populations. Both demonstrate achievement on a standardized, norm-reference test at the 50th percentile. Principals in both schools are also average, that is their abilities in 21 key leadership responsibilities are ranked at the 50th percentile. Now assume that the principal of school B improves her demonstrated abilities in all 21 responsibilities exactly one standard deviation. Our research findings indicate that this would translate into mean student achievement at school B that is 10 percentile points higher than school A (p. 166).*

Finally, studies conducted in school districts in Memphis, Tennessee; El Paso, Texas; and Long Beach, New York identify strong leadership as the key to improving student learning in poorly performing schools (Gates, Ross, & Brewer, 2003). "While schools make a difference in what students learn, principals make a difference in schools" (Lipham, 1981, p. 17).

Principal leadership extends beyond simple supervision. Positive correlational studies show that a powerful instructional leader sets a tone that permeates the entire educational institution. These leadership characteristics are consistent from school to school and district to district (Purkey & Smith 1982). "Of significant importance is the general instructional climate and instructional organization, with their significant effect on student outcomes" (Halliger, 1990, p. 4). Thus, while the connection between principal leadership and student achievement is not simple to establish, the vast majority of studies do validate the linkage. Given this connection linking principal leadership to student achievement, appropriate principal leadership becomes critical for the success of all schools and the collaborative school management model more significant.

School climate

School climate has been described as "the set of internal characteristics that distinguish one school from another and influence the behaviors of each school's members" (Hoy, Smith, & Sweetland, 2005, p. 1). In the landmark study by Brookover, Schneider, Beady, Flood, and Wisebaker (1978), school climate was found to be a more significant factor in student achievement than the variables of race and socioeconomic status. Finally, in a study by Taylor (1995), aspects of school climate emerged as stronger predictors of job satisfaction than did the elements of decision participation.

Kottkamp, Mulhern, and Hoy (1987), used factor analytic techniques to develop five factors to measure school climate on a Likert type scale:

a. Supportive principal behavior (principal works hard and offers constructive criticism),

b. Directive principal behavior (principal supervises teachers closely and rules with an iron fist),

c. Engaged teacher behavior (teachers support each other and are friendly with students),

d. Frustrated teacher behavior (paperwork is burdensome and nonteaching duties are excessive), and

e. Intimate teacher behavior (teachers are close friends and socialize regularly) (p. 41).

It is interesting to note that school climate is often thought to include student attitudes and perceptions as well, but this landmark study did not address that issue.

Many believe school climate is closely associated with efficacy of the school discipline system. In a recent article the connection seemed to be demonstrated: "Nevertheless, school climate explained a substantial percentage of the variance in all measures of school disorder, controlling for the effects of community characteristics and school student composition. Schools in which students perceived greater fairness and clarity of rules had less delinquent behavior and less student victimization" (Academic OneFile, 2004, p. 4).

When researcher Kathleen Cotton (1996) examined the research, she found several key factors in effective school-wide discipline: commitment, high expectations, clear rules, a supportive environment, a visible and supportive principal, delegation of authority to teachers, and close ties to the community. Other findings suggest that a healthy school climate requires innovation, consistent enforcement of a written code of conduct, and teaching of social competency. One study linked lower levels of misconduct to increased levels of daily academic challenge and increased student perceptions of success.

Classroom Management Defined

In a survey conducted among 34 randomly selected practicing administrators and teachers, the following statement was identified by 94% of the respondents as most important for classroom teaching success: "A consistently implemented discipline system, the appropriate use of student relevant curriculum, and the skillful use of pedagogy, are all equally important to successful classroom management" (Kurth, 2011, p. 2). Clearly, over the last 50 years, educational research has moved away from focusing on controlling student behavior and has focused more on ways to increase our knowledge of what effective classroom managers do and how they do it (Evertson & Harris, 1992).

Harry Wong offers a comprehensive definition of classroom management when he states that "Classroom management refers to all of the things a teacher does to organize students, space, time, and materials so student learning can take place" (2009, p. 23). Rosas and West (2009), add, "Teachers must possess the skills to create a safe learning environment that promotes academic growth" (From the abstract).

The start of the school year is key to having an effective classroom (Harry Wong, 2009; Marzano, 2003; Emmer, et al., 1980, Evertson & Emmer, 1982). Teachers who are effective managers prepare, plan classroom rules and procedures, clearly communicate expectations, establish routines, and procedures, and teach them along with expectation for appropriate performance. They also systematically monitor student work and behavior, and provide feedback about academic performance and behavior. Teachers who take the time to set up this type of system have a smooth running classroom that results in improved student achievement. If misbehavior does occur, a teacher that provides a structured environment with clear expectations of behavior will be able to quickly and effectively address it (Wong, 2009).

Another study concerning the specific methods employed to facilitate classroom management concludes that classroom management skills can be identified and learned. Data from this program evaluation indicate that teachers implement a number of classroom management strategies at higher levels after participating in sustained professional development for two or more years as provided by content experts and when the school's leadership is perceived as supportive. In addition, levels and degrees of program implementation in middle grades schools were found to be associated with improved school climate and student outcomes, again, with school leadership being a covariate. Attendance, behavior, and academic achievement as measured by state assessments and other adequate yearly progress criteria among high poverty middle grades schools were found to be associated with levels of implementation and supportive school leadership. The model used to support this finding is robust whenever 50% or more teachers in high poverty middle grades schools implement developmental designs for two or more years, student achievement improved. (Hough & Schmitt, 2011).

Student Relevant Curriculum

The general lack of research and inquiry on this topic is interesting, given the central importance practicing educators ascribe to the concept. However, the literature does show that competent teachers are able to identify student relevant curriculum and contend that student relevant curriculum should be seen as career-relevant or alternatively, culturally relevant. "Relevant, challenging, integrative, and exploratory all describe the curriculum desirable in middle school" (National Middle School Association, 2010). Career-relevant curriculum is one prominent strategy used since the 1970s to achieve these goals (Akos, Charles, Orthner, & Cooley, 2011, from the abstract). All of the relevant literature seems to agree that student relevant curriculum is a function of the individual child's needs. "To most experienced teachers a teachable moment is associated with whether a teacher's Teachable Moment is relevant to the learner's "learning moment,".... and was based on careful observation and interaction with children, an ability to recognize and interpret their observations according to their understanding of child development, and strong beliefs about what is important to teach (Hyun, 2002, p. 97).

John Dewey (1904/1964) at the turn of the twentieth century articulated a fundamental tension in the preparation of teachers—specifically, what is "proper relationship" of subject matter and pedagogy. "On one hand, to what extent does teaching—and hence, learning to teach—depend on the development of knowledge of subject matter? On the other, to what extend does it rely on the development of pedagogical method" (p. 208). In 1986, Shulman, Wilson, Grossman, and Richert introduced "pedagogical content knowledge" to the lexicon of research on teaching and teacher education. The term called attention to a special kind of teacher knowledge that links content and pedagogy. In addition to general pedagogical knowledge and knowledge of the content, Shulman and his colleagues argued that teachers needed to have additional information such as what topics children find interesting or difficult or the visual models most useful for teaching a specific content idea. This study contends that pedagogy may well be unique to both subject matter and audience. To be an effective teacher, one must understand how those concepts are interconnected.

Discipline

Jones says that "discipline, most simply stated, is the business of enforcing simple classroom rules that facilitate learning and minimize disruption" (1979; p. 268). Variations on this definition are offered by Duke (1989), Gettinger (1988), Strother (1989), and many others. Researchers, Lasley and Wayson (1982), note that some educators view disciplinary issues as "cultural factors, peer group pressure, or genotypic tendencies" (p. 29). They disagree with those educators and make the case that these activities are a natural part of the educational process. The article concludes by contenting that all faculty members and students must be involved in the behavior management process.

The pursuit of learning can be derailed in schools plagued by discipline problems. This is certainly not news to principals and teachers. Research confirms their intuitions about the connection between discipline and achievement. One recent study found that classroom behavior, rather than class size, was a primary factor associated with improved achievement. On the whole, research suggests that improvements in school discipline will create an environment more conducive to academic achievement.

So, how can discipline be improved in schools and classrooms? Research suggests a three-pronged approach: work to improve the general school climate, target interventions to students who seem to need them most, and train and support teachers in effective classroom management" (Smith, 2004, p. ii).

Discipline Programs

The following approaches to discipline focus almost entirely on the classroom and the individual, not the overall interactions of a comprehensive system.

1. Reality therapy—The focus of this program was to encourage students to make positive choices while making clear to the students that their behavior had consequences (Glasser, 1975).

2. A positive approach to discipline—Involves instilling in the students a sense of responsibility for their behavior (Scarlett, Ponte, & Singh, 2009).

3. Teacher effectiveness training—Students are taught problem-solving techniques and negotiation techniques (Gordon, 1982).

4. Transactional analysis—Students with behavior problems are given exercises to identify the problem and to find ways to make changes (Goldhaber, 1976).

5. Assertive discipline—the program focuses on giving the right of the teacher to teach and the student to learn. Student behavior that interferes is not tolerated (Canter, L. & Canter, M., 1976).

6. Adlerian approach—Getting the teachers to understand the student's reason for his discipline and to teach the teacher to cope with the problem (Oberst, 2003).

7. Student team learning—Teaching how the student could work in cooperative groups (Davis, 1995).

8. Capturing kids' hearts—This program featured a workshop that lasted two days. The focus was to build a strong bond between the students and develop a behavior contract (Middleton, 2007).

Successful administrators

Administrators dealing with discipline have a different task than their teaching colleagues, and researchers have identified some of the behaviors that lead to a successful discipline process. Successful administrators:

1. Maintained visibility with the teachers, staff, and students,

2. Reached out to the community,

3. Were involved with their students,

4. Fostered good school/parent communication,

5. Were aware of the people's lives,

6. Set high standards, and

7. Were clear about what was expected for student behavior (Meyers & Pawlas, 1989).

This imposing and ambiguous list is symptomatic of what is wrong with school wide management approaches. One might well wonder how anyone could be a successful administrator, particularly if the school is a large one. The Collaborative School Management model suggests an answer.

▶ The Collaborative School Management Model

The Collaborative School Management model is driven by seven basic postulates. The postulates direct administrative behavior, and require that faculty, building administration, and the district office agree on the entire building management process. The community should be invited to the discussion table when building climate issues are discussed.

Postulate One: Administrators must assign a very high priority to helping all teachers understand the interactive nature of the principles of classroom management.

Postulate Two: Administrators must assign a very high priority to collaboratively developing school wide expectations for discipline, pedagogy, and relevant subject matter.

Postulate Three: There are four audiences that will be observing administrative educational decisions. They are faculty and staff, students, the community, and the district office. Administrators must evaluate the consequences of administrative decisions using each of these groups' perspectives before taking action.

Postulate Four: The administrator will voice collaborative school management concerns directly to the teachers before voicing them elsewhere.

Postulate Five: The administrator must understand that disciplinary actions that are in the best interests of the organization may not be in the best interests of the individual student.

Postulate Six: The objective for any discipline system is behavior change, not punishment. Punishment is understood to be one of several tools that may precipitate behavior change.

Postulate Seven: Expectations generated from the discipline flow chart will be followed. If there is an exception to this process, before any action is articulated or imposed, the administrator will walk to the teacher's classroom to explain why the exception is appropriate.

▶ Implications

The power in the Collaborative School Management model is two-fold. First, it promotes common expectations system wide. Second, it helps administration understand the needs of colleagues and to provide consistent administrative decisions. The following examples are instructive.

Scenario One

A fistfight has occurred between two close friends who are honor students. After interviewing the students, it is clear to the assistant principal that the friends have made up and that there is no continuing danger of injury to anyone. Additionally, the students have an important lecture in calculus in one hour. Should the students be allowed to attend the class? After all, it is in the students' best interests to do so, and there is no danger to students or adults.

Application of the collaborative school management model is instructive. Administrative Postulate Three requires that we examine the possible perceptions of the audiences that will review the discipline decision. If we return the fighters to class within the hour, the student audience will rightly conclude that the fighting rule won't be enforced, or worse, that good students receive special treatment. The faculty, community and the district audiences will conclude the same thing. Clearly, the organization requires implementation of the agreed upon consequences.

The model's direction does not stop here. Administrative Postulate Five says the administrator must understand that disciplinary actions that are in the best interests of the organization may not be in the best interests of the individual student. The sanction agreed upon as part of the seamless discipline process must be imposed, although doing so may well not be in the students' best interest.

Scenario Two

An angry parent shows up in the assistant principal's office late Friday afternoon. Her daughter, Sally, did not turn in a required permission slip for the dance when it was due, and was told that she could not attend. The mother takes responsibility saying, "I was sleeping and couldn't wake up to sign that stupid slip. Since it is my fault, you should let my daughter go to the dance. I'm not leaving here until you agree she can."

Administrative Postulate Three is applied. The audience viewpoint is considered. Assessing the faculty viewpoint here is sufficient, although those of students, community, or district office are equally compelling. The administrator can be sure that faculty will note the rule was not enforced, making the following interaction highly probable. On the Monday following the dance, the social studies department chair comes to the office and inquires sweetly, "Could faculty please have a list of the school rules we are not going to enforce. We want to know the ones to ignore so we can do our job more effectively." This perspective alone makes the decision clear. The girl may not attend the dance, even if the assistant must go through an unpleasant scene.

➡ Conclusion

There are two major and constant problems associated with providing leadership to realize a positive school educational climate. One is that the expectations of the teacher, student, community, and/or the administrator are often not synchronous. The second is that the administrator can be unsure as to which course of action will promote maximum school efficacy. Given the collaborative school management model, administrators can systematically make decisions in a way that maximizes the long-term positive payoff to all stakeholders, and promotes the best interests of the organization. Additionally, administrators need to be aware of the powerful audience groups, whose perceptions often have great impact on the school climate, and be consistent and clear in their management decisions.

Discussion Questions

1. The collaborative school management model is predicated on the perception that there is a disconnect in expectations and communication between school administration, teachers, district administration, and the school community. Looking at your school district specifically, do you find this sort of disconnect is present? If so, list four major areas where you believe the model's application could help develop a better educational environment. If you don't see a disconnect, what is your school or district doing that is successful?

2. A worried parent comes to you and confesses finding marijuana in his son's room. The son is a star athlete on the basketball team. Clearly, having marijuana at home is a violation of the athletic code enforced at your school. What are your first thoughts concerning a course of action? Apply the model. Does it suggest a different course of action? Do you agree or disagree with the postulates of the model?

3. One of the model's postulates requires that you may have to adopt a course of action that is in the best interests of the organization but not in the best interests of the individual student. Can a committed and professional educator ethically apply this postulate?

4. Are all of the model's identified "audiences" required to be involved in its application to effectively improve the school educational climate?

5. A parent comes to your office and tells you that her child, Monique, is dying of leukemia. She asks that you violate school rules and allow Monique to participate in graduation next month. There is a strictly enforced school rule that says seniors may not walk in the graduation ceremony if they do not have the credits needed to graduate. Monique does not have the required credits. Would you strictly apply the management model, or allow Monique to participate in graduation?

Activity

Gather into a group and have each member present a difficult situation they have dealt with in school/classroom management. The situation should involve multiple levels of building personnel. Then spend some individual time analyzing the difficult situation using the collaborative school/classroom management model. Finally, have each individual present the solution to the difficult situation to the group for discussion. The solution should demonstrate application of the model's postulates.

Background of the Author

Dr. Kurth has spent more than 35 years as a public school teacher and administrator. He was recognized as the Phoebe Apperson Hearst Teacher of the Year, was nominated by his students for the California Chemistry Teacher of the Year and for the American Chemical Society "Catalyst Award." He was the Principal of the Year in the Seamount League in both 1999 and 2000 and a member of the Washington State Principal's Representative Council. For 17 years he has been a principal at both the elementary and secondary level. Dr. Kurth holds teaching credentials in mathematics, chemistry and social studies, as well as the Professional Administrative Credential. His academic training includes a BA in Political Science (University of California at Irvine), a MA degree in Curriculum and Instruction, (Cal State Long Beach) and a EdD in Organizational Leadership from the University of La Verne. He is currently an Associate Professor, Masters' Degree Program Lead, Course Lead, and Lead Faculty in Educational Administration at National University, San Bernardino.

References

Akos, P., Charles, P., Orthner, V., & Cooley, D. (2011). Teacher perspectives on career-relevant curriculum in middle school. *Research in Middle Level Education Online*, 34(5), 1–9.

Bridges, Edwin M. (1982). Research on school administrator: Evidence from US high schools 1967–1980. *Economics of Education* (18): 12-33.

Canter, L., & Canter, M., (1976). Assertive discipline: *A take charge approach for today's education*. Los Angeles, CA: Canter and Associates.

Cotton, K. (1996). School size, school climate, and student performance: *Northwest Regional Educational Laboratory*. Portland, OR.

Davis. J., & James, B. (1995). *Interdisciplinary courses and team teaching: new arrangements for learning*. Phoenix, AZ: American Council on Education and the Oryx Press.

Dewey, J. (1964). The relation of theory to practice in education. R. Archambault (Ed.) *John Dewey on Education*, 313–338.

Duke, D. (1989). School organization, leadership and student behavior. *Strategies to Reduce Student Misbehavior*. O. C. Moles (Ed.) Washington, DC: Office of Educational Research and Improvement, 31–62. ED 311 608.

Emmer, E., Evertson, C., & Anderson, L. (1980). Effective classroom management at the beginning of the school year. *Elementary School Journal*, 80 (5), 219–231.

Evertson, C. M., & Emmer, E. T. (1982). Effective management at the beginning of the school year in junior high classes. *Journal of Educational Psychology*, 74 (4), 48–498.

Gettinger, M. (1988). Methods of proactive classroom management. *School Psychology Review*, 14(8), 22-242.

Glasser, W. (1975). *Reality therapy: a new approach to psychiatry*. New York: Harper and Row.

Goldhaber, M. (1976). *Transactional analysis: principles and applications*. Boston: Allyn and Bacon.

Gordon, T., & Burch, N. (1982). *T.E.T. teacher effectiveness training*. Retrieved (September 9, 2011) from http://scholar.google.com/scholar?cluster=1744456059940880022&hl=en

Hallinger, P., & Heck, R. (1998). Exploring the principal's contribution to school effectiveness: 1980-1995, *School Effectiveness and School Improvement*, 2, 157–191.

Hough, D., & Schmitt, V. (2011). *Middle Grades Research Journal*, 6 (3), 163–175.

Jones, F. (1979). The gentle art of classroom discipline. *National Elementary Principal* (58), 266–322.

Krug, S. (1992). *Instructional leadership, school instructional climate, and student learning outcomes*. Urbana, GA: National Center for School Leadership.

Kurth, D. (2011). A survey of practicing educator's perception of successful classroom management skills. *National University OIRA*.

Lasley, T., & Wayson, W. (1982). Characteristics of schools with good discipline. *Educational Leadership*, 28–31.

Lipham, J. (1981). *Effective principal, effective school*. Reston, Virginia: National Association of Secondary School Principals.

Marzano, R., & Marzano, J. (2003). The Key to Classroom Management. *Educational Leadership*. September, ASCD.

Meyers, K., & Pawlas, G. (1989). The principal and discipline, elementary principal series 5. *Phi Delta Kappa Foundation*, 66, 1–28.

Middleton, M. (2007). *Capturing kids' hearts: Session 4 an aid in child development*. Retrieved from www.flippengroup.com/education/edupress3.html

Oberst, U., & Stewart, A. (2003). *Adlerian psychotherapy: an advanced approach to individual psychology*. New York: Brunner-Routledge.

Purkey, S., & Marshall S., (1982). Highlights from research on effective schools. *Association for Supervision and Curriculum Development* 12, no. RIEFEB1984: 9.

Rosas, C., & West, M. (2009). Teacher beliefs about classroom management: Pre-service and in-service teachers' beliefs about classroom management. *Phi Delta Kappa Foundation*, 76, 34–66.

Rowan, B., & Denk, C. (1984). Management succession, school socioeconomic context and basic skills achievement. *American Educational Research Journal* (21). 17–537.

Scarlett, W., Ponte I., & Singh J. (2009). *A Positive approach to discipline*. Thousand Oaks CA: Sage Publications.

Strother, D., Wayson, W., DeVoss, G., Kaeser, S., Lasley, T., & Pinnell, G. (1989). Practical applications of research. *Phi Delta Kappa Foundation*, 66, 728.

Waters, T., Marzano, J., & McNulty, B. (2003). *Balanced leadership: What 30 years of research tells us about the effect of leadership on student achievement*. Aurora, IN: Mid-Continent Research for Education and Learning.

Wong, H., & Wong, R. (2009). *The first days of school—How to be an effective teacher*. Mountain View, CA: Harry K. Wong Publications, Inc.

Principal Expectations and Why Telling Makes a Difference

Michele Pecina EdD, National University

ISLLC Standard 1: Facilitating the development, articulation, implementation, and stewardship of a vision of learning that is shared and supported by the school community.

▶ Abstract

This paper explored Standard One of the Interstate School Leaders Licensure Consortium (ISLLC) standards. The case study presentation followed the author's journey in developing a vision, communicating the vision, implementing the vision, and monitoring and evaluating the vision. This paper examined Bryan Smith's research on building a shared vision and Erlinda Teisinger's contributions to school leadership. The actual Principal Expectations document used in the researcher's work is presented in detail and explained for application.

▶ Why Telling Makes a Difference

It could strike the reader that "telling" might not be the best approach for a school administrator in today's highly accountable schools. Recently, however, Marc Johnson, an award winning superintendent of schools from Sanger Unified School District, Sanger, California stated as he addressed a group of future administrators at a Phi Delta Kappa event, that he is convinced the success of his schools comes from his direct order that all of the district's schools would follow the Professional Learning Communities (PLC) model. He came back from a Professional Learning Communities training before school started in 2009 and immediately bought the book on PLCs, gave it to his school administrators, and then told all of his principals to have it in place on the first day of school. The district has been very successful since using the PLC model in the academic achievement of its students. This example can be utilized as the school administrator reflects on the expectations they may have for their schools.

New principals today face a myriad of challenges posed by the demands of accountability requirements under federal laws of No Child Left Behind (California Department of Education, 2006) and the State of California's Public School Accountability Act (PSAA, 1999). These challenges include raising test scores on a consistent basis, data studies, and motivational strategies for staff and students to improve. School principals are held accountable in that their dismissal is a very real possibility if Academic Performance Index (API) demands are not met (California Department of Education, 2006). The question can then be asked as to how a principal should prepare for each school year's vision to best meet accountability demands?

As a school administrator reflects on the beginning of a school year, it comes to the forefront on how he or she will lead to make a difference in the academic achievement that is her responsibility. The first strategy that should be developed is building a shared vision. The five stages recommended by Smith (1993) are telling, selling, testing, consulting, and co-creating. The first stage relates to the Marc Johnson example previously given. The superintendent knew what the vision should be and he required his administrators to follow it and transfer that vision to their schools. The telling approach is one of the main tools a principal has in creating a vision for the school. Bryan Smith (1993) explains this approach as one to be used in times of crisis. "We've got to do this. It's our vision. Be excited about it, or reconsider your vision for your career here" (p. 315). The selling and testing of the vision comes with the presentation of the principal expectations followed by break out discussion groups so it can be determined how much of the vision is taking hold. The National Association of Elementary School Principals emphasizes the sharing of the vision. "Learner-centered leaders help others understand that they are part of something greater than themselves and provide hope and the belief that, by working together, everyone's performance can improve" (p. 24). Consulting enhances the vision with small school teams viewing information on progress. Data collection with tools, such as, benchmark data, classroom walk-throughs with school profiling, and professional learning communities' discussion results provide consulting opportunities. The last stage of co-creating according to Bryan Smith (1993) results in people being satisfied in being part of a process in shaping the vision. He further posits that each organization will gravitate towards a stage. The stage described in the following case study is the telling stage to establish the vision because of the demanding times public school administrators find themselves in today's accountability environment and that the sense of urgency is a constant factor.

▶ Case Study

A case study of the author's personal journey with establishing a vision, principal expectations, and achieving school accountability is presented here. Approximately, eight years ago, the author realized that school performance was essential with the attention being given to accountability. As an elementary school vice-principal and principal serving in five different school districts in the state of California, the author concluded that a strong leadership role was needed to achieve in demographically challenged schools. The author's administrative practices have included wide reading in the field and participating in select trainings to enhance her repertoire. The author attended a training in 2003 that would profoundly influence her successes as an administrator. The training was conducted by Erlinda Teisinger (2003) and entitled "Instructional Leadership That Reproduces Leadership." The principle of Kaizen was presented as a process of ongoing improvement by everyone in the school community and is a way of thinking to assure continuous improvement (Imai, 1986). The Plan Do Check Act cycle (PDCA) was emphasized with various other strategies to achieve continuous improvement. The DuFours (1992) recommend this approach in their Professional Learning Communities trainings. The highly effective instructional leader according to Teisinger (2003) was one who used essential characteristics of reproduction, institutionalization, and legitimization, which were proposed initially by (Hanson, 1996). The author determined from these characteristics that the principal expectation piece introduced would be able to be reproduced from year to year and institutionalized. Most importantly, these expectations would communicate the vision of the school. The author would further conclude that she would be upfront each school year thereafter and she would formalize the process at the first school meeting of the year by telling what she expected as the school leader.

The first category to be reviewed would be the expectations for student achievement. The majority of public schools in the state of California serve large populations of English Language Learners. The expectation would be that all ELLs would gain one proficiency level in English each academic year. The next expectation under student achievement was that all learners would advance to the next level on the California State Standards tests in language arts and mathematics. These levels on the standards scale were far below basic, below basic, basic, proficient, and advanced. In order to secure academic achievement in the school, these expectations had to happen and the staff concurred. Of course, Professional Learning Communities and the use of Plan, Do, Check, Act Cycle as part of the PLCs sustained work on the vision.

The next titled area of expectations had the emphasis on teaching in the classroom and school wide practices. A walk-through model was known in the school. These were done throughout the month. It was expected that a daily schedule would be posted during these informal walkthroughs. The members of the walk through group including administrators and teachers would make note of the evidence on direct instruction techniques. Evidence would be gathered in the form of a checklist and notations were also made on the different strategies in the teacher repertoire that were being utilized. The strategies recorded were English Now! (Teisinger, 2000) during the designated ELD block and Steps For Success, a student metacognition model (Brallier, 2006). The emphasis here is that teachers regularly received professional development for their repertoire and in turn were asked to regularly use their training to advance the vision of helping students advance academically.

The last principal expectation related to a professional classroom environment. As the administrator, the author believed that the environment of each classroom had to project the vision of maximum student achievement.

First, all classrooms were to be clean, organized, and attractive.

Second, the California State Standards in reading and math were the basis of all lessons taught in those subjects and a monthly display was put up in those two subjects of student work. Each teacher was to have displayed behavior standards, a class mission statement, direct instruction standards, and objectives written for students for a particular lesson, daily schedule including a dedicated ELD block. The behavior standards were submitted at the beginning of each school year and were based generically on Canter's (1990) assertive discipline model. A class mission statement gives the teacher and students a focus for each school day. Direct instruction lesson models with standard and objective on the board were a regular expectation for math and language arts lessons. The posting of the daily schedule took the place of a formal lesson plan book and the monitoring of that tool. The ELD block was to be observed on this schedule. A student goal-setting model was used based on the work of O'Neill and Conzemius (2006). Students under teacher guidance regularly posted their own goals for reading and math for that quarter on their desks. The classroom environment reflected with evidence the principal expectations and vision of the school to academically achieve.

Monitoring and evaluating the vision took place on a regular basis using the principal expectation chart. Each teacher received feedback and a discussion time every two weeks on the progress of the vision. This was done by having a roving substitute come with the principal. The substitute would take over the class while a conference took place in the back of the room on components of the expectations. Benchmark data was shared and frequently discussed. A school profile or update was done on the principal expectations four times a year. This update was done as a state of the school address.

In conclusion, the tool of principal expectations greatly enhances the administrator's capacity to guide a school's vision for academic achievement. The author personally found that this tool helped new administrators at their interviews and of course when they received their individual school assignments. The schools that used this approach for their school vision had continuous growth as evidence in benchmark and standardized test growth. The tool can also be personalized for areas of emphasis and maximize collaboration after it is "told."

Discussion Questions

1. Explain what "telling" means and how it influences school leadership.

2. What are the major steps in the development of a school's vision?

3. How would the Professional Learning Communities (PLCs) work in a typical school setting?

4. What principal expectations should be addressed for student achievement in today's schools?

5. What principal expectations should be addressed for teaching and learning?

6. What principal expectations should be addressed for the classroom environment?

Leadership Activity

Background

A new principal has been hired. The school has been performing poorly on standardized tests and issues of discontent among faculty exist because of continued low academic performance. The school needs a new vision and direction.

Activity Directions

1. Have everyone assume the role of a new principal in this situation.

2. Divide the group into three sections to address the development of principal expectations for student achievement, teaching and learning, and classroom environment.

3. Have each group give a 20 minute charted response to the activity.

Activity Critique

1. How useful would these principal expectations be for the new principal?

2. From the school faculty's perspective, would there be a focus after the principal expectations were presented?

Background of the Author

Dr. Michele Pecina is currently Core Adjunct Faculty for the School of Education, Educational Administration at National University in Fresno, California. She has a BA in Social Sciences from Fresno State, a MA in School Administration from La Verne University, and an EdD from Alliant University. She served in the California public schools for 38 years as a teacher and school administrator. In 2003, she was selected as the NAESP Elementary Principal of the year representing the State of California in Washington, D.C. She also was recognized by the Association of California School Administrators (ACSA) in 2008 as the Elementary principal of the year for her service.

Principal's Expectations

Student Achievement

By the end of the school year

1. All English Language Learners will have gained an average of one proficiency level in English.

2. All learners will have advanced to the next level in language arts and mathematics on the standards scale (Far Below Basic, Below Basic, Basic, Proficient, Advanced).

Teaching and Learning

School Wide and Classroom Strategies

There is evidence of direct instruction and use of a teacher repertoire by every classroom teacher during whole class lessons and small group instruction.

Classroom Environment

1. All classrooms are clean, organized, and attractive.

2. Sixty percent of walls have displays of currently standards-based student work.

3. All of the following will be in evidence:

   a. behavior standards,

   b. class mission statement,

   c. direct instruction standard/objective written on front board,

   d. daily schedule showing core instructional blocks, including a dedicated ELD time

5. Student Goal Setting cards (Grades 2–6)

S.M.A.R.T. Goals

Ask yourself: "Is My Goal _____ "

S = Strategic and Specific?

M = Measurable?

A = Attainable?

R = Results – based?

T = Time – bound?

Closing the Achievement G.A.P.

Goals Are Possible

Reading Goal: I will _____

Math Goal: I will _____

I will reach my goal by _____

Name: _____

References

Brallier, K. (2006). *Steps To Success.* San Jose: Literature Connection.

California Department of Education. (2006, May). *NCLB frequently asked questions.* Retrieved (March 24, 2008) from http://www.cde.ca.gov/nclb

California Department of Education. (1999) *Public schools accountability act of 1999.* Retrieved (August 6, 1999), from http://www.cde.ca.gov/ta/ac/pa/overview.asp

Canter, L. (1990). *Back to school with Assertive discipline/Grades K-6.* Canter. Santa Monica, CA: Lee & Associates.

Hanson, M. E. (1996). *Educational Administration and Organizational behavior* (4th ed.). Needham Heights, MA: Allyn and Bacon.

Imai, M. (1986). *Kaizen: The key to Japan's competitive success.* New York, NY: Random House.

National Association of Elementary Principals (NAESP). (2001). *Leading learning communities: NAESP standards for what principals should know and be able to do.* Alexandria, VA:.

O'Neill, J., & Conzemius, A. (2006). *The power of smart goals.* Bloomington, IN: Solution Tree.

Senge, P., & Smith, B. (1994). *The fifth discipline fieldbook.* New York: Doubleday.

Teisinger, E. V. (2003). *Instructional leadership that reproduces leadership.* Fresno, CA.: LitConn.

Using Web-Cams and Online Enhancements to Provide Feedback to Teachers and Students Using Remote Access Technology

Dan Cunniff, PhD, Loren Naffziger, EdD, National University, La Jolla, California

ISLLC Standard 2: Advocating, nurturing and sustaining a school culture and instructional program conducive to student learning and staff professional growth

▶ Abstract

Universities and school districts are taking advantage of today's technologies to enhance teaching and staff development on all fronts. From smart boards to videos, instructors, principals, and other educational leaders are taking advantage of the numerous applications available using the internet. Online programs are now standard in most universities. In order to make these programs more student-friendly and promote more student engagement, program organizers have turned to greater use of audio and visual opportunities. This paper presented a few of the enhancements used in online programs including the application of a secure online tool called IRIS Connect. The paper included a report of a student and instructor satisfaction survey connected to the IRIS enhancement.

Key words: Interns, evaluation, credential, remote observation, video, professional development, IRIS Connect.

▶ Introduction

IRIS Camera

Assuming that funding will not be available in the future to support the supervision and evaluation of interns in the San Diego and Riverside area school districts, National University's School of Education has begun to explore cost saving measures. With the help of a grant by the California Commission on Teacher Credentialing, they have purchased ten remote controlled observation cameras called IRIS Cameras. These cameras can send and receive as well as record audio and video from the classroom to any off-site location. Their purpose is to record student teacher and interns working toward a teaching credential in live classroom settings. The university supervisor can then critique the lesson with the student intern and his or her school supervisor after the observed class lesson. It can also be used to record best practices to be shared with other students and teachers for staff development purposes. Institutional Review Board (IRB) permission was required along with school district, parent, student and supervising teacher release forms being signed (Holt & Naffziger, 2010).

Most teacher licensure/certification programs require some practice teaching under the supervision of an experienced teacher prior to awarding a credential. Typically, practice teachers must be observed and evaluated several times during the practice period. This process can be both time consuming and costly with marginal results. This requirement becomes even more complex with distance education and international teacher certification programs. To reduce the high cost of face-to-face observations and skill assessment, National University in southern California, USA, has been using a secure online tool called IRIS Connect. This system links a remote live video stream and audio controls with observation and data collection tools for capturing information used to inform the teacher assessment and remediation of performance, all at a distance.

IRIS Connect dashboard facilitates a remote 360-degree field of vision in the classroom, with pan, tilt, zoom capabilities, a variety of audio and editing capability. With the dashboard tools, an evaluator and practice teacher can view and discuss the skills observed and those needing remediation in a confidential environment. The system is also proving to be ideal for creating scenario-based professional development materials for experienced teachers and other school personnel.

National University (NU) is the State of California's largest provider of teacher education coursework and clinical practice. The observation and evaluation of the clinical practice of these teacher candidates is as a part of the State of California credentialing program. This process can be both time consuming and costly with the results on improving the teaching practices of the candidates being marginal. NU is conducting a pilot project which utilizes an Internet-connected remote viewing, communication, and evaluation system that operates through a secure web site known as IRIS Connect. The use of "thereNow" (a US company that provides the equipment, software, and IRIS Connect access) Internet Connected Equipment and their proprietary Web site are central to the discussion of how this interactive program can improve the development of teacher credential candidates (see fig. 1).

The specific group of teacher candidates who are participants in this project are interns at multiple school districts throughout the southern region of California. The interns' areas of concentration for their studies include general education, special education, and work with the deaf and hard of hearing populations in the public school system ranging from kindergarten to the twelfth grade. In an effort to improve upon

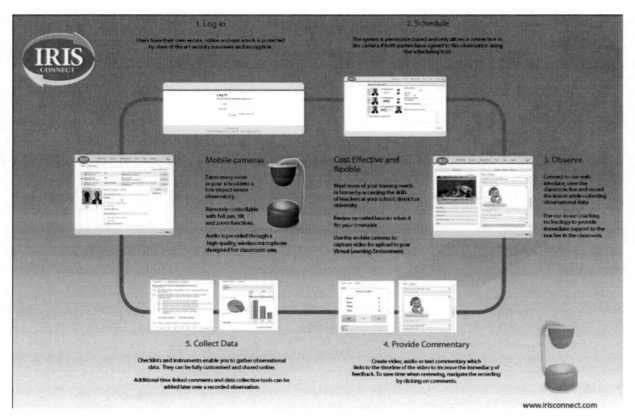

Figure 1: IRIS Connect system overview – sequence of usage

the clinical practice process, the use of Internet-based system is undergoing a pilot test to determine if the technology expenditures are cost effective for improving the intern' teaching performance.

The impetus for conducting this project includes the recent economic downturn and the desire to improve the teacher practice development of the candidate. California has been one of the states suffering the impact of the economic recession, which includes the loss of funding for special programs. The benefits of recording the pedagogical practices of interns teaching candidates for analysis, reflection, and the development of a video library are present in the literature. The following section provides a synoptic review of the literature that pertains to the use of remote observation and videotaping of those involved in the development of professional teaching practice.

■ Best Practices for Remote Observation and Videotaping

Beck, King, and Marshall (2002) suggest that the use of videotaping to develop cases has an "intuitive" component, which relates to the use of the recording of actual classroom interactions (p. 346). According to the authors, pre-service teachers are better able to make the cognitive transition from theory to practice as real-life situations create the opportunity to discover instructional problems. The recognition of diversity, the need to differentiate instruction, and the development of alternative pedagogical strategies are a part of the benefits of videotaping. In addition, the richness of the multimedia stream that includes visual and auditory elements creates an environment for interpreting the "events and contexts" in an authentic environment (p. 347). In summarizing their findings, the authors make the following statement in regards to the use of videotaping by pre-service teachers:

> These cognitive processing experiences may have extended and deepened videocase makers' understanding of teaching and learning, and consequently increased their ability to identify, interpret, and analyze manifestations of exemplary teaching during observation beyond that of the preservice teachers whose cognitive processing of observations was limited to their classroom experience. In turn, videocase makers' increased ability to read teaching-learning ideas in what they observed could have influenced their ability to identify, interpret, and analyze manifestations of exemplary teaching later in the video test situation (Beck et al., p. 358).

Comparable to Face-to-Face Observations

Supporting the idea that the Internet system can efficiently reduce costs, Dyke, Harding, and Liddon (2008) report that a "strong correlation in professional judgments of teaching performances by both online and in-class observers (p. 45). The dual observation camera system that the authors discuss utilizes a two-way visual and audio scheme. In this system, the teaching candidate and the observer can see and talk to each other over an Internet-anchored software application. The design of the pre-observation, observation, and post-observation procedures was conducive to creating a collaborative environment, which was conducive to a strong teacher candidate performance. The findings of these researchers support the premise that online viewing of a teaching candidate is as reliable as the face-to-face observation of their teaching practices.

A major component of the remote teacher observation is to capture moments that will enhance the teaching practices of those entering the profession. Waxman, Tharp, and Hilberg (2004) note that, "One of the most important purposes of systematic classroom observation is to improve student teacher's classroom instruction" (p. 90). The feedback that observers provide helps teacher candidates understand their own strengths and weaknesses and consequently enables them to improve their instructional methods and strategies drastically.

Face-to-face classroom observations of student teachers versus remote classroom observation of student teachers can be cost efficient for all involved, and the outcomes are beneficial. When conducting face-to-face classroom observations, the supervising teacher or the university incurs expenses that range from mileage to travel time, and in some cases, overnight housing. In comparison, while using remote classroom observation, the supervising instructor does not experience any of those expenses. In fact, the supervising instructor can observe the student teacher from any location that Internet access is available.

Another benefit of using the remote observation is that the recording and archiving of the observation, which allows for reviewing at any time (see fig. 2). Having the availability to review the observation will provide a visual enhancement for the teaching candidate. Videos allow the teaching candidate to see his or her errors or areas that need improvement with the feedback that the supervising instructor provides. The pricing of the equipment and software associated with the use of remote classroom observation may be high; however, the return on your investment is worthwhile according to Waxman et al. (2004).

Figure 2: IRIS Connect observation window with panel for comments

Online Discussions with Peers

Lee and Wu (2006) describe a case study that includes a comprehensive use of an Internet-based computer mediated communication system involving the videotaping of instructional activities. In the first semester, the intern or student teacher candidate made videotapes of his or her microteaching sessions and met in small groups of peers with a mentoring faculty member to review their practices. During the second semester, the inclusion of lesson plans, handouts, and self-evaluations were additions to the videotaping of teaching performances. The utilization of an online discussion forum with all of the second semester student teaching materials was conducive to a thorough evaluation of the candidate's performances. The findings of the study point out that the ability for an intern or student teacher to "review their performances in an online environment is more convenient, leads to better self-evaluation, and improves learning through the collaborative interactions of peers" (p. 376-377). The authors suggest that future uses of the Internet-based system may incorporate the use of peer collaborations, which would align to the NU pilot project.

Additional Considerations

In addition to the remote observation and video recording of the intern or student teacher, other aspects for the use of the Internet-based system warrant consideration for future projects. Reflective practices, small peer group collaboration, cognitive coaching, and the development of the social, affective, psychomotor, and cognitive domains are possibilities with the system. This accumulation of benefits to the using of the system could have positive effects on the overall performance of the teacher candidate in the beginning of their educational career.

Reflective Practices

Rosaen, Lundeberg, Cooper, Fritzen, and Terpstra (2008) present the findings of the case study that include the value of utilizing the videotaping of intern's teaching segments for reflective practice training. By utilizing small "chunks" and smaller "segments," the authors report that the interns were better able to make specific observations on their pedagogical practices as compared to memory-based reflections. The researchers report that the ability to move from general classroom management to specific pedagogical practices; center on the children's responses to instruction; and the capacity for the teacher candidates to connect to the evidence improves significantly by the use of videotaping (see fig. 3).

Small Group Collaboration

Teacher candidates who were a part of a pilot project utilizing joint reflection methods for reviewing videotapes of their instructional practices were successful in forming a strong professional identity. In this pilot study, the use of a collaborate team of teacher educators, in-service teachers, and student teachers was beneficial to the credential candidate. The conclusions of the study indicate that teaching candidates developed strong professional collaboration skills as well as the formation of individual and social identities were positive outcomes in this study. The authors summarize their findings in this statement:

> It is our belief that the reflections that we observed benefited the student teachers by increasing their confidence, enthusiasm, and professional training. The student teachers commented on how much they appreciated the opportunity to work over an extended time with a team of teaching professionals, and how beneficial that opportunity was for their professional training (p. 58).

Cognitive Coaching

Crasborn, Hennissen, Brouwer, Korthagen, and Bergen (2008) discuss the improvement of supervisors in promoting dialogue with their mentees as opposed to being didactic through the implementation of a specific training program. The video recording of the mentor-mentee discussions of the teaching candidates' performance provides an additional opportunity for analyzing the quality of the relationship. The author's report is specific to a supervisory training analysis, but the implications for the use of the Internet-based system are evident. Specifically, the analysis of the mentor-mentee relationships through the feedback provided in the IRIS Connect web site may lend itself to the improvement of training of university and school support personnel.

Social, Affective, Psychomotor, and Cognitive Domains

Yung, Yip, Lai, and Lo (2010). provide an analysis of the literature on the use of videotaping for professional development as well as teaching pre-service applications. They conclude that the best practices for the use of videotaping would incorporate the social, affective, psychomotor, and cognitive domains in the desirable learning outcomes. The importance of developing a collaborative community that allows the participants to reflect on their skills and strategies will promote cognitive development. This growth in the cognitive domain will enhance the participants' development of professional attitudes and values with confidence.

Professional Development

Lundeberg et al. (2008) present the findings of a case study in professional development that concludes that teaching professionals find it valuable to analyze videos of their practices as well as those of their peers. The researchers' discoveries include qualitative data that supports the construction of a video library that allows teachers to identify new strategies and observe their changes in practices. The reflections, which were a part of the participants' procedures in this study, were reportedly analogous to 'having a mirror placed in my face" (p. 11). The teachers in this study also report that the use of videos allowed them to see the effects that their teaching methods have on their students. Collaboration within the group of participants also was beneficial to their professional development.

The participants note that there was an enhancing effect to the reflections when the colleagues were able to provide their input, which they refer to as being like a "double mirror" (Lundeberg et al., 2008, p. 13). A comment by one of the participants presents the consensus that the researchers report: "I enjoyed the comments and suggestions about how I would be able to do things better" (p. 13). The researchers report that the teachers found the "positive, trusting climate" to be a critical feature of their learning community (p. 14). In addition to this aspect of the study's methodology, the participants gained valuable knowledge as to how the students in their classrooms interact.

The ability to view and analyze small group interactions presented the teachers with new information on the students. One participant reports, "It helped me to see a side of small group discussion that you don't normally see in day-to-day teaching" (p. 15). One of the interesting findings of this study was that teachers who were focusing on student interfacing "recommend the use of video in professional development programs" (p. 30). The consensus of opinion that came from the surveys and focus groups interviews was that the collection and collaborative discussion of videotapes was beneficial to their professional development.

Literature Review Summary

The Internet-based system is a vehicle for promoting reflective practice, developing a collaborative community, improving supervisory practices, and creating an effective arena for promoting the development of the four domains. By carefully guiding the teacher candidate, those in supervisory roles can provide the tools for the candidates to develop their reflective practices. The IRIS Connect web site allows the candidate to review their pedagogical practices at times and locations that can be conducive to the reflective practice. If teacher candidates are encouraged to discuss and review their video captured moments with their peers, they will develop the type of collaborative community that can create synergistic outcomes. Specifically, the group may encourage and strengthen each other's ability to analyze teaching practices that will promote the individual candidate's ability to perform at higher levels of pedagogical proficiency.

The Internet-based system allows the supervisors to access the candidates' observations and evaluate them using a number of criteria. The standardization of these criteria through the use of specific tools and protocols will allow NU to train the supervisory team in the best practices for the use of the items. In alignment with the work of Crasborn, Hennissen, Brouwer, Korthagen, and Bergen (2008), it is also advisable to consider training the supervisors on the best practices for facilitating discussions with the candidates that allow them to reflect on their performances.

By adding all of the previously discussed professional development skills to the candidates' experience, the expectation for growth in the four domains that Yung et al. discuss is certain. The candidates will have the benefit of a social community that will promote their ability to assess their teaching practices, which ensures their cognitive and affective domains undergoing transformative growth. The summation of these experiences can propel the candidates into a bright teaching career.

Live observation

If an observation has been correctly scheduled and the time to start has arrived then it will appear in the upcoming section of your observation library and be highlighted in green. Simply click on the 'Details' and then the 'Start' button to log in.

tip..
Try to make a single recording in your observation - this will mean that you have just one file to upload and all of your time linked comments will display correctly

Live video stream
Click on the screen where you want to centre the camera and use your mouse scroll wheel to zoom

Audio controls
Including the push to talk button for in-ear coaching

Record button !

Data collection tools
The page opposite has more info on how to create and use these..

Create live time linked comments
Type your note in the box and then on 'Add comment'
The note will then get added to the commentary time line underneath

Observation details, settings and adding supporting files

Figure 3: Multiple ways to convey evaluation details while viewing via the Internet

▶ Current Study

A study of the effectiveness of the Internet-based system is underway by a team of educational professionals at NU. The focus of the research is to examine the usability of the equipment and system as well as the impact of technology on the teacher candidates' performance. The essence of the research questions is to determine whether the use of the IRIS remote observation system is a viable alternative to the traditional face-to-face classroom observation and assessment system. To accommodate the use of the system by NU and school site supervisors modifications to IRIS Connect web site have been made (see fig. 4). These enhancements to the remote observations will allow the supervisors the ability to record multiple sets of data while observing or reviewing the teacher candidates' performance. This will provide additional feedback to the intern that can be valuable for making corrections to his or her teaching practices. The details of the research questions that will form this case study are as follows.

Technology Related Questions

1. What are the issues/problems of establishing observation cameras within school districts and specific school sites for the assessment of teacher candidates?

2. How well did the observation cameras work at each site? What were the problems (if any) encountered in the application of the technology? How were these resolved?

3. What is the ease of use of the remotely controlled observation cameras? Were the supervisors able to control the camera effectively in order to capture the lesson being taught?

4. What is the quality of the video captured during the teaching events?

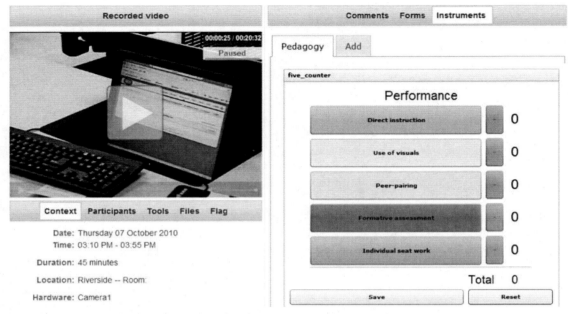

Figure 4: Modifications to enhance feedback by counting specific behaviors

5. Were interns and student teacher supervisors able to access the web site to view and provide immediate feedback to candidates? Were teaching credential candidates able to view video tape and feedback provided during observation? What problems (if any) were encountered accessing and using the IRIS web site?

6. How satisfied are study participants with the use of the technology to provide support and feedback on performance?

Consumer Related Questions

1. How effective were the cameras for observing teaching credential candidate performance? What were the candidates' perspectives? What are the intern and supervisor perspectives?

2. How effective was the web site for providing feedback to the teaching credential candidate following the observation? What is the teaching credential candidate perspective and supervisor perspective?

3. What kinds of issues/problems were encountered working with the technology in the classroom and on the web site?

4. Is the IRIS remote observation camera system a viable alternative to face-to-face classroom observations? If yes, why? If not, why?

5. How was teaching credential candidate reflection on their teaching performance enhanced or improved through use of the IRIS system of observation?

6. How satisfied were study participants with the use of the technology to provide support and feedback?

▶ Research methodology

The creation of a survey that addresses the research questions will be a part of the evaluation of the Internet-based observation, communication, and evaluation project. The survey will be sent to the interns,

NU-supervisors, and school site intern supervisors that consent to their participation in this study. The use of an Internet host (SurveyMonkey™) will allow the participants the ability to present their perspectives anonymously. The researchers will analyze the data as it pertains to the research questions and concerning the three primary stakeholder group perspectives. The three primary stakeholder groups are the interns, NU supervisors, and the school supervisors.

The second data set that will form a part of the qualitative data is the interviews with the individual participants. Each of the individual participants will have an opportunity to discuss their perceptions that relate to the research questions. This data will provide the stakeholders with additional opportunities to discuss their perceptions as to the strengths and challenges of using the technology. These private meetings will also allow the participants the opportunity to make additional suggestions for improving the use of the system.

Cost/Benefit Analysis

To assess the difference in costs between face-to-face and remote observation systems, the travel reimbursement payments to NU supervisors will need to be determined. In addition, the cost comparison between travel and lodging to the Imperial County school sites and the costs associated with the use of the system will add to the cost-benefit data. This quantitative data will form the third portion of the assessment of the Internet-based system.

Preliminary Findings

The specific collection of qualitative and quantitative data has not yet begun due to the short duration of the project's history. However, we can state that one of the biggest obstacles to implementing this project is the concern for the identity protection of the kindergarten through twelfth grade students in the various school districts. To date, we have sent letters to over 38 school district representatives with additional follow-up in the form of other communication to more than 25 of those individuals. We have been successful in placing the remote observation system equipment in four different school districts and two more governing school bodies are in the second phase of discussions. One intern and the corresponding NU supervisor are actively using the system with several more expecting to be online within the next 30 days.

Adaptations to Enhance School Site Control

The concern for the protection of K-12 student privacy creates the need to adapt our project to include the exclusive use of the asynchronous features of the Internet-based equipment and software. This assures the school district representatives that their employee (the intern teacher candidate) will be the one that controls the videotaping and uploading of recordings to the IRIS Connect web site. This additional layer of protection for K-12 student identities is a necessary step for at least one of the two districts now in the next phase of discussion for being a part of this study.

Additional Internet Technologies Available

Although the survey and follow-up meetings with the study participants has not taken place as of the writing of this report, there is some feedback from focus groups on the project coming through our work with the various school districts. The remote observation equipment requires the use of the host sites Internet. The requirements for the Internet use include the establishment of a static IP address that has public access for remote observations. The typical firewall configurations of today's school districts make this a challenging aspect to the use of the system. This challenge includes getting the proper administrative permissions, which can require multiple approvals from various levels of governance. The use of the IRIS Connect web site requires the downloading of their software and a PC check that may necessitate the downloading of Adobe's Flash Player updates. Older personal computers may not have the capacity to support this software and the requirements for the best operation of the remote viewing system. Broadband connections that allow for high rates of downloading are a requirement for optimal use as well.

Repositories

Repositories are information holding areas. There are many of these available to the consumer for a small fee and some who offer it as a free service within a corporation or educational institution.

Clouds

Clouds are online back-ups that involve downloading a company's software installed on your computer. The purpose of the software is to allow you to easily restore your computer if it crashed from hard drive failure, you accidently delete files on your laptop or iPad, or if they are stolen. There is usually a charge for this service. Some services include justcloud.com, zipcloud, mpcbackup.com, etc.

Faculty Community Networks

Some universities such as National University in La Jolla, California, have embarked on a network system called the National University Faculty Community Network. This is similar to an intranet system, where faculty and invited guests can enter the network to hold asynchronous discussions in area forums. The Faculty Community is a private and secure space designed specifically for new and experienced faculty of all technology and teaching skill levels. It provides a wealth of resources for faculty, including learning forums, discussions, content examples, teaching strategies, support resources, and links to other useful areas such as the catalog and online courses. The faculty can check back on a regular basis to add or retrieve new information, resources news and updates.

▶ Conclusions

The use of an Internet-based system for viewing, communicating, and evaluating teacher candidate performance is an effective alternative to the traditional face-to-face observations as case studies have shown. The current project underway at National University has the potential to improve upon this institution's teacher training practices by allowing supervisors the ability to communicate synchronously and asynchronously through a secure web site. The ability for the supervisors to provide critical feedback to the interns that corresponds to specific video segments will allow the candidates to gain greater insight into their teaching performance. In addition, the possibility to reduce costs associated with travel in terms of time and mileage is an advantage of using an Internet-based system.

Discussion Questions

1. Computers, cell phones, and other Internet devices are being acquired by individuals and families all over the world. Does this pose any special consideration for educators? Is this a problem or an opportunity? Explain.

2. Schools have not evolved as fast as other organizations in the use of computer technology. Why?

3. Administrative applications have progressed more steadily than instructional applications. Why? Will it change in the future? Explain.

4. Planning for computer and internet technology should center on the application rather than on only hardware, software, or other individual components. How and where in a district or school

should this planning occur? Who should be the major participants in planning for technology? Explain.

5. Equity issues and the use of technology relate to much broader societal issues involving minority, gender, and other socioeconomic factors that may be beyond the scope of most educational leaders' duties. What are some of these issues as they relate to technology in the schools? What strategies would you consider to lesson any inequalities that might exist?

Activity

Develop an action plan for the development and operation of a technology committee in your school or district. Be sure to involve all necessary stakeholders and the tasks necessary for the group to be effective.

Background of Authors

Dr. Dan Cunniff – see editors' biographies.

Loren Naffziger is an Instructional Technology Specialist, teacher education clinical practice lead supervisor, and professor. His dissertation work is an examination of the most effective practices of face-to-face, online, and hybrid teaching methods with an emphasis on blended learning. He is a former high school principal, which was the beginning of his work in teacher education, professional development, and blended or hybrid learning. His current involvements include the use of an Internet-based remote observation, communication, and evaluation system in teacher education. He has several ongoing pilot projects including the use of SMART Technologies in Higher Education, most effective practices for substitute teachers, and the use of video conferencing in teaching. His research interests span the areas of teacher education and the use of technology to improve education.

References

Beck, R. J., King, A., & Marshall, S. K. (2002). Effects of videocase construction on preservice teachers' observations of teaching. *The Journal of Experimental Education*, 70(4), pp. 345-361.

Berk, R. A. (2010). How do you leverage the latest technologies, including Web 2.0 tools, in your classroom? *International Journal of Technology in Teaching and Learning*, 6(1), 1-13.

California Department of Education. (2010). *Economic Impact Aid*. Retrieved (9-10-12) from http://www.cde.ca.gov/fg/aa/ca/eia.asp

Crasborn, F., Hennissen, P., Brouwer, N., Korthagen, F., & Bergen, T. (2008). Promoting versatility in mentor teacher's use of supervisory skills. *Teaching and Teacher Education*, 24, pp. 499-514.

Dyke, M., Harding, A., & Liddon, S. (2008). How can online observation support the assessment and feedback, on classroom performance, to trainee teachers at a distance and in real time? *Journal of Further and Higher Education*, 32(1), pp. 37-46.

Lee, G. C., & Wu, C. (2006). Enhancing the teaching experience of pre-service teachers through the use of videos in web-based computer-mediated communication (CMC). *Innovations in Education and Teaching International*, 43(4), pp. 369-380.

Lundeberg, M., Koehler, M. J., Zhang, M., Karunaratne, S., McConnell, T. J., & Eberhardt, J. (2008). *"It's like a mirror in my face": Using video analysis in learning communities of science teachers to foster reflection on teaching dilemmas.* Retrieved (9-10-12) from http://pbl.educ.msu.edu/wp-content/uploads/2008/04/lundeberg_et_al_march_2008.pdf

Maclean, R., & White, S. (2007). Video reflection and the formation of teacher identity in a team of pre-service and experienced teachers. *Reflective practice*, 8(1), pp. 47-60.

Marsh, B., Mitchell, N., & Adamczyk, P. (2010). Interactive video technology: Enhancing professional learning in initial teacher education. *Computers & Education*, 54, pp. 742-748.

Orozco, L. (2009). *"Leadership Innovation: Preparing Leaders Through Technology in Authentic Assessment."* Paper presented at the California Association of Professors of Educational Administration Fall Conference, Los Angeles, California.

Rosaen, C. L., Lundeberg, M., Cooper, M., Fritzen, A., & Terpstra, M. (2008). Noticing: How does investigation of video records change how teachers reflect on their experiences? *Journal of Teacher Education*, 59(4), pp. 347-360.

Waxman, H. C., Tharp, R. G., & Hilberg, R. S. (2004). *Observational Research in U.S. Classrooms*. New York, NY: Cambridge Press.

Yung, B. H. W., Yip, V. W. Y., Lai, C., & Lo, F. Y. (2010). *Towards a model of effective use of video for teacher professional development.* Paper presented at the International Seminar, Professional Reflections, and National Science Learning Centre, York, England.

Fostering Values for the Global Age: Refocusing Accountability to Ensure Success for All

R. D. Nordgren, PhD, Professor, National University, La Jolla, California

ISLLC Standard 6: Understanding, responding to, and influencing the larger political, social, economic, legal, and cultural context

▶ Abstract

"Race to the Top" incentives have followed the No Child Left Behind mandates, ostensibly to ensure the US graduates have the knowledge, skills, and dispositions to succeed in a global economy and society. This article, based on current scholarship and the author's personal experiences in US and Swedish schools, attempts to debunk the assumption that a set of mandates or incentives based on low-cognitive and low-skill assessments will allow this lofty goal to be reached. Instead, the school leaders should advocate a values-driven curriculum that may ensure the US and other nations reach this goal.

Key Words: Values, Accountability, Standards, Reform, Curriculum

▶ Introduction

In recent calls for accountability and school reforms, what is too often ignored is the need to develop citizens and workers who can do more than simply function in Industrial Age, "McDonaldized" positions (Ritzer, 2000) where the work is prescribed and supervision is direct and controlling (Partnership for 21st Century Skills; Zhao, 2009). What the future workforce needs are those who are capable of working collaboratively and unsupervised, and responding to continuously changing needs of the organization, its customers, its markets as well as the entire geopolitical landscape with which the organization must interact (Brady, 2011; Kohn, 2004; Wagner, 2008; Wolk, 2011). The current reform agenda calls for a system of assessments that seek low-cognitive levels of knowledge that may be incomplete, if not irrelevant, measures (Wolk, 2011; Zhao, 2009).

The development of this worker is an imposing task for P-12 education leaders, to be sure, but one at which we must succeed or our children will be doomed to toil in what are too often dead-end, low-paying jobs. We, as school leaders, are forced to focus on preparing our students for tests that require little more than regurgitation of memorized material. At the same time, we must also focus on predictable state academic standards that, although written in language that would connote a need for fairly high levels of learning (Bloom, 1956), are nonetheless too comprehensive, forcing us to question their attainability. This article suggests a different accountability focus and subsequent standards, a focus that would ensure our children are prepared for success in the global economy, one that front loads value-laden goals rather than academic.

▶ The Early Development of High-level Standards

In the early 1990s, I was asked to participate in writing content standards for my school district. As part of a group of 30 or so middle and high school teachers, we were to determine what students should *know, do, and be like* in the next millennium. Once we agreed upon the traits that we wanted our high school graduates to possess (what they should *be like*), we broke into content-area groups to determine how we, in my case language arts teachers, could help foster these traits in our students. We wrote standards based on what students should know and do using a list of verbs that corresponded to high levels of Bloom's Taxonomy of Learning Objectives (1956). We agreed not to write any standard that was at the lowest level, "knowledge," which is simple recall of facts that can be memorized and easily forgotten. Our product was a list of dozens of well-written standards in the categories of reading, writing, and literature; mathematics, science, and social studies had similar numbers of standards, also written toward high levels of learning. When our state content standards were published a couple of years later, many of my colleagues were surprised at how similar these were to the standards we had written. In fact, I examined state standards for high school social studies for the six largest states (California, Texas, New York, Florida, Illinois, and Ohio), representing over 40% of the US population (US Census Bureau, 2003). They are all quite comparable in content and language. When we hear calls for national standards such as the Common Core, one can argue that we already have them—the standards to which most of our students are held are essentially the same thanks in part to influential national content-area organizations such as the National Association of the Teachers of English.

So our "national" standards are written at high levels, but are our children held accountable to learning at these high levels? Writing standards to a high level of learning actually make assessment extremely difficult. To "analyze the relationships of pairs of words in analogical statements…and infer word meanings from these relationships" (Ohio Department of Education, p. 235) requires much more than a multiple-choice test that can be graded by a scanning machine. A teacher needs to use alternatives to multiple choice and true/false quizzes and tests to truly assess standards that ask students to "analyze" and "infer." These alternatives, such as essays and long-range projects, require much more time and intellect to assess—they are not as clean, cut-and-dried as a test requiring closed-ended answers. With this in mind, it is no wonder that teachers are hesitant to use other forms of assessment, and it is certainly no wonder why states assess students using multiple-choice and other easily-graded tests. Several states assess writing which, on the surface, would seem to require more burdensome grading practices, but these writing tests are highly structured so that the states can train assessors relatively easily to look for certain, prescribed aspects of the writing to determine differences between high and low-scoring essays (Florida Department of Education, 2004). The knowledge tested in this type of essay is not at a high level like that inferred by the content standards for writing in language arts. Although a student may be using analysis and synthesis in writing the piece, he or she is being assessed at only the application level—applies what was learned in the classroom into novel situation in the workplace (Bloom, Mesia, & Krathwohl, 1964).[1]

▶ Standards and Knowledgework

If the best our accountability system can do is assess students in their ability to apply the rules of writing a short, descriptive or persuasive piece, then are we truly determining whether or not our students are reaching levels of deep understanding, the type of learning that is essential for them to thrive as "knowledgeworkers"[2] in the global economy? Charles Handy (1995), a British business scholar, says that what

---

[1]   Also see International Center for Leadership in Education's Rigor-Relevance Framework at http://daggett.com/research.html. This framework uses overlies Bloom's Cognitive Taxonomy with levels of application.

[2]   Perhaps first used by Peter M. Drucker in *The Effective Executive*, published in 1967 by HarperCollins.

people really need to know in order to succeed as a knowledgeworker or "symbolic analysts" as described by Handy and Robert Reich (1992) is *how to conceptualize, coordinate, and consolidate knowledge*—Handy's "3 Cs." These verbs are not gained in the schools, but rather in the homes of the professional class, the knowledgeworkers, aiding the existence of a class system in the Western World, especially those cultures that favor vertical individualism (Triandis, 1995) where the division of social classes (and wealth) is not only accepted, but expected (e.g., US and Great Britain). The kind of knowledge Handy proposes is not what students can *know*, but what they *do* to show what they know. The crux of his argument is that formal schooling does nothing to ensure that knowledge is actually of any use, that a graduate must leave the school to determine if what he or she learned is of any value in the "real world." "[The 3 Cs] as we know from trying to develop them in adult life in organizations, need mentoring, small-group experience, and real-life problem solving. You have to live them to learn them" (1995, p. 208). Indeed, he is correct, but I will go one step further: students' meaningful knowledge and the actions that can demonstrate a true understanding of this knowledge emanate from values that they possess, or what they are *like*. And certain values have been determined to be crucial for success in the post-Fordist/Industrial Age economy as will be listed and described shortly.

▶ What Do We Want Them to be Like? Values to be Fostered.

Although teachers in my school district in the early 1990s wrote what we wanted our graduates to be like, we did little in the way of planning to assess our students for these values. If we wanted students to be effective collaborators in a team and to desire to be so, how would we know when they were? It will take much more than standardized paper-and-pencil testing. We must depend on the professionalism of educators to first foster these values, then accurately assess their existence in our children through the development of strong connections between teachers and students. These connections would require student-centered learning environments and a strengthening of the constructivist trend in schooling, a trend that is apt to die given the stringent requirements of the shortsighted accountability movement (Apple, 2001; Giroux, 2012; Kohn, 2004). But how can we as school leaders instill values while ensuring that our students are advancing academically? We can change how we conduct schooling by first developing, then accepting, a values-based curricula that ensure all students will possess the dispositions that are conducive to gaining the high-level learning necessary to flourish as knowledgeworkers.

▶ From Ages Four through Eight, Reduce the Emphasis on Academics?

Perhaps we are wasting valuable time on academics at an early age. Instead, perhaps we should concentrate on developing the values that are crucial for success in the global economy. A great contributor to the Achievement Gap between African-Americans and whites as well as between lower and high socioeconomic strata in the US is the amount of academic stimuli and learning a student gains at home (Hart & Risley, 1995). When students come to school without the literacy advantages of others, they are at great risk to be forever behind academically. Surprisingly, I found in Sweden that early elementary education emphasizes value development over academics, including literacy, and yet by the time Swedes are in high school, they score better than their US counterparts in math and science (NCES, 1999). This fostering of values in young children, values that provide the basis for self-regulated learning essential for the knowledgeworker of the Global Age (Partnership for 21st Century Schools; Zimmerman & Schunk, 2001), may be the key to the Swedes success in international comparisons. Once these basic values are established in students, the learning of academic matter may become less of a strain than what we presently experience in US schools. Students will flourish once they have the foundation they need to become responsible, life-long learners, which our children must be to succeed in an unpredictable global economy (Zimmerman & Schunk, 2001). And the Achievement Gap? By providing free or at least affordable pre-school for all children, pre-school that is focused on values rather than academics, the disparities between African-Americans, Hispanics and whites as well as the disparity between social classes may begin to close (Belfield, 2004).

What are these values and can everyone agree upon them? Absolutely. I give the reader the national curricula of Sweden as a prime example. The Swedes are experiencing a tremendous influx of immigrants from such impoverished nations as Vietnam, Kurdistan, Somalia, and China—nations that are culturally disparate from Sweden. Yet the Swedes concentrate on fostering values in their youth, leaving academic learning for later years. Some of the values they embrace are:

- Trust
- Personal Responsibility
- Democracy at all levels: classroom, school, community, and national
- Tolerance toward others who may differ from you in race, culture, and beliefs (Regeringskansliet, 1999).

What I have found in my studies in Swedish schools (2001; 2003) is that these values seemed to be the primary focus of early schooling and the results are extremely beneficial to the upper level teachers. For instance, when I asked high school teachers about classroom management problems, they didn't quite understand what I meant. They wanted to know why students would want to interfere with the learning of others. A Swedish principal visiting a school where I once worked was astounded that we had several personnel who worked exclusively with student discipline. She said that in Sweden when students weren't keeping up academically, they were merely counseled by their teachers. Did they ever misbehave? No, not really. My own observations in Sweden found that students did fall off-task and socialize, but because the learning activities were personally developed by the students based on their understanding of their own needs and a deep sense of personal responsibility, they would soon get back to their activity. In essence, the Swedish classrooms at all levels—elementary, middle, high schools—bore very little resemblance to what I've observed in the US.

Yes, Sweden has a much different culture from that of the US—and other nations. I have to add, however, that Swedish students behaved as they did out of design; the national curricula are value-based, explicitly calling for trust between adults and students as well as responsibility for both. And, yes, it is a different culture, but one that has opened its doors to immigrants and refugees from many other cultures as previously noted. The Swedish government feels compelled to ensure that certain values are shared by all its citizens (Sandahl, 1997). I have to admit that this is much easier for Swedes than for Americans due to the difference in how we perceive an individual. The Anglo-centered US culture is "vertically individualistic," accepting and perhaps embracing differences in class (Triandis, 1995), but we may be deluding ourselves that anyone can move up and down the social and economic ladder by sheer determination: the old Horatio Alger/pull-yourself-up-by-the-bootstraps theory of success. In contrast, the Swedes are horizontally individualistic, as are most Scandinavian cultures, in that while they celebrate the individual, the culture abhors distinct social strata. No one should be above anyone else. Swedish lore support this belief: for instance, the tallest blade of grass will be the first to be cut down. In other words, don't try to place yourself above others regardless of fame or fortune. *Lagom* is a term derived from an old Viking tradition of sharing. A millennium ago, Viking warriors would pass around a bowl of mead out of which no one person would drink more than his share; everyone deserved equal amounts (Sandahl, 1997). We in this country also celebrate the individual, of course, but we also don't truly believe in equality of services and support. The Jeffersonian notion of meritocracy (Barber, 1992) is celebrated in our American culture, but do we truly live by it? If we did, we wouldn't allow for the educational inequalities brought about by privilege contrasting with poverty. Of course neither we nor the Swedes can ensure that everyone gets absolute equal footing as too many variables exist in the lives of our students. As Handy points out, certain cultural advantages are given to those whose parents are of means. The Swedes, with their inherent belief of equality and their social democratic form of government, do not allow for vast differences between classes and appear embarrassed by the existence of classes at all. Because the US holds firm to a vertical individualism that doesn't truly embrace the notion of meritocracy, we must be even more vigilant in ensuring that all our children are instilled with the values that will enable them to obtain knowledgeworker positions in the post-Fordist economy. As Handy scolds:

> *A just, and sensible, society will do something about that accumulating difference between the children of the successful and the others. Since 80% of the young do not have symbolic analysts as parents, we have no choice but to use their early schooling as a substitute. That means intensive care and attention in the years from 4 to 10, when the [three Cs] skills are beginning to be formed (1995, p. 208).*

P-12 schooling—especially public school—is the only consistent factor in our culture, notwithstanding the growing trend to home school.

Tolerance, trust, responsibility, and democracy are fostered in Swedish schoolchildren and if they were also the focus of US schools, academic improvement may be the reward. These four values would make the lives of teachers and administrators much easier in that students would be better citizens—an explicit goal of the Swedes (Regeringskansliet, 1999). Discipline problems should decrease as time spent on academics would increase. What could also happen, as I witnessed in Sweden, is that our students would become more interested in democracy, especially at the local level such as deciding on classroom and school governance and in curricular decision making. The result could be an active participant in a public democracy in contrast to the private democracy where only a few can truly participate that Sehr (1997) convincingly argues is now the case in the US.

▶ More Values of Knowledgeworkers

From the prevailing literature on what students should know, do, and be like to succeed in the post-Fordist economy, I have extracted the following competencies from the literature on workforce:

- Teamwork: collaborating with others who may be diverse in culture, race, and beliefs
- Problem solving: both individually and collaboratively
- Pragmatic technical skills: especially those that are highly technical and transferable to various workplace environments
- Entrepreneurship: creativity and risk-taking.

Successful knowledgeworkers in the twenty-first century will collaborate effectively in a team setting and be able to solve problems both within a team and independently. Technical skills will be technology oriented and must be transferable from one profession and organization to another as workers do and will constantly change jobs. My initial contact with Swedish educators came when they visited US schools in 1999, many to determine what American schools did to promote creativity and risk-taking, the keys to becoming an effective entrepreneur. Unfortunately, for both them and us, they found our schooling does little to promote entrepreneurship except to maintain highly competitive environments that may contribute to antisocial behaviors (Glasser, 1998; Wagner, 2008; Zhao, 2009).

▶ Accountability Interfering with Success in the Global Age

Our accountability system in P-12 education is essentially ensuring more of the same with its dependence on testing of low-level knowledge and its inability to assess high-level learning as described by Bloom and his colleagues a half-century ago. Educational leaders must take back our schools from those who impose dumbed-down and teacher-proof curricula (Gatto, 2002; Brady, 2011) along with a dependence on testing as the only assessment instrument. The current focus of accountability does little or nothing to ensure that our children will be prepared for knowledgwork, thus, success in the global economy. Low-level knowledge regurgitated onto standardized tests does not hold accountable teachers and students for what is necessary in the post-Fordist economy except for low-paying, dead-end, "McDonaldized," and automated jobs that do not require complex knowledge, deep understanding, and life-long learning. Until we can embrace curricula and a form of schooling that promote values over low-level academic goals, we will never ensure that all our children will be successful in the Global Age.

Discussion Questions

1. The phrase "culture shock" is used by anthropologists, social psychologists, and sociologists to express one's unpreparedness for the environment into which she is suddenly thrust. Identify a time in your life when you were disoriented by your surroundings. What were your initial feelings? How did you rectify these feelings—or did you? What was one value in this environment with which you were uncomfortable? Why did this make you uncomfortable?

2. From your schooling experience as an educator (or as a student), recall a time when one of your students (or classmates) seemingly experienced culture shock. What signs of culture shock did this person exhibit? What values do you believe were the cause of this person's disorientation? Who, if anyone, helped him or her? What did they do to orient the student?

3. Let's assume that the US doesn't have the will or the means to ensure that a standard set of values is learned in our public schools where over 90% of school-age children attend. What other societal institutions can foster the values necessary for economic success and the proliferation of a public democracy? How will we ensure that each person gains a set of values that is compatible with others' sets of values?

4. Recall a lesson you've recently taught, observed being taught, or was taught to you. Were you asked to *conceptualize*, *coordinate*, and *consolidate* what you learned? If so, how were these assessed? If not, describe how this lesson could have been taught and assessed to meet Handy's "3 Cs."

5. John Dewey was a proponent of fostering democracy in our schools as he was convinced an autocratic school environment was not conducive to producing a graduate capable of engaging in a democracy. Using the lesson you recalled for item 4 above, how could this have been taught so that democracy was fostered in all students involved? Take into account the content, instructional methods, and the learning environment.

6. One of the values the author was studying in Sweden was entrepreneurship, a combination of creativity and risk-taking. What would a classroom look like that fostered entrepreneurship? What activities would be taking place, how would it be governed? How would it differ from the classrooms you experienced as a student in elementary, middle, and/or high school? And/or college?

Activity

You've been identified by the local university as a teacher who promotes "Twenty-first century values" in your classroom—that is, teamwork, problem solving, pragmatic technical skills, and entrepreneurship. Your principal knows you're interested in becoming a school administrator some day and asks you to develop a 30-minute interactive presentation to your colleagues on how you do this. Using PowerPoint and/or other media, develop such a presentation addressing curriculum, instructional methods, assessment, and learning environment.

Background of Author

R. D. Nordgren is a professor of Educational Administration at National University in La Jolla, California. He is the author or co-author of three books on school reform, curriculum, and teaching methods. Nordgren's current research interests are "non-cognitive variables" and college success, and national school reform.

References

Bloom, B. S., Mesia, B. B., & Krathwohl, D. R. (1964). *Taxonomy of Educational Objectives (vol.2)*. New York: Longman.

Brady, M. (2011). *What's worth learning*. Charlotte, NC: Information Age Publishing.

Florida Department of Education (2004). "Florida writing assessment program" (*Florida Writes!*). Retrieved (Oct. 4, 2004) from www.firn.edu/doe/sas/fw/fwapdesc.htm

Giroux, H. A. (2012). *Education and the crisis of public values: Challenging the assault on teachers, students, and public education*. New York: Peter Lang.

Handy, C. (1995). *The Age of Paradox*. Boston: Harvard Business School Press.

Hart, B., & Risley, T. R. (1995). *Meaningful differences in the everyday experience of young American children*. Baltimore: P.H. Brookes.

Kohn, A. (2004). *What does it mean to be well educated? And more essays on standards, grading, and other follies*. Boston: Beacon Press.

National Center for Education Statistics (NCES) (1999). Highlights of the Third International Mathematics and Science Study (TIMSS): Overview and Key Findings across Grade Levels. Washington: U.S. Department of Education.

Nordgren, R. D. (2001). *Democracy, trust, student responsibility, and global workforce competence*. Unpublished dissertation, DEPARTMENT, University of South Florida, CITY, FL.

Nordgren, R. D. (2003). *Making schooling relevant for the global age: Fulfilling our moral obligation*. Lanham, MD: Rowman Littlefield.

Ohio Department of Education (2004). Academic Content Standards: K-12 English Language Arts. Columbus, OH.

Partnership for 21st Century Skills. Framework for 21st century skills: life and career skills. Retrieved (March 7, 2011) from http://www.p21.org/index.php?option=com_content&task=view&id=266&Itemid=120

Reich, R. B. (1992). *The work of nations: Preparing ourselves for 21st century capitalism*. New York: Vintage Books.

Regeringskansliet (1999). *The 1994 Curriculum for the Non-compulsory School System (Lpf94)*. Stockholm, Sweden: Ministry of Education and Science.

Ritzer, G. (2002). *The McDonalization of Society*. Thousand Oaks, CA: Pine Forge Press.

Triandis, H. C. (1995). *Individualism & collectivism*. Boulder, CO: Westview Press.

U.S. Census Bureau (2003). "Annual estimates of the population of the United States, and for Puerto Rico: April 1, 2000 to July 1, 2003." Retrieved (October 4, 2004) from www.census/gov/prod/2202pubs/c2kprof00-us.pdf

Wagner, T. (2008). *The global achievement gap: Why even our best schools don't teach the new survival skills our children need—and what we can do about it*. New York: Basic Books.

Wolk, R. A. (2011). *Wasting minds: Why our education system is failing and what we can do about it*. Alexandria, VA: ASCD.

Zhao, Y. (2009). *Catching up or leading the way: American education in the age of globalization.* Alexandria, VA: ASCD.

Zimmerman, B. J., & Schunk, D. H. (Eds.). (2001) *Self-regulated Learning and Academic Achievement: Theoretical perspectives.* Hillsdale, NJ: Lawrence Erlbaum Associates

Chapter 4
Change Conditions with Entrepreneurial Leadership

"It is time for us to release ourselves from the simplistic and ineffective prescriptions; the time to dream is upon us."

—Carl Glickman

Introduction to Chapter 4

Wayne Padover, PhD, Associate Professor, National University, La Jolla, California

Innovative educational leadership in part is a visionary action to bring about organizational change encompassing an entrepreneurial spirit. As Glickman reflects in the previous quote, the leader must constantly assess the ongoing production of the organization on the basis of specific expectations of achieved results. With recognition of the terminology, "there is always room for improvement," the leader strives for a continuous improvement model. The improvement is measureable both quantitatively and qualitatively with use of the inquiry or action research model. The question becomes, "how may we use the data to structure and guide the leadership decisions needed to achieve our vision or expectations"?

The articles included in this chapter speak to the visionary talents of innovative educational leaders and some of the options available to them in restructuring the organizations they lead to bring about the desired change. The entrepreneurial way of thinking utilizes a systems approach to bring about change with the recognition of creating a new organizational structure which leads dynamically to the desired outcomes. In their articles, Dan and Judy Cunniff evoke a business community model to assist the leader in serving as a catalyst for organizational growth. Donna Elder and Wayne Padover encourage the development of local educational foundations to enhance the human and financial resources school organizations can bring about through a community development model. Finally, Donna Elder reviews the various school options representing changes to the traditional school organizational structure. She engages the reader to think of how an alternative school model might enhance the educational opportunities for students at their current educational organization.

A Basic Business Model for Innovative Educational Leaders

Daniel T. Cunniff, PhD and Judith R. Cunniff, MPA

ISLLC Standard 3: A school administrator is an educational leader who promotes the success of all students by ensuring management of the organization, operations, and resources for a safe, efficient, and effective learning environment.

▶ Abstract

This article discussed the importance of educational leaders being aware of a basic management cycle that can be used when confronted with situations and problems they will encounter as educational professionals. The process has been used by the authors as they worked in, or consulted for, major business organizations. The cycle may serve as a template for the administrator as he or she makes decisions on a daily basis. The system starts with the abstract and becomes more specific as a management action plan is developed.

▶ Introduction

The management skills the authors present are designed to assist the new administrator in having control over his or her work, which will enable him or her to get greater satisfaction and results from the position. Most administrators enter the profession with little or no management training for their position.

Innovative leadership involves drawing others into the active pursuit of the mission statement or strategic goals or organizational objectives. Researchers suggest that leadership ranges from vision, mission, purpose, direction, inspiration and management to implementing plans, arranging resources, coordinating effort, and getting things done (Cunningham, 1982). Some strong leaders are weak managers. Effective innovative leaders are good at both leadership and management.

One writer structures his university class to let the students take advantage of their life experiences on the job and develop and sharpen their skills of supervision and instructional leadership. He stresses that to develop control over your job and your people, you must first discover ways to greater self-control. Self-control is a key to the control of others. He asks the students to begin a process of self-study using journals, group discussion, problem solving, and action planning.

▶ The Management Cycle

Planning, implementing, evaluating, and reporting is the format the writers used as instructors, in developing and conducting their classes. This is referred to as "the management cycle."

As a former business analyst for Fortune 500 companies internationally for over ten years, Dr. Cunniff has been successful in being part of consultant teams that have saved companies millions of dollars through cost savings or cost avoidance using the talent within the organization. Ms. Cunniff has instructed managers in customer service and quality control for large companies, school districts, and universities in the problem solving process.

Success in using this management cycle technique led Dr. Cunniff to apply this as a practitioner in school districts as well as in the classroom as a university professor at Portland State University, California State at San Marcos, and at National University in California. This technique has worked well in both on ground and online classes.

It seemed obvious to the authors, that the same principles that achieved positive results in industries such as Boeing, McDonnell Douglas, Canadian National, and Peabody Coal Mines could easily be transferred to public school education.

This management cycle system included a basic problem solving process that culminated with a management action plan (MAP) that assures accountability in bringing a project to completion.

During the first instructional meeting, participants are introduced to the management cycle along with the course or program syllabus as to how the course or workshop is structured; this is then followed by a presentation of a modified Kepner Tregoe problem solving approach. Finally, a management action plan is presented which becomes the foundation of project management. A more detailed project or program schedule is derived from the management action plan or (MAP). This is the process used by many management consultants in business as they proceed to analyze and develop interventions to improve business practices. Educational administrative students or employees use this to help them to identify problems or issues confronting administrators (teachers, students and parents) in public or private education as well as in commercial businesses. As stated earlier in this book, leadership is defined as the ability to inspire and translate a vision into actions that can accomplish a goal. **Management is the process by which organizations reach their goal**.

The management cycle can be thought of as a basic system of the process through which the leader and the team achieve their ends (Katz & Kahn, 1978).

Planning yields to implementing then evaluation and reporting. This happens at every organizational level.

Planning

To think of an organization as a system in the planning stage assumes that some action will result (Barnard, 1938, p.77). Regardless of the level of the system being analyzed, all levels contain three universal elements including the willingness to cooperate, having a common purpose, and communication (Wren, 1994, p. 268).

Planning is the first step of the management cycle. Here the leader outlines and defines the problem, issues, or programs he or she desires to undertake. Often when the focus is on top management, the planning is directly related to the mission statement, organizational objectives, or the organizations core principles (Parsons, 1960). Consideration is given to methods, material and manpower needed to embark upon and complete the task selected. It is in this phase that the student or administrator identifies the people in and around the environment who can assist in the problem identification. In business it would be co-workers, supervisors, or managers. In the classroom it would be university support services such as writing, or math consultants, librarians, professors, school personnel in their districts, other outside agencies, or students in the class. The latter offer the most immediate source of support and tend to expedite the process.

Implementing

Perhaps **the most difficult part of the cycle is implementing**. Planning needs to be converted into action in this part of the cycle. A dictionary definition includes: (1) to give practical effect to and ensure actual fulfillment by concrete measures; (2) to provide instruments or means of expression (Webster's, 1979). This requires the coming together of multiple factors to successfully launch the endeavor. It is at this point where most projects get bogged down, usually through communication, relationship issues or financial miscalculations. Scheduling and conducting meetings involves having the means to locate contributing team members, finding a meeting location, and times that are convenient for all to attend. Accountability is the key in the implementation of any project and it is here that focused leadership comes into play. **Clearly defined roles and assignments are needed** to complete the many tasks needed to reach a successful conclusion. Simply stated, implementation is any activity necessary for the organization to translate planning into the intended accomplishment.

Evaluating

Key in completing projects is the evaluation of progress involving the critical factors or benchmarks on the path toward project completion. A critical look must be taken at several points in many of the selected issues. In thesis classes, for example, students review their topics with the instructor and use other students as proofreaders. A writing center and library staff provide additional evaluators in the quality control aspects of the research, writing development, and their management action plan.

Reporting

Problem research does not need to be accomplished in isolation. Depending on the class and extent of the research, the school district as well as the university has certain requirements and restrictions. Due to privacy laws, the university may have an Institutional Review Board (IRB) that must give approval to any studies or research involving human subjects. School districts have policies requiring employees to get approval from supervisors or boards. Keeping top-level administration informed and involved, if possible, will insure a successful outcome to any endeavor. Getting written approval of a management action plan is a tangible way to communicate to management that you respect its position and wish to follow the chain-of-command.

Once the project is completed, **there is the expectation that the results be shared** with management or the district, agency, professional organization, or foundation of your affiliation. This is especially beneficial when the results are positive or result in saving the organization money. This can also open the door to funds for future research, merit recognition, or promotion. These procedures have been stressed in businesses as well as in the classroom by most university professors.

Outcomes

Many students and educators realize the importance of this process of collaboration in the form of the management cycle and have written papers on leadership teams and the significance of team building and collaboration as school administrators. Several thesis and dissertations have been published emphasizing the high quality of results stemming from this method used in decision making.

Bringing employees, staff members and students to the conclusion that collaboration and consensus yields positive results has included a variety of experiential activities. Over the years, the writers have taken students on trust walks, where dyads blindfold each other and guide them through obstacles. Dividing the class into groups of six, the writers have simulated a spaceship crash landing on the dark side of the moon and had them decide, as a group, what to carry with them to rendezvous with the mother ship. These and other activities stressed the necessity for trust and consensus in building a team and solving problems.

In providing structure for their problem solving, the writers have used a modified scientific method and Kepner Tregoe problem solving and a root cause analysis technique. Here the writers provide the students or employees with a format, which includes six steps:

- Define the problem in one sentence
- State what is really happening now regarding the problem
- State the ideal situation that should occur
- List the barriers to reaching the ideal
- Develop a list of possible solutions to the barriers
- Create a management action plan (MAP)

Defining the problem is the most difficult of the six steps. The participants must narrow the problem and be very specific about what they can accomplish given their resources and time constraints. Most students take on very broad issues and require guidance in delineating their problem.

Stating what is really happening now regarding the problem or issue is usually not a problem. Most participants select an issue because they are passionate about the topic or have a vested interest in its resolution.

Stating the ideal situation that should occur on the surface seems like a straightforward matter, but as the student does further research and reviews the literature, this ideal tends to become more realistic given the resources available. It usually comes down to a financial concern.

Listing the **barriers to reaching the ideal can get out of hand**. Many students develop a laundry list of barriers that are either insignificant or beyond their control. Here is where advisors and university professors, supervisors, or managers can take an active role in keeping the student on track.

Developing a list of possible solutions to the barriers can be a daunting task that requires the aid of internal or external team members. Coming up with acceptable solutions that are politically correct in a given situation is touchy, and requires researching the impact decisions will have on all the stakeholders.

Creating a management action plan (MAP) is the backbone, roadmap, and culmination of the problem solving process. The MAP is the accountability element of the process that includes who is responsible for what, within a specific time frame. It is up to the team leader to insure that the activities listed in the MAP are realistic and attainable given the resources and time constraints. The creator of the MAP must get the buy-in from his or her key decision makers before the MAP is implemented. The team leader must be ready to answer the pentab questions of who? what? when? where? and why? Having these decision makers sign off on the plan is crucial in its implementation. It has been the writers' experience, if the MAP can show a dollar cost benefit in either cost savings or cost avoidance, the plan has a better chance of getting approval. This is especially true in times when money is tight and school districts or other organizations are looking for cost reductions in all areas of the budget.

▶ Conclusion

Innovative leadership guides the organization, inspiring its members with a sense of purpose. Management is the process of being accountable for all of the resources to make things happen. The innovative leader creates new alternatives to existing methods or problems. Effective leaders must leave their comfort zones to confront new and unknown challenges. They must value differences, and build on them to get to the destination (Covey, 1989). Businesses such as McDonnell Douglas, Boeing, General Electric, Amoco, Peabody Coal, Canadian National, and others, have realized **millions of dollars in cost savings** by using these techniques. Cadillac, Harley Davidson, and Federal Express have all won the prestigious recognition for quality in the form of the Malcolm Baldridge Award. There is no reason why our school district administrators cannot learn from their successes and use some of these very same ideas to increase not only productivity within the district, but student achievement as well. To the extent that universities, school districts, and businesses play a role in addressing the management cycle will determine the amount of success derived in raising the levels of fiscal responsibility and performance.

Discussion Items

1. Using your organization as an example, develop a list of your six most pressing issues. Present these issues in the form of a question and discuss the barriers toward reaching a solution.

2. Create an e-mail memo to your staff stating your primary organizational issue and the method you will use to create a solution.

3. Separate into groups and select a topic to resolve involving educational administration.

4. List the resources that are available for solving problems at the administrative level. How can the administrator be innovative in solving these problems?

5. In a group setting develop a management action plan to resolve a key problem concerning the school or organization.

6. Discuss the main sources of work-related stress and the impact on the organization as a whole.

Activity

Select an educational issue in your organization and develop a Management Action Plan to address the issue.

Background of the Authors

Daniel T. Cunniff PhD (See About the Editors)

Judith Garrod Cunniff MPA, a published author, with a BS from the University of Illinois and a MA in Public Administration from National University, Judith has had a diverse career in both business and education. Judith has worked as a dietitian, buyer/merchandiser for a major grocery food chain, supervisor, teacher, copywriter, paralegal, notary public, real estate agent, restaurant owner, co-innkeeper for a bed and breakfast/ranch, and an administrative assistant at K-12 and university levels. Ms. Cunniff is the lead author of "The Crisis of Methamphetamine and its Management" published in the *American Journal of Business Education, 2008.*

References

Barnard, C. I. (1938). *The functions of the executive*, Cambridge, MA: Harvard University Press.

Covey, S. R. (1989). *The 7 habits of highly effective people*. New York: Simon & Schuster.

Cunningham, L., & Hentges, G. T. (1982). *The American school superintendent*. Arlington VA: The American Association of School Administrators.

Katz, D., & Kahn, R. I., (1978). *The social psychology of organizations*. New York: Wiley.

Parsons, T. (1960). *Structure and process in modern societies*. Glencoe, IL: Free Press.

Webster's New Collegiate Dictionary. (1979). Springfield, MA: Merriam.

Wren, D.A. (1994). *The evolution of management thought* (4th Ed.). New York: Wiley.

It Takes an Innovative Educational Leader and a Village

Donna Elder, EdD, National University, La Jolla, California
Wayne Padover, PhD, National University, La Jolla, California

ISLLC Standard 3: A school administrator is an educational leader who promotes the success of all students by ensuring management of the organization, operations, and resources for a safe, efficient and effective learning environment.

ISLLC Standard 4: A school administrator is an educational leader who promotes the success of all students by collaborating with families and community members, responding to diverse community interests and needs, and mobilizing community resources.

▶ Abstract

Particularly during cycles when schools and school districts lack financial resources, the need for innovative educational leadership by administrators becomes all the more vital. The authors use the literature and their experiences as school site principals and school district superintendents as well as working with development officers at institutions of higher education to encourage educational leaders to form and support Local Education Foundations (LEFs). These entities can serve as vehicles to bring about needed financial, human, and in-kind services to their institutions.

Key Words: local education foundations, leadership, philanthropy, resource allocation

▶ Statement of the Issue

Public education has differed from higher education relative to the development of strategies to meet educational needs over time albeit particularly during financially climatic cycles of significant financial need. Historically, public educators have chosen a path of being passive, entitled recipients of goods and services provided to them. Higher education, on the other hand, has taken a more proactive stance, particularly independent organizations, in developing financial resources and in-kind services to address the educational needs of their organizations. Multi-million dollar endowments and fund development programs have been common-place for institutions of higher education (Bushaw & Lopez, 2012).

If public educational leaders viewed their roles as catalysts in a long-standing and likely to be continually longer-standing austere financial environment, the authors believe they would marshal human, financial, and in-kind resources to effectively provide leadership for their organizations. They would view their roles, not as victims of the political process and unfair bureaucracy but as dedicated, creative, innovative educational leaders who recognize they have a unique opportunity to serve students, teachers, staff, parents, and communities in bringing together opportunities for the benefit of all concerned. They would also recognize this is what skilled, creative, caring leaders do.

Review of the Literature

Historically, LEFs gained popularity in the early1980s as tax initiatives began to reduce funding to public schools in a variety of states across the United States. The National School Foundation Association represents LEFs as "privately operated, nonprofit organizations established to assist public schools" and which qualify as charitable organizations, "different from school districts, public institutions or local governments" (Clay, Hughes, Seely, & Thayer, 1985). A public school foundation "is designed to augment, supplement, or complement programs and activities currently being provided by the district" (McCormick, Baver, & Ferguson, 2001). Currently in the US there are over 6,500 school foundations in 14,500 school districts (McCormick et al., 2001). They have their own board of directors and their own staff, both paid and volunteer. Most school foundations operate as "an independent entity, with no formal, legal relationship to the school district" (De Luna, 1995, p.8). Foundations can specify in their bylaws whether the school board will be involved in voting.

Americans are generous in their giving. In 2011 charitable giving was over 298 billion dollars an increase of 4% over 2010. The largest percentage of giving, 32%, goes to religious organizations. Education is number two with 13% of charitable gifts (www.givingusareports.org). To many people's surprise, individuals are the largest percentage of charitable donors with about 75% of gifts coming from them.

In higher education, foundations have been a long standing tradition. Private institutions have had foundations for years. The 1960s and 1970s were very successful years for private college and university foundations. In the 1970s and 1980s, public institutions of higher learning became very active with the development of educational foundations. In the 1990s, community colleges began forming foundations. The 2000s became active years for the P-12 foundations. California has been a leader in the P-12 arena. In 2000, California Educational Foundations raised more than 30 million dollars effecting more than 3.5 million children (CCEF, 2011).

The California Consortium of Education Foundations (CCEF), one of the oldest state-wide coordinating entities in the country, describes LEFs as 501(c) (3) Internal Revenue Service Code nonprofit organizations whose boards represent local community and education leaders and who are financially accountable to their communities. Each is unique in its operation, its programs, and the resources it provides to its community, but all share a common commitment to improving education at the local level. They go on to state LEFs: (1) Serve as conveners with nonprofit agencies to address community issues relating to education, (2) Link people and organizations in their communities with public schools, developing awareness and resource support, (3) Increase teacher morale by making direct financial grants to teachers and by recognizing their importance in the community, and (4) Broaden support for public education and local schools with greater community awareness. In addition, some of the impact of LEFs in California have been: (1) In 2009, California education foundations raised more than 250 million dollars to benefit public schools and address the local needs of California's students, (2) LEFs sponsored programs as diverse as the communities they represent, ranging from teacher grants to purchases of instructional technology to funding after school enrichment, art and music programs to providing dental screenings, and (3) More than 36,000 community leaders served on the boards of LEFs as volunteers, bringing new ideas and perspectives to educational issues. These leaders serve as ambassadors for local schools and spokespeople for public education. Interesting to note, in some school districts 30 to 40% of currently serving school board members had previously served as LEF board members.

Utilizing Often Untapped Human Resources in the School Community

LEFs have many similarities as related to Parent-Teacher Associations (PTAs) and Parent-Teacher Organizations (PTOs). They both work with schools to assist them to meet their organizational goals. They are both fundraising organizations to some extent. They work with parents, school and school district administrators, and community members. Whereas parents compose the largest component of the PTAs and PTOs, that is generally not true as it relates to the composition of education foundations. With approximately 85% of the residents of most communities not having students attending local schools, the former parent leaders of the school community are often supportive of the local school and most often that support and talent is lost to the school and school district. It is particularly ironic not to make use of this bank of talented resources in local communities. Oftentimes, these older individuals have completed careers in a wide variety of services and professions and will likely have talents which can be utilized by the LEF. They often have valuable contacts in the community given the extended time they have lived there (Chmelynski, 1999). They often have more relaxed schedules than parents and are able to devote more time to specific support for the local education foundation. Older citizens new to the community will find the involvement with education foundations to be a very pleasing way to develop relationships with like-minded members of the community. One of the author's experiences helping to initiate a local educational foundation as the school district superintendent in a rural northern California community began by asking members of the community who they knew who might have interest and interpersonal and technical skills to offer leadership to the fledgling organization. A parent in the school district recommended a retired realtor who had served on the chamber of commerce in a suburban community. Marilyn Carrel and her husband, Bob, who had been a corporate executive, helped to get our LEF off to the right start. It was more than 20 years ago and the foundation continues to serve the students, parents, staff, administration, and the community. Interestingly enough, my relationship with Bob and Marilyn has continued all these years after. It underscores the point that an important part of the education foundation process is the social relationships which develop among those actively participating in the program i.e., altruistic citizens who welcome their responsibility and opportunity to actively contribute to their community through the vehicle of educational foundations.

Local foundations can raise large sums of money to support schools efforts. Working with one local foundation, one of the authors helped raise the annual fund contributions. The annual fund was a "direct ask" that was done each year. Every member of the school community was asked to contribute whatever they could from one dollar to large gifts. In year one of the annual fund $300,000 dollars were raised. By the end of year four, the fund had increased to one million dollars. All foundations do not have this capacity, but they do have the capacity to continually improve annual giving by establishing a culture of giving. This is a new concept in the public schools, but can be nurtured and developed. Many foundations have successful annual fund campaigns.

▶ Innovative Educational Leadership is about Community Development

For the innovative educational leader initiating or working with a LEF provides an opportunity to focus the resources of the community on the betterment of educational opportunities for the children of the community. At this point, the reader is clear about LEFs raising funds for schools and school districts. If the authors were to mention the dollars (and there were tens of thousands on an annual basis plus multi-million dollar grants-in-aid) brought to the educational organizations served were not the most impressive aspect of LEFs, the authors' sanity might be held in question. The most impressive aspect of the development of LEFs was having this entity serve as a catalyst for bringing together diverse members of the community across racial, ethnic, religious, educational, political, and socioeconomic lines. This kind of involvement would happen when the LEF would sponsor events, e.g. volunteering the labor, equipment and expertise to build a multi-use sports field or construction of a greenhouse for the science program or offering transportation and interpreter services for non-English speaking parents to attend parent-teacher conferences or sponsoring a Career Education Day while bringing in individuals to schools to make presentations about their work situations. At the same time, the composition of the LEF board needs to be representative of the community being served.

In addition, LEFs often will collaborate with other service groups in fundraising efforts. Here again, the level of diversity increases as individuals in a community come together on behalf of bringing about a higher level of educational services than was deemed available previously for the children of the community. In the suburban community in which I served, the local Lions Club determined they needed assistance to organize their signature fundraising event--a rodeo. They requested the LEF provide volunteers to assist in the operations aspects of the event and agreed to donate a large percentage of the profits to the LEF. That agreement has been in effect for the past ten years and hundreds of thousands of dollars have been raised. In a low socioeconomic school district in an urban community in which one of the authors' served, a local electrical technology company, which employed many parents in the school district, agreed to underwrite a pre-school program to benefit their employee's children and other children in the community (Grace and Wendroff, 2001).

LEFs can also be very helpful in providing spokespersons for schools in the community. They are a different voice than the school district personnel and give a different perspective about school district policies. LEFs can be very influential when districts are holding bond or parcel tax elections. There are many examples of LEFs which have assisted the district in passing bond and parcel tax elections. At the very least, LEFs can serve as a "convener" in bringing together members of the community for forums with regard to school-related issues.

▶ LEFs are Similar and yet Different

An innovative educational leader who has worked successfully with an LEF may expect all LEFs to operate in the same way. The authors' experience and the literature (Hicks, 2003) would not support that notion. To the contrary, the leadership and the workers of the urban school districts generally were the school and school district faculty and staff. They recognized the parents in low socioeconomic urban school districts were most concerned about having basic necessities to provide for their families and were not able to volunteer their time for LEF leadership activities. As a school district administrator, having a LEF also proved to be very beneficial on multiple occasions when applying for competitive grants-in-aid. Oftentimes competitive grant applications received extra credit toward obtaining the grant when an application indicated it had the support of a local parent-community entity, beyond that of a parent-teacher organization. The leadership of suburban school districts was most often parents of students. They were available to make donations to the LEF, encourage their friends and neighbors to participate and gain support of others in the community or other communities. Parents in suburban communities, often of mid to upper socioeconomic backgrounds, will have expanded contacts and fund-raising opportunities based on their professional and social relationships. Rural LEFs often have leadership which is composed of community leaders who often participate in community service organizations. They will involve a wide variety of friends from the town whose relationships are related to church and civic activities.

▶ Implications for Innovative Educational Leaders Who Choose to Work with LEFs

To an increasing extent schools and school district parent communities are recognizing the advantages they have when working with an administrator who has successful administrative experience with LEFs or is at least excited by the possibility of working with an existing LEF. Possibly, the administrator is interested in helping initiate an educational foundation in the new school community. The educational leader must understand a leadership style that is competent, communicative, transparent, visible, and forthright will be attractive to community members who have a successful LEF in operation or want to initiate an LEF in their school or school district. LEF-oriented volunteers want school personnel to be engaging and encourage the community members to feel ownership in the local schools. Personal connection is naturally about relationships and relationship-building is critical to the development of a successful educational foundation. How the educational foundation is perceived begins at the top with the school board and the district superintendent. When the board and superintendent are both supportive of the concept and willing to actively have roles in the various projects in the community sponsored by the educational foundation, very positive circumstances will follow. When the school and school district staff begin to develop relationships with members of the parent and other community members and a critical mass is achieved benefits to the school community will follow, both financial and in-kind services.

The Politics of Innovative Educational Leadership and LEFs

By definition, IRS 501(c)(3) designation of private, nonprofit organizations require the majority of the activity for these kinds of organizations not be politically-oriented. LEFs recognize the limits of their political activities; yet at the same time innovative educational leaders need to understand: (1) many of the individuals on LEF boards are influential people in the community, (2) from 20-30% of the LEF board members often become school district board members, (3) opportunities for educational leaders from principals to school district superintendents to develop "key communicator groups" can be important for the growth and development of the LEF and the educational institution.

Innovative educational leaders need to be politically astute and engaged with a wide variety of community members. Without knowing the political community and them knowing you, the working together relationship of the school and the community will be diminished and certainly not developed to the extent that would be most beneficial for the LEF and the school or school district. Although the LEF may choose not to take political positions in support of candidates or initiatives to not jeopardize its nonprofit status, their members can and often do provide aggressive support for political issues in the local community inclusive of local bond elections. The innovative educational leader must understand that political points of view in the local community can be positively influenced through the opinions of key communicators in the school community. These key communicators are individuals, such as the LEF board of directors and other active members of the school community, who often have relationships with influential members of the community. As difficult and controversial issues arise (as they inevitably will) the key communicators can offer information and perspective to members of the community, oftentimes ably representing the educational institution's perspective in a clear and straight-forward manner.

The Case against LEFs

If LEFs are so beneficial for students in the way they utilize untapped resources in the community, what are the arguments against them? Some would say, given the broad span of resources in various communities it is much easier to develop LEFs in high wealth suburban communities and therefore a disproportional amount of resources would go to those communities. All communities these authors have seen developed their unique ways to support students utilizing LEFs. As noted above, it may have been done in a wide variety of ways, but success consistently followed sound leadership and concerted effort in a wide variety of communities.

Others would say if communities raise financial and other resources for their students' education, the state and federal government will not be encouraged to provide adequate funding to schools and students. Innovative educational leaders cannot be willing to wait for adequate funding and support for students to come about while standing idly by. Naturally, utilizing all of the political processes available through local, state, and federal government as well as professional educational organizations, innovative educational leaders must continue the challenge to bring about needed resources for their students.

Some educational leaders, superintendents, school board members, and principals recognize that to work successfully with most LEFs, the leadership style, as mentioned above, needs to be open, communicative, and engaging with an entrepreneurial and partnership mentality. Those same leaders have not been trained to appreciate nor have experienced this engaging style of leadership and would prefer not to partake.

Activities

1. What would you do to help organize an LEF in your school district or school as:

    a. An assistant principal

    b. A principal

    c. A district superintendent

2. As an administrator (select the role from above) what would you say to the president of the Parent-Teacher Organization who feels threatened by the advent of an LEF?

3. As a site principal, how would you approach the school district superintendent who may or may not be supportive of the development of an LEF at your school or the school district?

4. Develop a point/counter-point discussion as related to the question: Do we need LEFs as part of the problem-solving mechanism of funding education in America?

    a. From a teacher's perspective

    b. From a parent's perspective

    c. From a student's perspective

5. After viewing the websites of the National School Foundation Association (www.NSFA.org) and the California Consortium of Education Foundations (www.cceflink.org) determine how the information provided could be helpful to an administrator working with an LEF.

References

Bushaw, W. J., & Lopez, S. J. (2012). Public education in the United States: A Nation Divided. Phi Delta Kappan, 93(9), p. 9-25.

California Consortium of Educational Foundations. (2001). *Starting an Educational Foundation.* Retrieved (September, 2003) from http//www.cceflink,org

Chmelynski, C. (1999). Nonprofit foundations raise millions for schools. *School Board News.* Alexandria, VA: Retrieved (July 2, 2012) from http://www.nsba.org/sbn/1999/022399-all.html

Clay, K., Hughes, K. S., Seely, J. G., & Thayer A. N. (1989). *Public school foundations: Their organization and operation.* Arlington, VA: Educational Research Service.

De Luna, P. (1995). *The education foundation: Raising private funds for public schools* (Report No. ISSN-0733-2548). Eugene, OR: Oregon School Study Council. (ERIC Document Reproduction Service No.390 152).

Grace, K. S., & Wendroff, A. L. (2001). High impact philanthropy: How donors, boards, and nonprofit organizations can transform nonprofit organizations. New York: Wiley & Sons.

McCormick, D. H., Bauer, D. G., & Ferguson, D. E. (2001). *Creating foundations for American schools.* Gaithersburg, MA: Aspen Publishers.

Starke, D. (2012). *Charitable giving: It's in the numbers.* Retrieved (October 23, 2012) from www.givingusareports.org

Views from the Fringes of Public Education

Donna Elder, EdD, Associate Professor, National University, La Jolla, California

ISLLC Standard 6: An education leader promotes the success of every student by understanding, responding to, and influencing the political, social, economic, legal, and cultural context.

Abstract

The article will review the various alternatives to the traditional public school. In the 1960s many different ways to meet the needs of a changing student population were formulated. Many of these are still part of the choices available to families today.

Key Words: magnet schools, vouchers, charter schools and homeschooling

As an innovative and entrepreneurial leader, it is important to be open to a variety of ways to think about the public school system. As we know, there is no easy way that works for every child. One has to open the mind to alternatives and options. This article will explore alternatives that have developed on the fringes of the public education system.

Alternative education is important in a democratic society. As groups feel more constrained by the public system, it is important to have alternative approaches to the mainstream system to provide choices to meet the needs of all students. Claussen (2010) states that after World War II government became more and more involved in the public educational system, which left some students feeling disenfranchised and that alternative education systems are essential to a democratic system. Alternative education has been available since colonial times (Koetke, 1999). Religious groups provided one form of an alternative with the establishment of religious schools. Private schools have offered another alternative, but outside of the public system. Within the public system, there are a number of alternatives from magnet schools, schools within a school, homeschooling, online schools, schools of choice within the district, and charter schools. All of these have provided parents and students with choices.

Magnet Schools

In the early 1950s alternative education was mostly for students who had dropped out of school or who had behavioral issues and needed to have an alternative placement. In the late 1970s, other alternatives began to be formulated. One of the alternatives was schools within a school and magnet schools. These schools were structured to offer programs that were different from the main stream high school. For example, the focus of the school could be on health services and provide opportunities for students to have internships in a local hospital. The majority of magnet schools are at the high school level.

At their inception, most magnet schools were formed to respond to desegregation and to avoid a court-ordered desegregation. Magnet schools provided an alternative that encouraged students from white backgrounds to attend schools that were heavily minority based. The first magnet school opened in Tacoma, Washington in 1968 (Rossell, 2005). Magnets continued to grow as a way to integrate schools by using student and parent choice. The magnet school concept then expanded across the nation and became an alternative to the traditional pubic school concept for many students. In addition the sustained growth of magnets was supported by federal funding through the Emergency School Assistance Act from 1972 to 1981 and then Chapter 2 block grants. Magnet schools were also funded under the No Child Left Behind Act of 2001. Magnet schools were seen as both choice and innovation. Magnet schools have seen a steady growth since their inception.

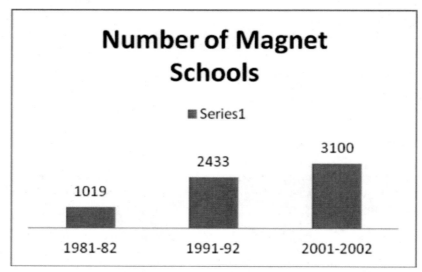

(National Center for Educational Statistics, 2007)

A thought to ponder is why did it take outside pressure to provide choice for students and parents in the public system? As an instructional leader are you forward thinking and looking for alternatives for your students or are you stuck in status quo thinking?

▶ Vouchers

Another response in the 1970s to either a perception or reality of failure of the public school system was the institution of vouchers. The thinking was that this option would level the playing field and give students in failing schools options to attend schools of their choice using vouchers to pay. This idea was proposed from a market-driven perspective that competition will improve schools as well as give parents' choices. The economist Michael Friedman was a proponent of the voucher system as a model for improving the public system. He felt that government was not the best way to run the education system (Gillespie, 2005). Vouchers continue to be a controversial issue today, being debated in the educational platform of the presidential candidates. In the 2012 election Mitt Romney was a proponent of the voucher model and President Obama supported using the money to support the public system. **There is no conclusive evidence that vouchers improve student achievement overall for students with vouchers or improves the public system** (Pons, 2012).

◗ Charter Schools

Charter schools are another attempt at finding an alternative delivery model to improve public education. In 1991, Minnesota passed the first charter school law. From this point charter schools have grown throughout the country. Charter schools were seen as the opportunity not only to provide an alternative for students, but also to improve the public schools by offering competition. The arguments are similar to those made for the voucher movement. Neither of these movements has delivered improvement to the public schools.

The Center for Research on Education Outcomes at Stanford (2009) found that only 17% of the charter schools had performance results that exceed the traditional public schools. Nearly 50% of the schools had the same performance levels as the traditional public schools and 37% underperformed the traditional public schools. Seventy percent of the nation's charter schools were included in this study.

Despite the failure to live up to the expectations of many, charter schools have provided opportunities for students that would not have been available in other situations. Parent choice makes a difference in how students perform and charter schools provide for parent choice. In addition to choice, charters have opened up a wide variety of educational delivery models which have not been available in the local public schools. Approximately **10% of the students across the nation attend charter schools** (Center for Education Reform, 2010). For many of these students, charter schools have opened up opportunities and supports that were not available in their local public school. **The real story for charter schools lies in the individual school and the effect it has on individual students**.

Charter Examples that Work

New Orleans tells a successful charter school story for an entire city. After hurricane Katrina, the school district underwent massive reform. Charter schools were a major part of the reform movement. In 2005 Orleans Parish was the second-worst-performing school district in the state (Newsweek, 2010). As of 2010 there are 42 charters throughout the city. Before Katrina two-thirds of the schools were failing and in the 2010-11 school year only one-third of the schools were failing (Newsweek 2010). Progress is being made and charters have a role in this turn around.

SciAcademy located in New Orleans is a good example of why charters can be successful. The faculty had a fairly traditional approach to education and learning planned when they opened their doors. They soon discovered this was not serving their students well and were able to change their approach and better reach their students. The principal, Ben Marcovitz, explains it like this, "They have to learn to read better first. SciAcademy added a literacy program, with classes in phonics and fluency. The entire curriculum basically changed over a weekend" (Newsweek, 2010). "The vision of SciAcademy is to prepare all scholars for college success equipped with the passion and tools to begin innovative and world changing pursuits" (http://www.sciacademy.org/index.php/about_us/our_values/).

As you think about this vision, you can see where the principal and faculty had to rethink what they were doing to be able to reach this vision. If they had continued to pursue the original course, students would not be ready for college or other pursuits. Their test results on the state exam in Algebra I, a gatekeeper for college entrance, surpassed the state scores with 34% of the students at the mastery and advanced levels while only 12% were at mastery and advance levels statewide (http://www.sciacademy.org/index.php/our_program/results/).

Another story takes place in the Los Angeles area. The district was a K-8 district and the parents did not want to send their students to the local high school district. The community had tried for years to become a K-12 unified district, but State Board of Education would not approve them becoming a unified district. The district had an entrepreneurial leader who decided that the solution was to form a charter. A founding group worked together with the school district board and had a charter approved to form a high school to serve the district students as well as others in surrounding areas. The school opened in fall of 2009. Since then, they have opened two high schools; one has a science and math focus, the second has a design focus. In 2011 they opened an innovative K-8 school to meet the needs of the non-traditional younger student. One of the advantages of charter schools are that they are nimble and can respond quickly to the needs of the communities they serve.

Even though as a movement charter schools did not turn around public education, there are many examples of outstanding charter schools that have made a difference in their communities. They offer an opportunity for innovation and change.

➡ Homeschooling

Although homeschooling has been an alternative since the founding of the United States, it did not become problematic for parents to choose until the 1850s when compulsory attendance laws came into effect. As with other alternative schooling, it was reinstituted and became allowable by law in many states in the 1960s (http://www.aophomeschooling.com/blog/homeschool-view/homeschoolings-roots-in-america/). Homeschooling is a growing movement and has continued to maintain a sizeable population of students over time. It is estimated that **over two million students are homeschooled**. The homeschooling population is growing about 15 to 20% a year (McDowell and Ray, 2000). Homeschooled children have a unique profile. In 1999, compared to non-homeschooled students, homeschooled students were more likely to be white, to have families with three or more children in the household, to have two parents (especially when only one parent was in the labor force), and to have parents whose highest level of educational attainment was a bachelor's degree or higher (http://nces.ed.gov/pubs2006/homeschool/characteristics.asp). In the 2003 study, the profile remained the same. Homeschooling is a niche for certain types of families. As you think about the challenges of homeschooling, it does require that at least one parent be at home and have the skills necessary to educate the children in the family. In addition, states have rules and regulations that parents must meet to homeschool their children. Each state is different, but these regulations make homeschooling more complex than it was in the early years of the nation. Homeschooling is selected by many families as a way to educate their children and it could be called the silent alternative as it is not debated in the political or educational arenas.

The question to ponder is why does change have to come on the fringes of the system? Why cannot school leaders change the system from within? In 1969 *Teaching as a Subversive Activity* was written by Neil Postman and Charles Weingartner. Postman and Weingartner (1969) argue for changing the educational system. The system as they saw it, was not meeting the needs of students and that the way to fix it had to be subversive, because the educational establishment was not going to fix it. All of these alternative schooling models speak to this idea. When the system is not meeting the needs of the students it serves, change needs to occur. SciAcademy is a good example of how the school turned the curriculum delivery model around over a weekend. As leaders, we need to be on the cutting edge and be the promoters of change to innovate in the system rather than holding on to what exists.

Activities

1. Visit a Magnet school in your community. Determine how successful it is working and why it is successful or is not successful.

2. If your school district operates a homeschooling division, visit the division. How do they meet the needs of the students they serve? Why have students and parents selected this option of schooling?

3. Locate a charter school petition on a charter school website. Review its petition and determine the focus of the school. Either by reviewing the website or visiting the charter, analyze how closely aligned the charter is to the practice at the school.

4. In your educational setting, which of these innovations could be created to better meet the needs of students? Do you have a totally different idea that could improve the education of students in your school or district?

Homeschool view: Homeschooling's roots in America. (2012, November) *Alpha Omega Publications*. Retrieved (October 1, 2012) from http://www.aophomeschooling.com/blog/homeschool-view/homeschoolings-roots-in-america/

National Center for School Statistics. (2009). Retrieved (November 10, 2012) from Fast Facts: http://nces.ed.gov/fastfacts/display.asp?id=30

Postman, N., & Weingarnter, C. (1969). *Teaching as a subversive activity*. New York: Dell Publishing.

Rossell, C. (2005). Magnet schools: No longer famous, but still. *Education Next*, 5(2), pp. 1-10.

Small Learning Grants

Dorothy Payne, Associate Faculty, National University

ISLLC Standard 4: Collaborating with families and community members, responding to diverse community interests and needs, and mobilizing community resources.

Many challenges face today's educational leader. Current school budgets are barely enough for salaries and basic classroom supplies. **To improve the school programs, the innovative administrator needs to turn to other sources** such as foundations, corporations, and state agencies that offer grant awards to solve these financial shortcomings. As stated in the July 1997 issue of *Social Work in Education*, funding is at the heart of school-linked services and that there is a relationship between quality services and the financing of these services (Nancy Feyl Chavkin, "A Beginner's Guide to Grantwriting", July 1997). Teachers and administrators who truly wish to try new ideas need to develop skills in grant writing.

▶ Review of the Literature

Grants are proposals for funding a project that the school or organization feels needed and necessary. As pertaining to the K-12 school site, the grant most often pursued by educators is the small learning grant. Small learning grants are proposals to solve a need that an educator sees in the classroom or school site. The most successful grants are part of the school's overall fundraising plan. These grants may be from a variety of sources (private or public), but most require the same information. The disbursement awards are generally $1,000 to $20,000. Small grants are generally ten to twenty pages and can take a manageable amount of time to complete the proposal. Federal grants, on the other hand, can be over fifty pages and take a good deal of time to prepare. Because the small learning grants are less cumbersome, the time involved in writing these grants is not overwhelming to the K-12 educator.

The kinds of projects that get funded are those that offer a creative response to a problem or need as well as have the potential for sustaining the project and its outcomes after the grant period ends. The grant proposal identifies the problem and offers a solution. The need must be real and documented with supporting data.

▶ The Grant Writing Team

The start of the grant process begins with organizing the team. Grants can be written by individuals, but the process is not as cumbersome or time consuming if a team is on board to help with the many details of the grant. Ideally, there should be two writers, one reader, one administrator, and one researcher.

The Administrator

School administrators "have to understand the process of applying for grants, but they also need to understand what information is typically found in a grant (Ruskin and Achilles, 1995). Local businesses and organizations need to be contacted by the administrator to determine if they offer grants for school programs. In addition, as a school leader, the administrator is responsible to help with any red tape or information needed to write the grant. **The administrator supplies information to the team and works closely with the writers**. Grant applications (also called "Request for Proposals") need to be followed exactly. They require the following information, which needs to be kept on file for any other future grant writing endeavors:

a. An Internal Revenue Service (IRS) Letter of Determination, proving that the school organization is tax-exempt. The IRS can be contacted directly (1-877-829-5500). They can advise if a grant is currently exempt under Section 501c3 of the Internal Revenue Code. The letter of determination is NOT the same as an "ein" – nine digit number. The "ein" is the employer identification number, also known as a TIN.

b. A copy of the school budget from the current and last year.

c. The type of school and number of students enrolled.

d. The ethnicity and the percentage of school's students who receive a free lunch or reduced lunch.

e. The net amount of money the school raised last year or in a similar year.

The Researcher

In addition to local businesses and corporations, a weekly search of the Internet is necessary for grants that align with the school's mission and/or project. Some online sites that are valuable are Fundsnet Services, The Grantsmanship Center, and ED.gov. In addition, the National School Boards Association (www.nsba.org) and the US. Department of Education (www.sdoe.org) list websites and periodicals that offer grant opportunities. Included in the appendices of this article are other websites of interest to grant writers.

The Reader

The reader assists the writers by asking pertinent questions. Does the project make sense as written? Is it grammatically and linguistically correct? This individual keeps the writer(s) on task and provides overall assistance with the grant project. The readers need to be acquainted with the grant's Request for Proposal's guidelines. There can be more than one reader involved in the grant writing project.

The Writer

This individual writes the grant. The project identifies and articulates school-based needs and/or problems. Outcomes need to be measurable and realistic, and the proposal needs to clearly articulate the methods to achieve those outcomes. If possible, use research to support the goals of the project. When describing the project, include a timeline. Most grant awards are for one year. If the project in the grant is to be extended, describe how will it be funded and how it will be sustained. Identify and articulate school-based needs and/or problems that the project will solve. The school and its mission need to be outlined as well.

Every organization that offers funding has a contact person to assist grant writers. The writer needs to establish a relationship with this individual to answer any questions, etc. regarding the guidelines, rubrics, and timeline of the proposal (D. Fernandez, 1999). A sample funding agency's rubric is available in the appendix of this article. For the beginning grant writer, it is recommended to peruse grants that have been written and funded. Kurzweil Educational Systems, (A Sample Grant Proposal, 2002), shows a paper grant application. Other funders request that the grant is both accessed and submitted online. All grant applications have guidelines on how to apply, information needed, etc. The grant application may contain some or all of the following categories:

The Grant Abstract

This is the part of the grant application that convinces the funder "that what you propose to do is important and that your organization is the right one to do it" (Fritz, 2011). The abstract describes the need for the project and the demographics it will serve. The goals and objectives are briefly outlined as well as how the project will be evaluated to measure its success. Also included is how the project will continue after the funding has expired.

A Statement of Need

This describes the problem that the project will address and solve. If possible, cite references that might pertain to other similar studies that were successful. If pertinent equipment is to be used, refer to the successes of that equipment or curriculum at other campuses. **Make sure the need can be supported with testimony or data before writing the proposal**. Never write a grant just because you need money for your classrooms (Smith and Tremore, 2011).

The Program Description

This provides information regarding the project. It explains how the project will be implemented and who is involved. The description identifies and responds to a need at the school and offers a resolution to that problem or need. It helps to start with the outcomes of the project, be specific in what needs to be achieved and design the project back from these outcomes.

Goals and Objectives

These are described in measurable terms that address both academic and/other needs of the students. These need to be cited in the timeline of the grant application.

The Budget

This must include all expenses needed for the project, including necessary training costs, and materials. Mention any funding received from other sources, such as grants and school budgets. Check the Request for Proposal (RFP) to see if matching funds are required. Many districts will not have the money to match your project even if you are awarded the grant. However, volunteers count as "in kind" contributions. When you list salaries, check with your district concerning salaries for any individuals working on the project. Many districts require that you account for benefits in your funding model.

The Evaluation

Specify how you will determine the effectiveness of the project and how you will measurably show what you will accomplish.

The Cover Letter

The letter must be neatly typed, free of errors, and signed by the principal. Put everything together with your cover sheet and a cover letter. Online applications will have a space in their format that will be checked or have the title typed into the proper section of the application.

► Case Study

Two years ago, in Newbury Park, Manzanita Elementary School, Conejo Unified School District, CA transitioned into a Magnet School—EARTHS. The school's mission dealt with environmental issues. The principal, Jennifer Boone, organized a grant-writing team to supplement her school budget. Her team consisted of herself, a staff member, and parents. Three of the parents had experience in grant writing, but many of the other volunteers did not. The team met twice each month and several of the members worked in teams or independently. The school obtained grant awards from both public and private foundations (Amgen, US Forestry Services, Boeing, and Lowes). Many of the grant funders established school partnerships with EARTHS and were honored at various school assemblies. Parent members of the grant writing team gained valuable experience and were awarded "Treasure Hunter" certificates. The school continues to write grants and has established both local and organizational partnerships.

► Conclusion

Grant writing is both a partnership and a team effort. It reduces the stress on the school administrator to balance the budget, but at the same time accommodates innovation. Grants do not need to be repaid, but the educational leader must learn to think like a business person and be creative in developing a program or a project that can continue without grant monies. Planning for the long term is a necessary component prior to seeking grant funds.

Trends in funding show changes in priorities among both government and private foundations. During the 1980s and early 1900s, children's issues (child abuse, neglect, early childhood education, etc.) were focus projects (Smith & Tremore, 2011). While that focus has not disappeared, the trends have shifted to new priorities. In the mid-to-late 1990s, closing the digital divide became a new funding priority, particularly at the federal government level. Software that improves student learning, such as passing state and federal requirements are of interest as well as using technology to drive instruction. Other trends are for projects that support professional staff development, evaluations and training. Projects that address bullying and aggression are also being funded.

If you are fortunate to have a proposal funded, send a thank you note to the grantor. Keep the funding agency informed about your activities, progress and accomplishments. Invite them to come and see your program in operation. Send your funder reports that tell how you are using the funds. Make the grantor your partner in education. Send photographs of your project in action. Include the local newspaper in your activities as well. **Build on your successes** and include them in your next grant application.

Discussion Questions

1. What role does the educational leader hold on the grant writing team?

2. What trends today influence grant writing?

3. What components are important to include in the grant budget?

Activity

Look into the procedure of applying for a small learning grant for your school or district. What area seems the most likely, and who would you need to research and complete an application?

Background of the Author

Dorothy Payne is a member of the Core Adjunct Faculty for the School of Education, and Coordinator of the Education Administration Program for the Camarillo Center, at National University. She holds a BS in Urban Planning and a MS in Education Administration from California State University. She has been an educator and administrator (K-12) for the Los Angeles Unified School District. As a grant writer, she has written proposals funded by the California State Department of Education, JPL-NASA, Toyota Foundation, Los Angeles Educational Partnership, and Lowes Department Stores. She is a member of Associate Administrators of Los Angeles (AALA) and Association of California School Administrators (ACSA).

References

Cunningham, W., & Cordeiro, P. A. (2012). *Educational leadership: A Bridge to improved practice*. New York: Pearson.

Fernandez, D. *Ten grant writing tips*. Retrieved (May, 2011) from http://www.k12grants.org/tips/10_tips.htm

Fritz, J. *Eight grant proposal writing tips*. Retrieved (May, 2011) from http://www.About.com

Grant Savvy Blog. *A practical know-how for grant writing and proposal development*. Retrieved (May, 2011) from http://grantsavvy.blogspot.com/2011/04/grant-research-using-online-databases.html

Kelly, M. *Grant writing tips*. Retrieved (May, 2011) from www.About.com

Kurzweil Educational Systems. *A sample grant proposal*. Retrieved (April, 2011) from http://www.kurzweiledu.com

Ruskin, K. B., & Achilles, C. M. (1995). *Grant writing, fundraising and partnerships. Strategies that work!* Thousand Oaks, CA: Corwin Press.

Chapter 5
INNOVATION THROUGH TIME

"Yesterday is gone. Tomorrow has not yet come.
We only have today. Let us begin"

—*Mother Teresa*

Introduction to Chapter 5

Daniel T. Cunniff, PhD, Associate Professor, National University, La Jolla, California

Knowledge and respect for history can deepen the leaders' understanding of important, current issues. Even though this book presents a variety of innovative leadership concepts, the foundations of these ideas are resting on the fundamental truths about people relationships, and organizations.

The evolution of the Internet was built on the basic technologies of the past. The World Wide Web has been the launching platform for thousands of new organizations and products. It has become a means for social communication and in some cases calls for action creating mass gatherings and revolutions. The electronic culture has opened the door to globalization with the promise of prosperity for many.

As we embrace new, innovative ideas, we must remember where they came from and the culture and traditions that enabled them to grow and be applied to present day problems, products, and processes.

Louis Wildman in his article on "Building on the Past: The Basic Antinomy" believes we need to educate our teachers to encourage their students to learn from the past in order that they might benefit from previous mistakes and failures. He invites the reader to step back and think about innovation as it relates to history. He uses the descriptor "antinomy" as the opposition between one principle and another or a contradiction between laws such as retaining past ideas, yet wanting to innovate on those ideas. There is an antinomic or contradictory relationship to keep in mind as a re-inventive or innovative educational leader in the cycle of change.

Dr. Edmund Sass presents the American Educational History for us in his timeline dating from 1607 to present. All these events are reminders of the contributions made by those who came before us. History now waits to see who or what will be added to this on-going list. Many of you will be contributors to this timeline in one way or another.

It is the authors' hope and desire that you will do your part as situations present themselves, in a positive, meaningful, creative, and innovative manner, keeping in mind the best interests of those who believe and follow your lead.

Building On the Past: The Basic Antinomy

Louis Wildman, EdD, California State University, Bakersfield

ISLLC Standard 2: A school administrator is an educational leader who promotes the success of all students by advocating, nurturing, and sustaining a school culture and instructional program conducive to student learning and staff professional growth.

▶ Abstract

There is a basic antinomy (or fundamental opposition) in social-psychology between the desire to preserve the past and the desire to be open to change. That antinomy in education has a long history, dating from classical Greek education. Today, the desire to preserve the past is manifest in pre-defined curriculum standards, such as the Common Core State Standards. These standards represent what we want to pass on from the past to the next generation. However, we also want to be open to change—developing the unique talents and abilities of each child. Both sides of this antinomy are important.

Key Words: antinomy, curriculum, education

The social-psychologists, Edward Jones and Howard Gerard, identified a fundamental division of approaches toward information in the human organism: "There is a basic antinomy between openness to change and the desire to preserve a pre-existing view or conviction" (Jones & Gerard, 1967). This fundamental antinomy pits stability and self-maintenance on the one hand against openness to change and stimulation on the other. As Jones and Gerard point out: "If either side of this antinomy should become completely dominant, it is hard to see how the individual could survive as an intact, effective organism" (1967).

Applying this fundamental antinomy to education, we see that both sides strengthen the curriculum. Faculty desire to pass on to students preexisting views, as well as encourage students to develop their talents and abilities. The antinomy partitions education into two types: expository education where the faculty wants students to learn about the experiences of the past in order that students might benefit from previous mistakes and failures, and investigatory education where the faculty wants to help, assist, and coach students pursue their talents, interests, and creativity.

That fundamental antinomy in social-psychology explains much in education. As Immanuel Kant said, ". . . education partly teaches man something and partly merely develops something within him . . . " (Kant, 1803). Or, as Deborah Inman much more recently has observed: ". . . educators have debated the merits of two contrasting models of learning. One is teacher-centered and based on the idea that learning occurs as a result of the transmission of knowledge from the teacher to students. The other is child-centered and assumes that learning is a process of the discovery of knowledge by the students. The pendulum of practice has swung back and forth over the years between these two one-sided models" (Inman, 1998).

The history of this debate really starts with the Greeks in fifth century BC. Even then there were two sides or views on what constituted a liberal education. Isocrates (a pupil of Socrates and an oratory teacher) emphasized the importance of grammar and rhetoric—informing students about knowledge and virtue. On the other hand, Socrates, Plato, and Aristotle helped students search for knowledge and virtue. The Socratic method of instruction involved dialectic—the art of examining opinions logically, often through asking questions in the search for truth.

Roman education emphasized informing students, as so much of K-12 education today emphasizes teaching students pre-defined standards. In contrast, life in the great medieval universities involved participating in disputations—great debates among faculty and students in search of knowledge.

At the end of the nineteenth century, the humanist Matthew Arnold professed that education should include the best that had been thought and said, by studying classical texts, "proper" standards for the formation of culture and personality, and an accumulation of scientific facts. On the other side, the scientist Thomas Huxley thought education should be dedicated to increasing human knowledge by use of the scientific method as the sole method for reaching truth.

Today in K-12 education, most teaching is directed toward student attainment of specific standards. Very little teaching is intended to help, aid, and assist students develop their individual talents and abilities. Most often not recognizing this fundamental antinomy, schools spend much too little time developing the creativity of individual students. "Factory model" schools concentrate almost exclusively on teaching to required tests, and do so in an inefficient manner. Schools could be using instructional software and shared video conferencing among schools to systematically teach most predefined standards, allowing teachers to devote the time saved to individual student development.

To get student knowledge up to world-class competitive levels it is increasingly apparent that we will have to utilize multimedia educational technology. For example, fourth-grade teachers at PS. 100 in New York City use a computer-based math program produced by Time to Know Inc. A study showed that 93% of a cohort of fourth-graders using the program met or exceeded standards, whereas only 66% of those who didn't use the program met or exceeded standards. The researchers felt that the animation and sounds of the computer characters captured the students' attention in ways that would have been much more difficult for teachers to do on their own (Wall Street Journal, 2010, October 19).

Present student achievement expectation levels are too low. Agreed upon "treaties" between students and their teachers, as well as between schools and local communities need to be radically realigned in light of much higher international academic standards and new job requirements. Fortunately, the use of educational technology can help us set higher requirements, because educational technology is not so easily persuaded by social pressure.

For a start, faculty and curriculum coordinators can identify the great movies, plays, ballets, musicals, scientific experiments, and historic events that all students should see, and schedule films of these classics at appropriate grade levels. Watching these important films could be done in a large auditorium setting or at individually convenient times on computer monitors.

Twenty-first century schools should invest sufficiently in the school's wireless network. The bandwidth should allow the use of multifunctional e-readers like the iPad. Students with disabilities should have equal access to education technologies, such as e-readers, with a text-to-speech function that reads words aloud. If the school library is not also the community public library, a partnership should be formed, to share resources.

Clearly, the present generation is well-acquainted with cell phones and laptop computers. In impoverished areas, schools can purchase inexpensive netbooks—the Littleton, Colorado School District now has 4,600 netbooks—and utilize free open source educational software and participate in the development process. In many upper- and middle-class neighborhoods, every 12-year-old has his or her own lap-top. They compose music, make multi-media animations, use meta-search engines, and write a lot, because they've been word-processing since they were five. Hence, we should utilize computer assisted instruction now available, for example, through the CaliQuity e-Learning Platform (http://www.caliquity.org) to teach most of those national standards. We could also offer courses not commonly available in public schools, such as anatomy, physiology, and DNA technology, through Virtual High School.

Virtual High School is a nonprofit accredited school with 11,000 students enrolled from 662 schools in 33 US states and 32 countries. It offers 336 courses (www.govhs.org). When students are absent, upon their return they can continue where they left off. When students don't understand an idea they can replay an explanation, ask an aide, talk with others in the course through the use of online chat rooms, or obtain help from a teacher on duty or a teacher who may not be on-site. This learning mode will allow schools to offer rarely taught foreign languages and other specialized courses otherwise unavailable.

Of course we will also be able to design multiple strategies to teach those national standards, giving students a choice. The construction of those strategies, as well as the further elaboration of those strategies, can occasionally be done by students, who can sometimes better understand student learning difficulties since they are closer to the problem. While this will require students to learn an authoring system, so that they are not merely the users of software, writing instructional software is a good vocational skill to possess. Further, when one teaches someone else, they often learn the material better, themselves. On the other hand, for more difficult learning problems, professional instructional teams, including teachers, media experts, and scholars, as well as older students, can be hired to improve the success ratio.

In 2008, Clayton Christensen, Michael Horn, and Curtis Johnson wrote *Disrupting Class: How Disruptive Innovation Will Change the Way the World Learns.* Coming from a business background, they conceived of education in terms of a "factory model." Hence, they only stressed teaching students pre-defined standards measured in terms of test score performance.

Their understanding of education may be described in terms of a feedback model whereby instructional objectives are identified, taught in ways tailored to the individual, evaluated as to how well the objectives have been learned, the results analyzed to determine what should be done next, and then the cycle is repeated if the results do not meet desired expectations. They are correct in predicting that high-quality multi-media online computer assisted instruction is already available, so that students can choose which way (or even ways) they would like to learn.

Christensen, Horn, and Johnson understand that the "categorizing [of] students by age into grades and then teaching batches of them with batches of material—was inspired by the efficient factory system that had emerged in industrial America" (2008). Utilizing this understanding of the educational process, they too foresee tremendous educational improvement over current whole-class instruction. They see this coming technological "disruption" of the typical public school, which they call an "industry," analogous to what has happened to so many businesses: Apple disrupted Digital Equipment Corporation; Toyota disrupted General Motors; Sony disrupted RCA; Canon disrupted Xerox; Sony disrupted Kodak; and so on. They point out that "success with disruptive innovations always originates at the simplest end of the market, typically competing against non-consumption." In education they see this happening first by offering specialized courses (e.g. Arabic and AP courses) online to small, rural, and urban schools, as well as to school districts where budgets have been severely cut, as well as to homeschooled students and students who need special tutoring or who cannot keep up with a regular school schedule. Their research on disruptive innovation typically produces a graph which looks like an "S-curve." Initially the disruption "pace is slow, then it steepens dramatically, and, finally, it asymptotically approaches 100 percent of the market." Hence, if their analogy holds, six years from now computer assisted instruction will be providing instruction for half the K-12 students, disrupting public education as we know it.

In the author's judgment, the Christensen, Horn, and Johnson analysis is correct, and educators should take note. When silent films were replaced by movies with sound, the orchestral musicians in every theatre lost their jobs. Significantly improved computer assisted online instruction could do the same to many educators if we only conceive of education in terms of a factory model just intent upon teaching students pre-defined standards—particularly a common set throughout the nation.

The author welcomes improved computer-assisted online instruction. However, the author believes teachers should insist that the teaching time thereby saved be devoted to coaching, aiding, and assisting students develop their individual talents and abilities. We should remember the two sides to education. We cannot ask students to spend their K-12 years focused on pre-determined standards, and then expect them to suddenly become creative.

▶ Conclusion

The Chinese, with several thousands of years of experience with a total emphasis upon standards-based instruction, now know that a total emphasis upon standards-based instruction is wrong and are trying to change (Zhao, 2009).

We should pay attention to how Singapore classrooms have moved from a predominantly expository-transmission model, to a twenty-first century investigatory model where students engage in complex knowledge construction (Tucker, 2011).

Singapore has one of the best-performing education systems in the world. Their students now regularly place at the top on international comparison tests, such as TIMSS (the Trends in International Math and Science Study) and PISA (the Programme for International Assessment). How did this happen? Their education system progressed through three stages: a phase (1959-1978) focused on expanding basic education as quickly as possible; then a phase (1978-1996) focused on expository-transmission (like what is happening presently in schools here in the United States); and now a phase (1997-present) focused on innovation, investigations, creativity, and research. By the 1990s, their expository efficiency driven education system had improved test scores, but they realized that the world economy was becoming a global knowledge economy.

Singapore is a country with no natural resources. To be competitive, they envisioned becoming a global scientific hub. They realized that national progress was increasingly being determined by the discovery and application of new, marketable ideas. They realized that they needed expository and investigatory education.

Prime Minister Lee Hsieu Loong said they needed to promote "a different learning paradigm in which there is less dependence on rote learning, repetitive tests and instruction, and more engaged learning, discovery through experiences, differentiated teaching, learning of lifelong skills, and the building of character through innovative and effective teaching approaches and strategies" (Tucker, 2011).

Whereas teaching time saved by computer-assisted online instruction should be devoted to conducting project-based learning, many educators fear that educational technology will be used as a cover for an efficiency scheme which ignores individual student development. Christensen, Horn, and Johnson (2008) envision huge savings in the cost of public education devoted to teaching a common core of national standards. They forget the importance of teaching that enables students to make independent moves on their own initiative; teaching viewed as a liberating process; teaching which helps, aids, assists, and facilitates student interests and talent, and develops self-directed learners. In other words, they forget the basic antinomy.

Discussion Questions

1. Explain the following quotation in terms of the basic antinomy:

   American education is at a turning point. There are considerable pressures to move very sharply in the direction of "uniform schooling"; there is also the possibility that our educational system can embrace "individual-centered schooling" (Gardner, 1993).

2. Explain how online instructional software might teach the following eighth-grade language arts Common Core State Standard: "Form and use verbs in the active and passive voice."

3. Explain the following quotation in terms of the basic antinomy:

   We need, for the continuance of our society, education in conformity—*that is, training in the standardized procedures of learning such as reading, writing, science, mathematics, language, and logic, to provide for everyone a decent competency for citizenship and the daily problems of living. This meets the Jacksonian test. We also need* education in creativity *that develops the individual, encourages creators, leaders, even nonconformists. This meets the Jeffersonian test—and it is the kind of education that we are most in danger of neglecting today (Hungiville, 1995).*

4. Presently there is such a strong movement supporting outcomes-based education that many educators have lost sight of the needed balance, suggested by the basic antinomy. Many of those who know that we need a balanced curriculum don't know how to legitimize the investigatory side. Here are some topic examples of investigatory education: "What makes plants grow?" (primary grades); "Investigating the property of water weight: sink or float" (second grade); "Friction" (third grade); "Predicting changes in the weather" (fourth grade); "Creating an ad campaign" (sixth grade); "Planning a trip to Washington, DC" (middle school grades); "Family history (seventh grade); "Owl pellet reconstruction" (biology); "Comparative shopping" (home economics); and "Creating an individual exercise program" (physical education). Develop a similar list. Investigatory education permits the student to begin creating their own context, gradually taking over responsibility for self-directed lifelong learning. The investigatory approach helps, aids, assists, and facilitates student development. It encourages students to examine unexpected avenues that invite exploration.

5. Research tutorial instruction at Oxford and Cambridge. How is a typical tutorial conducted?

6. Visit the web sites for Deerfield Academy and Phillips Academy, which both have 5/1 student/teacher ratios. Report on the emphasis you find there on investigatory education.

7. In April of 1990, Chester Finn wrote a widely influential article ("The Biggest Reform of All") in *Phi Delta Kappan* which provided strong motivation for the "No Child Left Behind" Act. He said:

   When embarking on any given reform today ... it will be judged a success only to the extent that it boosts educational outcomes ... it is these learning outcomes by which society will appraise their efforts.

   The author used the basic antinomy to respond, which was also published in *Phi Delta Kappan* (October 1990):

   If education involves both passing on to the next generation what we think is of most worth, as well as facilitating individual student talent, then Chester Finn is terribly wrong. He presents a simplistic conception of the former part, while ignoring the larger latter part. Mr. Finn speaks of outcomes, but doesn't realize that artists and scientists do not attain eminence by pursuing the most efficient trail towards passing an exit exam. Rather, they linger to investigate an idea or pursue a special talent.

Do we want students to rush through their elementary and secondary years, accumulating facts and skills in order to pass even an improved GED? The author does not. Assuming that we will realize tremendous teaching efficiencies through technological means, Finn assumes that we would then lay off millions of educators, leaving a few evaluators, like himself, to assess students. Quite to the contrary, the realization of technological efficiencies would allow educators to devote more time to helping students with investigatory pursuits.

Today, many politicians measure education in terms of achievement test scores. Argue the issue, with those agreeing with me arguing in favor of Chester Finn's position, and those who agree with him, arguing in favor of my response. (Note: by arguing in favor of a position you personally do not support, you will be forced to consider the deeper issues and underlying assumptions.)

Background of the Author

Louis Wildman received a BA from Lewis & Clark College, a MMusEd from the University of Portland, and an EdD from the University of Washington. His musical career included nine seasons with the Portland, Oregon Symphony Orchestra, including several solo performances. He has served as a junior high math teacher, a college mathematics instructor, principal, curriculum coordinator, superintendent, and professor of educational administration. He received *Quest Magazine's* "Giraffe Award" as a superintendent, for "sticking his neck out for small schools;" the California Association of Professors of Educational Administration's "Outstanding Service and Dedication" Award; the California State University-Bakersfield School of Education "Service (1999)," "Teaching (2000)," "Research (2006)," and "Leadership (2009, 2010)" Awards; the Association of California School Administrators' "California Professor of Education of the Year" Award; and the National Council of Professors of Educational Administration "Living Legend" Award. His lecture/concert, "Ten Ideas Countering the Assault on Public Education," is available at http://www.youtube.com/channel/UC7vRDgECapObCF0oRUJSvMw/videos?view=1

References

Christensen, C., Horn, M. B., & Johnson, C. W. (2008). *Disrupting class: How disruptive innovation will change the way the world learns.* New York: McGraw Hill.

English, F., Papa, R., Mullen, C. A., & Creighton, T. (2012). *Educational Leadership at 2050.* Lanham, NY: Rowman & Littlefield Publishers, Inc.

Finn, C. (1990). The biggest reform of all. *Phi Delta Kappan.* 71(8), 584-92.

Gardner, H. (1993). *Multiple intelligences: The theory in practice.* New York: Basic Books.

Hungiville, M. (1995). Russel Nye: The professor in public life. *Academe, 81*(3), 24-27.

Inman, D. (1998). High performance learning communities. *The Policy Forum, 1*(2). US Dept. of Education.

Kant, I. (1803). *Lecture notes on pedagogy.* New York: Lippincott.

Kimball, B. (1995). *A history of the idea of liberal education.* New York: College Entrance Examination Board.

Tucker, M. (2011). *Surpassing Shanghai: An agenda for American education built on the world's leading systems.* Cambridge, MA: Harvard Education Press.

Zhao, Y. (2009). *Catching up or leading the way.* Alexandria, VA: ASCD.

American Educational History: A Hypertext Timeline

Last updated January 18, 2013.

Index: 1600–1699, 1700–1799, 1800–1899, 1900–1999, 2000–Present

1607 – The first permanent English settlement in North America is established by the <u>Virginia Company</u> at <u>Jamestown</u> in what is now the state of Virginia.

1620 – The <u>Mayflower</u> arrives at Cape Cod, bringing the <u>Pilgrims</u> who establish the <u>Plymouth Colony</u>. Many of the Pilgrims are <u>Puritans</u> who had fled religious persecution in England. Their religious views come to dominate education in the <u>New England colonies</u>.

1635 – The first Latin Grammar School (<u>Boston Latin School</u>) is established. <u>Latin Grammar Schools</u> are designed for sons of certain social classes who are destined for leadership positions in church, state, or the courts.

1635 – The first "free school" in Virginia opens. However, education in the <u>Southern colonies</u> is more typically provided at home by parents or tutors.

1636 – <u>Harvard College</u>, the first higher education institution in what is now the United States, is established in Newtowne (now <u>Cambridge</u>), MA.

1638 – The <u>first printing press in the American Colonies</u> is set up at Harvard College.

1640 – <u>Henry Dunster</u> becomes President of Harvard College. He teaches all the courses himself!

1642 – The <u>Massachusetts Bay School Law</u> is passed. It requires that parents assure their children know the principles of religion and the capital laws of the commonwealth.

1647 – <u>The Massachusetts Law of 1647</u>, also known as the Old Deluder Satan Act, is passed. It decrees that every town of at least 50 families hire a schoolmaster who would teach the town's children to read and write and that all towns of at least 100 families should have a Latin grammar school master who will prepare students to attend Harvard College.

1690 – <u>John Locke</u> publishes his *Essay Concerning Human Understanding*, which conveys his belief that the human mind is a *tabula rasa*, or blank slate, at birth and knowledge is derived through experience, rather than innate ideas as was believed by many at that time. Locke's views concerning the mind and learning greatly influence American education.

1690 – The first <u>New England Primer</u> is printed in Boston. It becomes the most widely-used schoolbook in New England.

1692 – The Plymouth Colony merges with the Massachusetts Bay Colony. About 50 miles to the north, in Salem, the infamous <u>Salem Witchcraft Trials</u> take place.

1693 – John Locke's *Some Thoughts Concerning Education* is published, describing his views on educating upper class boys to be moral, rationally-thinking, and reflective "young gentlemen." His ideas regarding educating the masses are conveyed in *On Working Schools*, published in 1697, which focused on the importance of developing a work ethic.

1693 – The College of William and Mary is established in Virginia. It is the second college to open in colonial America and has the distinction of being Thomas Jefferson's college.

1698 – The first publicly supported library in the US is established in Charles Town, SC. Two years later, the General Assembly of South Carolina passes the first public library law.

1710 – Christopher Dock, a Mennonite and one of Pennsylvania's most famous educators, arrives from Germany and later opens a school in Montgomery County, PA. Dock's book, *Schul-Ordnung* (meaning school management), published in 1770, is the first book about teaching printed in colonial America. Typical of those in the middle colonies, schools in Pennsylvania are established not only by the Mennonites, but by the Quakers and other religious groups as well.

1734 – Christian von Wolff describes the human mind as consisting of powers or faculties. Called Faculty Psychology, this doctrine holds that the mind can best be developed through "mental discipline" or tedious drill and repetition of basic skills and the eventual study of abstract subjects such as classical philosophy, literature, and languages. This viewpoint greatly influences American education throughout the nineteenth century and beyond.

1743 – Benjamin Franklin forms the American Philosophical Society, which helps bring ideas of the European Enlightenment, including those of John Locke, to colonial America. Emphasizing secularism, science, and human reason, these ideas clash with the religious dogma of the day, but greatly influence the thinking of prominent colonists, including Franklin and Thomas Jefferson.

1751 – Benjamin Franklin helps to establish the first "English Academy" in Philadelphia with a curriculum that is both classical and modern, including such courses as history, geography, navigation, surveying, and modern as well as classical languages. The academy ultimately becomes the University of Pennsylvania.

1752 – St. Matthew Lutheran School, one of the first Lutheran charity schools in North America, is founded in New York City by Henry Melchior Muhlenberg, after whom Muhlenberg College in Allentown, PA is named.

1754 – The French and Indian War begins in colonial America as the French and their Indian allies fight the English for territorial control.

1762 – Swiss-born Jean-Jacques Rousseau's book, *Emile, ou l'éducation*, which describes his views on education, is published. Rousseau's ideas on the importance early childhood are in sharp contrast with the prevailing views of his time and influence not only contemporary philosophers, but also twentieth century American philosopher and educational reformer John Dewey.

1763 – The French are defeated, and the French and Indian War ends with the Treaty of Paris. It gives most French territory in North America to England.

1766 – The Moravians, a protestant denomination from central Europe, establish the village of Salem in North Carolina. Six years later (1772), they found a school for girls, which later becomes Salem College, a liberal arts college for women with a current enrollment of approximately 1100.

1775 – The Revolutionary War begins.

1776 – The <u>Declaration of Independence</u> is adopted by the Continental Congress on July 4th. Written by <u>Thomas Jefferson</u>, the document serves notice to <u>King George III</u> and the rest of the world that the American Colonies no longer considered themselves part of the British Empire.

1779 – <u>Thomas Jefferson</u> proposes a two-track educational system, with different tracks for "the laboring and the learned."

1783 – The <u>Revolutionary War</u> officially ends with the signing of the <u>Treaty of Paris</u>, which recognizes US independence and possession of all land east of the Mississippi except the Spanish colony of Florida.

1783 to 1785 – Because of his dissatisfaction with English textbooks of the day, <u>Noah Webster</u> writes *A Grammatical Institute of the English Language* , consisting of three volumes: a spelling book, a grammar book, and a reader. They become very widely used throughout the United States. In fact, the spelling volume, later renamed the *American Spelling Book* and often called the *Blue-Backed Speller*, has never been out of print!

1784 – The <u>Ordinance of 1784</u> divides the Western territories (north of the Ohio River and east of the Mississippi) into ten separate territories that would eventually become states and have the same rights as the 13 original states.

1785 – The <u>Land Ordinance of 1785</u> specifies that the western territories are to be divided into townships made up of 640-acre sections, one of which was to be set aside "for the maintenance of public schools."

1787 – <u>The Constitutional Convention</u> assembles in Philadelphia. Later that year, the constitution is endorsed by the Confederation Congress (the body that governed from 1781 until the ratification of the US Constitution) and sent to state legislatures for ratification. The document does not include the words education or school.

1787 – The <u>Northwest Ordinance</u> is enacted by the Confederation Congress. It provides a plan for western expansion and bans slavery in new states. Specifically recognizing the importance of education, Act 3 of the document begins, "Religion, morality, and knowledge, being necessary to good government and the happiness of mankind, schools and the means of education shall forever be encouraged." Perhaps of more of practical importance, it stipulates that a section of land in every township of each new state be reserved for the support of education.

1787 – The <u>Young Ladies Academy</u> opens in Philadelphia and becomes the first academy for girls in America.

1788 – <u>The US Constitution</u> is ratified by the required number of states.

1791 – <u>The Bill of Rights</u> is passed by the first Congress of the new United States. No mention is made of education in any of the amendments. However, the Tenth Amendment to the Constitution states that powers not delegated to the federal government "are reserved to the States, respectively, or to the people." Thus, education becomes a function of the state rather than the federal government.

1801 – <u>James Pillans</u> invents the <u>blackboard</u>.

1812 to 1815 – The <u>War of 1812</u>, sometimes called the "Second War of Independence," occurs for multiple reasons, including American desires for territorial expansion and British harassment of US merchant ships. The war begins with an unsuccessful invasion of Canada by US forces. Though the <u>Treaty of Ghent</u>, signed on December 24, 1814, supposedly ends the war, the final battle actually takes place January 8, 1815 with <u>US forces defeating the British at New Orleans</u>.

1817 – The <u>Connecticut Asylum at Hartford for the Instruction of Deaf and Dumb Persons opens</u>. It is the first permanent school for the deaf in the United States. <u>Thomas Hopkins Gallaudet and Laurent Clerc</u> are the school's co-founders. In 1864, Thomas Gallaudet's son, Edward Miner Gallaudet, helps to start <u>Gallaudet University</u>, the first college specifically for deaf students.

1821 – The first public high school, <u>Boston English High School</u>, opens .

1823 – <u>Catherine Beecher</u> founds the <u>Hartford Female Seminary</u>, a private school for girls in Hartford, CT. She goes on to found more schools and become a <u>prolific writer</u>. Her sister, <u>Harriet Beecher Stowe</u>, an influential abolitionist, is the author of *Uncle Tom's Cabin*.

1827 – The state of <u>Massachusetts passes a law</u> requiring towns of more than 500 families to have a public high school open to all students.

1829 – The <u>New England Asylum for the Blind</u>, now the Perkins School for the Blind, opens in Massachusetts, becoming the first school in the United States for children with visual disabilities.

1836 – The first of <u>William Holmes McGuffey's</u> readers is published. Their secular tone sets them apart from the Puritan texts of the day. The <u>McGuffey Readers</u>, as they came to be known, are among the most influential textbooks of the nineteenth century.

1837 – <u>Horace Mann</u> becomes secretary of the newly formed Massachusetts State Board of Education. A visionary educator and proponent of public (or "free") schools, Mann works tirelessly for increased funding of public schools and better training for teachers. As editor of the *Common School Journal*, his belief in the importance of free, universal public education gains a national audience. He resigns his position as secretary in 1848 to take the congressional seat vacated by the death of John Quincy Adams and later becomes the first president of <u>Antioch College</u>.

1837 – Eighty students arrive at <u>Mount Holyoke Female Seminary</u>, the first college for women in the United States. Its founder/president is <u>Mary Lyon</u>.

1837 – The <u>African Institute</u> (later called the Institute for Colored Youth) opens in Cheyney, PA. Now called <u>Cheyney University</u>, it the oldest institution of higher learning for African Americans.

1839 – The first state funded school specifically for teacher education (then known as <u>normal schools</u>) opens in Lexington, MA.

1848 – <u>Samuel Gridley Howe</u> helps establish the <u>Experimental School for Teaching and Training Idiotic Children</u>, the first school of its kind in the United States.

1849 – <u>Elizabeth Blackwell</u> graduates from Geneva Medical College, becoming the first woman to graduate from medical school. She later becomes a pioneer in the education of women in medicine.

1851 – The <u>New York State Asylum for Idiots</u> opens.

1852 – Massachusetts enacts the <u>first mandatory attendance law</u>. By 1885, 16 states have compulsory-attendance laws, but most of those laws are sporadically enforced at best. All states have them by 1918.

1853 – Pennsylvania begins funding the <u>Pennsylvania Training School for Feeble-Minded Children</u>, a private school for children with intellectual disabilities.

1854 – The <u>Boston Public Library</u> opens to the public. It is the first major tax-supported free library in America.

1854 – Ashmun Institute, now Lincoln University, is founded on October 12, and as Horace Mann Bond, the university's eighth president states in his book, *Education for Freedom: A History of Lincoln University*, it becomes the "first institution anywhere in the world to provide higher education in the arts and sciences for male youth of African descent." The university's many distinguished alumni include Langston Hughes and Thurgood Marshall.

1856 – The first kindergarten in the United States is started in Watertown, Wisconsin, founded by Margarethe Schurz. Four years later, Elizabeth Palmer Peabody opens the first formal kindergarten in Boston, MA.

1857 – The National Teachers Association (now the National Education Association) is founded by 43 educators in Philadelphia.

1859 – Charles Darwin's *The Origin of Species* is published on November 24, introducing his theory that species evolve through the process of natural selection, and setting the stage for the controversy surrounding teaching the theory of evolution in public schools that persists to this day.

1860 – Abraham Lincoln, an anti-slavery Republican, is elected president.

1861 – The US Civil War begins when South Carolina secedes from the union and along with ten other states forms the Confederate States of American. The shooting begins when Fort Sumter is attacked on April 12. With the exception of the First Morrill act of 1862, educational progress is essentially put on hold until the war's end.

1862 – The First Morrill Act, also known as the "Land Grant Act" becomes law. It donates public lands to states, the sale of which will be used for the "endowment, support, and maintenance of at least one college where the leading object shall be, without excluding other scientific and classical studies and including military tactics, to teach such branches of learning as are related to agriculture and the mechanic arts, in order to promote the liberal and practical education of the industrial classes in the several pursuits and professions in life." Many prominent state universities can trace their roots to this forward-thinking legislation.

1863 – President Lincoln signs the "Emancipation Proclamation" on January 1.

1865 – The 13th Amendment is passed, abolishing slavery.

1865 – The Civil War ends with Lee's surrender at Appomattox Courthouse. Much of the South, including its educational institutions, is left in disarray. Many schools are closed. Even before the war, public education in the South was far behind that in the North. The physical devastation left by the war as well as the social upheaval and poverty that follow exacerbate this situation.

1865 – Abraham Lincoln is assassinated, and Andrew Johnson, a southern Democrat and advocate of state's rights, becomes President.

1866 – The 14th Amendment is passed by Congress as one of the reconstruction amendments. If ratified by three-fourths of the states, it would give all persons born or naturalized in the United States citizenship and equal protection under the law.

1867 – The Department of Education is created in order to help states establish effective school systems.

1867 – After hearing of the desperate situation facing schools in the South, George Peabody funds the two-million-dollar Peabody Education Fund to aid public education in southern states.

1867 – Howard University is established in Washington DC to provide education for African American youth "in the liberal arts and sciences." Early financial support is provided by the Freedmen's Bureau.

1867 – <u>Christopher Sholes</u> invents the modern typewriter. Known as the <u>Sholes Glidden</u>, it is first manufactured by <u>E. Remington & Sons</u> in 1873.

1867 & 1868 – The four <u>Reconstruction Acts</u> are passed over <u>President Andrew Johnson's</u> veto. They divide the South into military districts and require elections to be held with freed male slaves being allowed to vote.

1868 – In spite of opposition by southern states, the <u>Fourteenth Amendment to the US Constitution</u> is ratified and becomes law. It guarantees privileges of citizenship including due process and equal protection under the law including the right to vote for freed male slaves. It becomes the basis for the rulings in <u>Brown v. Board of Education</u> and <u>Pyler v. Doe</u> as well as many other important court cases.

1869 – Congress passes the <u>15th Amendment</u>. It prohibits states from denying male citizens over 21 (including freed slaves) the right to vote.

1869 – Boston creates the <u>first public day school for the deaf</u>.

1873 – The <u>Panic of 1873</u> causes bank foreclosures, business failures, and job loss. The economic depression that follows results in reduced revenues for education. Southern schools are hit particularly hard, making a bad situation even worse.

1873 – <u>The Society to Encourage Studies at Home</u> is founded in Boston by <u>Anna Eliot Ticknor</u>, daughter of Harvard professor <u>George Ticknor</u>. Its purpose is to allow women the opportunity for study and enlightenment and becomes the first correspondence school in the United States.

1874 – The Michigan State Supreme Court rules that <u>Kalamazoo may levy taxes to support a public high school</u>, setting an important precedent for similar rulings in other states.

1875 – The <u>Civil Rights Act</u> is passed, banning segregation in all public accommodations. The Supreme Court rules it unconstitutional in 1883.

1876 – <u>Edouard Seguin</u> becomes the first President of the Association of Medical Officers of American Institutions for Idiotic and Feebleminded Persons, which evolves into the <u>American Association on Intellectual and Developmental Disabilities</u>.

1876 – <u>Meharry Medical College</u> is founded in Nashville, TN. It is the <u>first medical school in the south for African Americans</u>.

1876 – The <u>Dewey Decimal System</u>, developed by <u>Melvil Dewey</u> in 1873, is published and patented. The DDC is still the world's <u>most widely-used library classification system</u>.

1877 – <u>Reconstruction formally ends</u> as <u>President Rutherford B. Hayes</u> removes the last federal troops from the south. The foundation for a system of legal segregation and discrimination is quickly established. Many African Americans flee the South.

1879 – The <u>first Indian boarding school</u> opens in Carlisle, PA. It becomes the model for a total of <u>26 similar schools</u>, all with the goal of assimilating Indian children into the mainstream culture. The schools leave a controversial legacy. Though some see them as a noble, albeit largely unsuccessful experiment, many view their legacy to be one of <u>alienation and "cultural dislocation."</u> The <u>Carlisle Indian Industrial School</u> closes in 1918. Famous athlete <u>Jim Thorpe</u> is among the school's thousands of alumni.

1881 – <u>Booker T. Washington</u> becomes the first principal of the newly-opened <u>normal school in Tuskegee, AL</u>, now <u>Tuskegee University</u>.

1884 – The first practical fountain pen is patented by Lewis Waterman.

1887 – The Hatch Act of 1887 establishes a network of agricultural experiment stations connected to land grant universities established under the First Morrill Act.

1889 – Jane Addams and her college friend Ellen Gates Starr found Hull House in a Chicago, Illinois neighborhood of recent European immigrants. It is the first settlement house in the United States. Included among its many services are a kindergarten and a night school for adults. Hull House continues to this day to offer educational services to children and families.

1890 – The Second Morrill Act is enacted. It provides for the "more complete endowment and support of the colleges" through the sale of public lands, Part of this funding leads to the creation of 16 historically black land-grant colleges.

1891 – Stanford University is founded in 1891 by former California governor and railroad tycoon Leland Stanford in memory of his son, Leland Jr.

1892 – Formed by the National Education Association to establish a standard secondary school curriculum, the Committee of Ten, recommends a college-oriented high school curriculum.

1896 – Homer Plessy, a 30-year-old African American, challenges the state of Louisiana's "Separate Car Act," arguing that requiring blacks to ride in separate railroad cars violates the 13th and 14th Amendments. The US Supreme Court upholds the Louisiana law stating in the majority opinion that the intent of the 14th Amendment "had not been intended to abolish distinctions based on color." Thus, the Supreme Court ruling in the case of Plessy v. Ferguson makes "separate but equal" policies legal. It becomes a legal precedent used to justify many other segregation laws, including "separate but equal" education.

1898 – The Spanish American War makes Theodore Roosevelt a hero, and the United States becomes an international power.

1900 – The Association of American Universities is founded to promote higher standards and put US universities on an equal footing with their European counterparts.

1901 – Joliet Junior College, in Joliet, Illinois, opens. It is the first public community college in the United States.

1903 – Ivan Pavlov reads his paper, *The Experimental Psychology and Psychopathology of Animals*, at the 14th International Medical Congress in Madrid, explaining his concept of the conditioned reflex, an important component of classical conditioning.

1904 – Mary McLeod Bethune, an African American educator, founds the Daytona Educational and Industrial Training School for Negro Girls in Daytona Beach, Florida. It merges with the Cookman Institute in 1923 and becomes a coeducational high school, which eventually evolves into Bethune-Cookman College, now Bethune-Cookman University.

1905 – Alfred Binet's article, "New Methods for the Diagnosis of the Intellectual Level of Subnormals," is published in France. It describes his work with Theodore Simon in the development of a measurement instrument that would identify students with mental retardation. The Binet-Simon Scale, as it is called, is an effective means of measuring intelligence.

1905 – The Carnegie Foundation for the Advancement of Teaching is founded. It is charted by an act of Congress in 1906, the same year the Foundation encouraged the adoption of a standard system for equating "seat time" (the amount of time spent in a class) to high school credits. Still in use today, this system came to be called the "Carnegie Unit." Other important achievements of the

Foundation during the first half of the twentieth century include the "landmark 'Flexner Report' on medical education, the development of the Graduate Record Examination, the founding of the Educational Testing Service, and the creation of the Teachers Insurance Annuity Association of America (TIAA-CREF)." See the Carnegie Foundation's home page for additional information.

1909 – Educational reformer Ella Flagg Young becomes superintendent of the Chicago Public Schools. She is the first female superintendent of a large city school system. One year later she is elected president of the National Education Association.

1911 – The first Montessori school in the US opens in Tarrytown, New York. Two years later (1913), Maria Montessori visits the United States, and Alexander Graham Bell and his wife Mabel found the Montessori Educational Association at their Washington, DC, home

1913 – Edward Lee Thorndike's book, *Educational Psychology: The Psychology of Learning*, is published. It describes his theory that human learning involves habit formation, or connections between stimuli (or situations as Thorndike preferred to call them) and responses (Connectionism). He believes that such connections are strengthened by repetition ("Law of Exercise") and achieving satisfying consequences ("Law of Effect"). These ideas, which contradict traditional faculty psychology and mental discipline, come to dominate American educational psychology for much of the twentieth century and greatly influence American educational practice.

1914 – The Smith-Lever Act establishes a system of cooperative extension services connected to land grant universities and provides federal funds for extension activities.

1916 – Louis M. Terman and his team of Stanford University graduate students complete an American version of the Binet-Simon Scale. The Stanford Revision of the Binet-Simon Scale becomes a widely-used individual intelligence test, and along with it, the concept of the intelligence quotient (or IQ) is born. The Fifth Edition of the Stanford-Binet Scales is among the most popular individual intelligence tests today. For additional information on the history of intelligence testing, see A.C.E. Detailed History of the I.Q. Test.

1916 – The American Federation of Teachers (AFT) is founded. So is the American Educational Research Association (AERA).

1916 – John Dewey's *Democracy and Education. An Introduction to the Philosophy of Education* is published. Dewey's views help advance the ideas of the "progressive education movement." An outgrowth of the progressive political movement, progressive education seeks to make schools more effective agents of democracy. His daughter, Evelyn Dewey, coauthors *Schools of To-morrow* with her father, and goes on to write several books on her own.

1916 – The Bureau of Educational Experiments is founded in New York City by Lucy Sprague Mitchell with the purpose of studying child development and children's learning. It opens a laboratory nursery school in 1918 and in 1950 becomes the Bank Street College of Education. Its School for Children is now "an independent demonstration school for Bank Street College." This same year (1916), Mrs. Frank R. Lillie helps establish what would become the University of Chicago Nursery School.

1917 – The Smith-Hughes Act passes, providing federal funding for agricultural and vocational education. It is repealed in 1997.

1917 – As the US enters WWI, the army has no means of screening the intellectual ability of its recruits. Robert Yerkes, then President of the American Psychological Association and an army officer, becomes chairman of the Committee on Psychological Examination of Recruits. The committee, which includes Louis Terman, has the task of developing a group intelligence test. He and his team of psychologists design the Army Alpha and Beta tests. Though these tests have little impact on the war, they lay the groundwork for future standardized tests.

1918 – World War I ends on 11 November.

1919 – The Treaty of Versailles is signed on June 28. It officially ends the state of war between Germany and the Allied Powers. However, the terms of the treaty are tragically flawed, and instead of bringing lasting peace, it plants the seeds for World War II, which begins 20 years later.

1919 – The Progressive Education Association is founded with the goal of reforming American education.

1919 – All states have laws providing funds for transporting children to school.

1920 – John B. Watson and his assistant Rosalie Rayner conduct their experiments using classical conditioning with children. Often referred to as the Little Albert study, Watson and Rayner's work showed that children could be conditioned to fear stimuli of which they had previously been unafraid. This study could not be conducted today because of ethical safeguards currently in place.

1920 – The 19th Amendment is ratified, giving women the right to vote.

1921 – Louis Terman launches a longitudinal study of "intellectually superior" children at Stanford University. The study continues into the twenty-first century!

1922 – The International Council for Exceptional Children is founded at Columbia University Teachers College.

1922 – Abigail Adams Eliot, with help from Mrs. Henry Greenleaf Pearson, establishes the Ruggles Street Nursery School in Roxbury, MA, one of the first educational nursery schools in the United States. It becomes the Eliot-Pearson Children's School and is now affiliated with the Eliot-Pearson Department of Child Development at Tufts University.

1924 – Max Wertheimer describes the principles of Gestalt Theory to the Kant Society in Berlin. Gestalt Theory, with its emphasis on learning through insight and grasping the whole concept, becomes important later in the twentith century in the development of cognitive views of learning and teaching.

1925 – Tennessee vs. John Scopes ("the Monkey Trial") captures national attention as John Scopes, a high school biology teacher, is charged with the heinous crime of teaching evolution. The trial ends in Scopes' conviction. The evolution versus creationism controversy persists to this day.

1926 – The Scholastic Aptitude Test (SAT) is first administered. It is based on the Army Alpha test.

1929 – Jean Piaget's *The Child's Conception of the World* is published. His theory of cognitive development becomes an important influence in American developmental psychology and education.

1929 – The Great Depression begins with the stock market crash in October. The US economy is devastated. Public education funding suffers greatly, resulting in school closings, teacher layoffs, and lower salaries.

1931 – Alvarez vs. the Board of Trustees of the Lemon Grove (California) School District becomes the first successful school desegregation court case in the United States, as the local court forbids the school district from placing Mexican-American children in a separate "Americanization" school.

1932 – Franklin Delano Roosevelt is elected president and begins bold efforts to initiate his New Deal and spur economic recovery. His wife, Eleanor, becomes a champion of human rights and forever transforms the role of American First Lady.

1935 – Congress authorizes the <u>Works Progress Administration</u>. Its purpose is to put the unemployed to work on public projects, including the construction of hundreds of school buildings.

1938 – <u>Ladislas Biro</u> and his brother Georg patent the <u>ballpoint pen</u>.

1939 – <u>Frank W. Cyr</u>, a professor at Columbia University's Teachers College, organizes a national conference on student transportation. It results in the <u>adoption of standards for the nation's school buses, including the shade of yellow</u>.

1939 – The Wechsler Adult Intelligence Scale (first called the Wechsler-Bellevue Intelligence Scale) is developed by <u>David Wechsler</u>. It introduces the concept of the "<u>deviation IQ</u>," which calculates IQ scores based on how far subjects' scores differ (or deviate) from the average (mean) score of others who are the same age, rather than calculating them with the <u>ratio (MA/CA multiplied by 100)</u> system. Wechsler intelligence tests, particularly the <u>Wechsler Intelligence Scale for Children</u>, are still widely used in US schools to help identify students needing special education.

1941 – The US enters <u>World War II</u> after the Japanese attack <u>Pearl Harbor</u> on December 7. During the next four years, much of the country's resources go to the war effort. Education is put on the back burner as many young men quit school to enlist; schools are faced with personnel problems as teachers and other employees enlist, are drafted, or leave to work in defense plants; school construction is put on hold.

1944 – The <u>GI Bill</u> officially known as the <u>Servicemen's Readjustment Act of 1944</u>, is signed by FDR on June 22. Some 7.8 million World War II veterans take advantage of the <u>GI Bill</u> during the seven years benefits are offered. More than two million attend colleges or universities, nearly doubling the college population. About <u>238,000 become teachers</u>. Because the law provides the same opportunity to every veteran, regardless of background, the long-standing tradition that a college education was only for the wealthy is broken.

1945 – <u>World War II ends</u> on August 15 (VJ Day) with victory over Japan.

1946 – At one minute after midnight on January 1, <u>Kathleen Casey-Kirschling</u> is born, the first of nearly 78 million <u>baby boomers</u>, beginning a generation that results in unprecedented school population growth and massive social change. <u>She becomes a teacher!</u>

1946 – In the landmark court case of <u>Mendez vs. Westminster and the California Board of Education</u>, the US District Court in Los Angeles rules that educating children of Mexican descent in separate facilities is unconstitutional, thus prohibiting segregation in California schools and <u>setting an important precedent for Brown vs. Board of Education</u>.

1946 – The computer age begins as the <u>Electronic Numerical Integrator And Computer (ENIAC)</u>, the first vacuum-tube computer, is built for the US military by <u>Presper Eckert and John Mauchly</u>.

1946 – With thousands of veterans returning to college, <u>The President's Commission on Higher Education</u> is given the task of reexamining the role of colleges and universities in post-war America. The first volume of its report, often referred to as the <u>Truman Commission Report</u>, is issued in 1947 and recommends sweeping changes in higher education, including doubling college enrollments by 1960 and extending free public education through the establishment of a network of <u>community colleges</u>. This latter recommendation comes to fruition in the 1960s, during which <u>community college enrollment more than triples</u>.

1946 – Recognizing "the need for a permanent legislative basis for a school lunch program," the 79th Congress approves the <u>National School Lunch Act</u>.

1947 – In the case of <u>Everson v. Board of Education</u>, the US Supreme Court rules by a 5-4 vote that a New Jersey law which allowed reimbursements of transportation costs to parents of children who rode public transportation to school, even if their children attended Catholic schools, did **NOT** violate the Establishment Clause of the First Amendment.

1948 – In the case of <u>McCollum v. Board of Education</u>, the Supreme Court rules that schools cannot allow "<u>released time</u>" during the school day, which allows students to participate in religious education in their public school classrooms.

1950 – <u>Public Law 81-740</u> grants a federal charter to the <u>FFA</u> and recognizes it as an integral part of the program of vocational agriculture. The law is revised in 1998 and becomes <u>Public Law 105-225</u>.

1952 – Public Law 550, the <u>Veterans Readjustment Assistance Act of 1952</u>, modifies the GI Bill for veterans of the <u>Korean War</u>.

1953 – <u>Burrhus Frederic (B.F.) Skinner's</u> *Science and Human Behavior* is published. His form of behaviorism (<u>operant conditioning</u>), which emphasizes changes in behavior due to reinforcement, becomes widely accepted and influences many aspects of American education.

1954 – On May 17th, the US Supreme Court announces its decision in the case of <u>Brown v. Board. of Education of Topeka</u>, ruling that "<u>separate educational facilities are inherently unequal</u>," thus overturning its previous ruling in the 1896 case of <u>Plessy v. Ferguson</u>. Brown v. Board of Education is actually a <u>combination of five cases</u> from different parts of the country. It is a historic first step in the long and still unfinished journey toward equality in US education.

1955 – <u>Rosa Parks</u>, a Montgomery, Alabama seamstress, refuses to give up her seat on the bus to a Caucasian passenger and is subsequently arrested and fined. The <u>Montgomery bus boycott</u> follows, giving impetus to the <u>Civil Rights Movement</u>. A year later, in the case of <u>Browder v. Gale</u>, the US Supreme Court rules that segregated seating on buses unconstitutional.

1956 – The *Taxonomy of Educational Objectives: The Cassification of Educational Goals; Handbook I: Cognitive Domain* is published. Often referred to simply as "<u>Bloom's Taxonomy</u>" because of its primary author, <u>Benjamin S. Bloom</u>, the document actually has four coauthors (M. D. Engelhart, E. J. Furst, W. H. Hill, and David Krathwohl). Still widely used today, Bloom's Taxonomy divides the <u>cognitive domain</u> into six levels: knowledge, comprehension, application, analysis, synthesis. *Handbook II: Affective Domain*, edited by Krathwohl, Bloom, and Masia, is published in 1964. Taxonomies for the <u>psychomotor domain</u> have been published by other writers.

1957 – The <u>Civil Rights Act of 1957</u> is voted into law in spite of <u>Strom Thurmond's filibuster</u>. Essentially a voting-rights bill, it is the first civil rights legislation since reconstruction and is a precursor to the <u>Civil Rights Act of 1964</u> and the <u>Voting Rights Act of 1965</u>.

1957 – Federal troops enforce integration in Little Rock, Arkansas as the <u>Little Rock 9</u> enroll at Central High School.

1957 – The Soviet Union launches <u>Sputnik</u>, the first satellite to orbit the earth. Occurring in the midst of the Cold War, it represents both a potential threat to American national security as well as a blow to national pride.

1958 – At least partially because of Sputnik, science and science education become important concerns in the United States, resulting in the passage of the <u>National Defense Education Act (NDEA)</u>, which authorizes increased funding for scientific research as well as science, mathematics, and foreign language education.

1959 – The ACT Test is first administered.

1960 – First grader Ruby Bridges is the first African American to attend William Frantz Elementary School in New Orleans. She becomes a class of one as parents remove all Caucasian students from the school.

1962 – First published in 1934, Lev Vygotsky's book, *Thought and Language* is introduced to the English-speaking world. Though he lives to be only 38, Vygotsky's ideas regarding the social nature of learning provide important foundational principles for contemporary social constructivist theories. He is perhaps best known for his concept of "Zone of Proximal Development."

1962 – In the case of Engel v. Vitale, the U. S. Supreme Court rules that the state of New York's Regents prayer violates the First Amendment. The ruling specifies that "state officials may not compose an official state prayer and require that it be recited in the public schools of the State at the beginning of each school day…"

1963 – In the cases of School District of Abington Township, Pennsylvania v. Schempp and Murray v. Curlett, the US Supreme Court reaffirms Engel v. Vitale by ruling that "no state law or school board may require that passages from the Bible be read or that the Lord's Prayer be recited in the public schools…even if individual students may be excused from attending or participating . . ."

1963 – Samuel A. Kirk uses the term "learning disability" at a Chicago conference on children with perceptual disorders. The term sticks, and in 1964, the Association for Children with Learning Disabilities, now the Learning Disabilities Association of America, is formed. Today, nearly one-half of all students in the United States who receive special education have been identified as having learning disabilities.

1963 – President John F. Kennedy is assassinated. Schools close as the nation mourns its loss. Lyndon Johnson becomes president.

1963 – In response to the large number of Cuban immigrant children arriving in Miami after the Cuban Revolution, Coral Way Elementary School starts the "nation's first bilingual public school in the modern era."

1964 – The Civil Rights Act becomes law. It prohibits discrimination based on race, color, sex, religion, or national origin.

1965 – The Elementary and Secondary Education Act (ESEA) is passed on April 9. Part of Lyndon Johnson's "War on Poverty," it provides federal funds to help low-income students, which results in the initiation of educational programs such as Title I and bilingual education.

1965 – The Higher Education Act is signed at Southwest Texas State College on November 8. It increases federal aid to higher education and provides for scholarships, student loans, and establishes a National Teachers Corps.

1965 – Project Head Start, a preschool education program for children from low-income families, begins as an eight-week summer program. Part of the "War on Poverty," the program continues to this day as the longest-running anti-poverty program in the United States.

1965 – Lyndon Johnson signs the Immigration Act of 1965, also known as the Hart-Cellar Act, on October 3. It abolishes the National Origins Formula and results in unprecedented numbers of Asians and Latin Americans immigrating to the United States, making America's classrooms much more diverse.

1966 – The <u>Equality of Educational Opportunity Study</u>, often called the <u>Coleman Report</u> because of its primary author <u>James S. Coleman</u>, is conducted in response to provisions of the Civil Rights Act of 1964. Its conclusion that African American children benefit from attending integrated schools sets the stage for school "busing" to achieve desegregation.

1966 – <u>Jerome Bruner's</u> *Toward a Theory of Instruction* is published. <u>His views regarding learning</u> help to popularize the cognitive learning theory as an alternative to behaviorism.

1966 – Public Law 358, the <u>Veterans Readjustment Benefits Act of 1966</u>, provides not only educational benefits, but also home and farm loans as well as employment counseling and placement services for Vietnam veterans. More than <u>385,000 troops</u> serve in Vietnam during 1966. From 1965-1975, more than nine million American military personnel are on active military duty, about 3.4 million of whom serve in Southeast Asia.

1968 – <u>Dr. Martin Luther King</u>, Nobel Prize winner and leader of the American Civil Rights Movement, is <u>assassinated in Memphis, Tennessee</u> on April 4. The <u>Martin Luther King, Jr. Holiday</u>, observed on the third Monday of January, celebrates his "<u>life and legacy</u>."

1968 – The <u>Bilingual Education Act</u>, also know as Title VII, becomes law. After many years of controversy, the <u>law is repealed</u> in 2002 and replaced by the <u>No Child Left Behind Act</u>.

1968 – The "Monkey Trial" revisited! In the case of <u>Epperson et al. v. Arkansas</u>, the US supreme Court finds the state of Arkansas' law prohibiting the teaching of evolution in a public school or university unconstitutional.

1968 – <u>Shirley Anita St. Hill Chisholm</u>, an African American educator, becomes the first African American woman to be elected to the US Congress.

1968 – <u>McCarver Elementary School</u> in Tacoma, Washington becomes the nation's first <u>magnet school</u>.

1969 – <u>Herbert R. Kohl's</u> book, *The Open Classroom*, helps to promote <u>open education</u>, an approach emphasizing student-centered classrooms and active, holistic learning. The conservative back-to-the-basics movement of the <u>1970s</u> begins at least partially as a backlash against open education.

1969 – On April 30, the number of US military personnel in Vietnam stands at <u>543,482</u>, the most at any time during the war. College enrollments swell as many young men seek student deferments from the draft; <u>anti-war protests</u> become commonplace on college campuses, and <u>grade inflation</u> begins as professors realize that low grades may change male students' draft status.

1969 – <u>ARPANET</u> (Advanced Research Projects Agency Network), the first "packet-switching" network and precursor of the internet, is created by the US Defense Department. Its <u>first message</u> is sent October 29, at about 10:30 pm. For alternate perspectives on the origins of the internet, see <u>So, who really invented the internet?</u>

1970 – <u>Four students are killed by Ohio National Guard troops</u> on May 4 during an anti-war protest at Kent State University in Ohio.

1970 – In his controversial book, <u>*Deschooling Society*</u>, Ivan Illich sharply criticizes traditional schools and calls for <u>the end of compulsory school attendance</u>.

1970 – <u>Jean Piaget's</u> book, *The Science of Education*, is published. His <u>Learning Cycle model</u> helps to popularize discovery-based teaching approaches, particularly in the sciences.

1970 – The case of <u>Diana v. California State Board</u> results in new laws requiring that children referred for possible <u>special education placement be tested in their primary language</u>.

1971 – In the case of <u>Pennsylvania Association for Retarded Children (PARC) v. Pennsylvania</u>, the federal court rules that students with mental retardation are entitled to a free public education.

1971 – <u>Michael Hart</u>, founder of <u>Project Guttenberg</u>, invents the <u>e-Book</u>.

1972 – <u>Texas Instruments</u> introduces the first in its line of electronic hand-held calculators, the <u>TI-2500 Data Math</u>. TI becomes an <u>industry leader</u> known around the world.

1972 – The <u>Indian Education Act</u> becomes law and establishes "a comprehensive approach to meeting the unique needs of American Indian and Alaska Native students."

1972 – The case of <u>Mills v. the Board of Education of Washington, D.C.</u> extends the PARC v. Pennsylvania ruling to other students with disabilities and requires the provision of "adequate alternative educational services suited to the child's needs, which may include special education . . ." Other similar cases follow.

1972 – <u>Title IX of the Education Amendments of 1972</u> becomes law. Though many people associate this law only with girl's and women's participation in sports, Title IX prohibits discrimination based on sex in all aspects of education.

1972 – The <u>Marland Report to Congress</u> on gifted and talented education is issued. It recommends a broader <u>definition of giftedness</u> that is still widely accepted today.

1973 – US involvement in the Vietnam War ends on January 27. More than <u>58,000 US service personnel are killed in action</u> during the war. The fighting continues until April 30, 1975 when South Vietnam surrenders to the communist North Vietnamese forces.

1973 – <u>Marian Wright Edelman</u> founds the <u>Children's Defense Fund</u>, a non-profit child advocacy organization.

1973 – The <u>Rehabilitation Act</u> becomes law. <u>Section 504</u> of this act guarantees civil rights for people with disabilities in the context of federally funded institutions and requires accommodations in schools including participation in programs and activities as well as access to buildings. Today, "<u>504 Plans</u>" are used to provide accommodations for students with disabilities who do not qualify for special education or an IEP.

1974 – In the <u>Case of Lau v. Nichols</u>, the US Supreme Court rules that the failure of the San Francisco School District to provide English language instruction to Chinese-American students with limited English proficiency (LEP) is a violation of the <u>Civil Rights Act of 1964</u>. Though the case does not require a specific approach to teaching LEP students, it does require school districts <u>to provide equal opportunities for all students</u>, including those who do not speak English.

1974 – The <u>Equal Educational Opportunities Act</u> is passed. It prohibits discrimination and requires schools to take action to overcome barriers that prevent equal protection. The legislation has been particularly important in <u>protecting the rights of students with limited English proficiency</u>.

1974 – <u>Federal Judge Arthur Garrity orders busing</u> of African American students to predominantly white schools in order to achieve racial integration of public schools in Boston, MA. <u>White parents protest</u>, particularly in South Boston.

1975 – The <u>Education of All Handicapped Children Act (PL 94-142)</u> becomes federal law. It requires that a free, appropriate public education, suited to the student's individual needs, and offered in the least restrictive setting be provided for all "handicapped" children. States are given until 1978 (later extended to 1981) to fully implement the law.

1975 – The <u>National Association of Bilingual Education</u> is founded.

1975 – *Newsweek's* December 8 cover story, "Why Johnny Can't Write," heats up the debate about national literacy and the back-to-the-basics movement.

1977 – Apple Computer, now Apple Inc., introduces the Apple II, one of the first successful personal computers. It and its offspring, the Apple IIe, become popular in schools as students begin to learn with computer games such as Oregon Trail and Odell Lake.

1980 – The Refugee Act of 1980 is signed into law by President Jimmy Carter on March 18. Building on the Immigration Act of 1965, it reforms immigration law to admit refugees for humanitarian reasons and results in the resettlement of more than three million refugees in the United States including many children who bring special needs and issues to their classrooms.

1980 – President Jimmy Carter signs the Refugee Education Assistance Act into law as the "Mariel Boat-lift" brings thousands of Cuban and a small number of Haitian refugees to Florida.

1980 – Ronald Reagan is elected president, ushering in a new conservative era, not only in foreign and economic policy, but in education as well. However, he never carries out his pledge to reduce the federal role in education by eliminating the Department of Education, which had become a cabinet level agency that same year under the Carter administration..

1981 – John Holt's book, *Teach Your Own: A Hopeful Path for Education*, adds momentum to the home-schooling movement.

1981 – IBM introduces its version of the personal computer (PC) with its Model 5150. Its operating system is MS-DOS.

1982 – In the case of Edwards v. Aguillard, the US Supreme Court invalidates Louisiana's "Creationism Act," which requires the teaching of creationism whenever evolution is taught, because it violates the Establishment Clause of the First Amendment to the Constitution.

1982 – Madeline C. Hunter's book, *Mastery Teaching*, is published. Her direct instruction teaching model becomes widely used as teachers throughout the country attend her workshops and become "Hunterized."

1982 – In the case of Plyler v. Doe, the US Supreme Court rules in a 5-4 decision that Texas law denying access to public education for undocumented school-age children violates the Equal Protection Clause of the 14th Amendment. The ruling also found that school districts cannot charge tuition fees for the education of these children.

1982 – In the case of Board of Education v. Pico, the US Supreme court rules that books cannot be removed from a school library because school administrators deemed their content to be offensive.

1983 – The report of the National Commission on Excellence in Education, A Nation at Risk, calls for sweeping reforms in public education and teacher training. Among their recommendations is a forward-looking call for expanding high school requirements to include the study of computer science.

1984 – Public Law 105-332, the Carl D. Perkins Vocational and Technical Education Act, is passed with the goal of increasing the quality of vocational-technical education in the United States. It is reauthorized in 1998 and again in 2006 as the Carl D. Perkins Vocational and Technical Education Act (PL 109-270).

1984 – The Emergency Immigrant Education Act is enacted to provide services and offset the costs for school districts that have unexpectedly large numbers of immigrant students.

1985 – In the case of <u>Wallace v. Jaffree</u>, the US Supreme Court finds that Alabama statutes authorizing silent prayer and teacher-led voluntary prayer in public schools violate the <u>First Amendment</u>.

1985 – <u>Microsoft Windows 1.0</u>, the first <u>independent version</u> of Windows, is released, setting the stage for subsequent versions that make MS-DOS obsolete.

1986 – <u>Christa McAuliffe</u> is chosen by NASA from among more than 11,000 applicants to be the first teacher-astronaut, but her mission ends tragically as the <u>Space Shuttle Challenger explodes</u> 73 seconds after its launch, killing McAuliffe and the other six members of the crew.

1987 – In the case of <u>Edwards v. Aguillard, et al.</u> the US Supreme Court strikes down a Louisiana law requiring <u>creation science</u> be taught along with evolution. Will this controversy ever be resolved?

1989 – The <u>University of Phoenix</u> establishes their "online campus," the <u>first to offer online bachelor's and master's degrees</u>. It becomes the "<u>largest private university in North America</u>."

1990 – <u>Tim Berners-Lee</u>, a British engineer and computer scientist called by many the <u>inventor of the Internet</u>, writes the first web client-server protocol (Hypertext Translation Protocol or http), which allows two computers to communicate. On August 6, 1991, he puts the first web site on line from a computer at the <u>CERN (the European Organization for Nuclear Research)</u> in order to facilitate information sharing among scientists. So . . . does this mean that <u>Al Gore didn't invent the internet</u> after all?

1990 – <u>Public Law 101-476, the Individuals with Disabilities Education Act (IDEA)</u>, renames and amends Public Law 94-142. In addition to changing terminology from handicap to disability, it mandates transition services and adds autism and traumatic brain injury to the eligibility list.

1990 – The <u>Milwaukee Parental Choice</u> program is initiated. It allows "students, under specific circumstances, to attend at no charge, private sectarian and nonsectarian schools located in the city of Milwaukee."

1990 – <u>Teach for America</u> is formed, reestablishing the idea of a <u>National Teachers Corps</u>.

1990 – <u>The Immigration and Nationality Act of 1990</u>, the first comprehensive reform since 1965, is enacted on November 29 and increases annual immigration to 700,000 adding to the diversity of our nation and its schools. Specific aspects of the law provide for family-sponsored visas; employment-based visas for priority workers, skilled workers, and "advanced professionals"; and 55,000 diversity visas "<u>allocated to natives of a country that has sent fewer than 50,000 immigrants to the United States over the previous five years</u>."

1991 – Minnesota passes the first "<u>charter school</u>" law.

1991 – The <u>smart board (interactive white board)</u> is introduced by <u>SMART Technologies</u>.

1992 – <u>City Academy High School</u>, the nation's first charter school, opens in St. Paul, Minnesota.

1993 – <u>Jacqueline and Martin Brooks'</u> *In Search of Understanding: The Case for Constructivist Classrooms* is published. It is one of many books and articles describing <u>constructivism</u>, a view that learning best occurs through active construction of knowledge rather than its passive reception. <u>Constructivist learning theory</u>, with roots such as the work of Dewey, Bruner, Piaget, and Vygotsky, becomes extremely popular in the 1990s.

1993 – The <u>Massachusetts Education Reform Act</u> requires a common curriculum and statewide tests (Massachusetts Comprehensive Assessment System). As has often been the case, other states follow Massachusetts' lead and implement similar, high-stakes testing programs.

1993 – <u>Jones International University</u> becomes the first university "to exist completely online."

1994 – The <u>Improving America's Schools Act (IASA)</u> is signed into law by <u>President Bill Clinton</u> on January 25. It. reauthorizes the <u>ESEA of 1965</u> and includes reforms for Title I; increased funding for bilingual and immigrant education; and provisions for public charter schools, drop-out prevention, and educational technology.

1994 – As a backlash to illegal immigration, California voters pass <u>Proposition 187</u>, denying benefits, including public education, to undocumented aliens in California. It is challenged by the ACLU and other groups and eventually <u>overturned</u>.

1994 – <u>Jim Clark and Mark Andreesan found Mosaic Communications</u>. The corporation is later renamed Netscape Communications. On December 15, they release the <u>first commercial web browser, Mozilla 1.0</u>. It is available without cost to individuals and non-profit organizations. By the summer of 1995, <u>more than 80%</u> of internet users are browsing with Netscape!

1994 – <u>CompuHigh</u> is founded. It claims to be the first online high school.

1994 to 1995 – <u>Whiteboards find their way into US classrooms</u> in increasing numbers and begin to replace the blackboard.

1995 – <u>Georgia becomes the first state</u> to offer universal preschool to all 4-year-olds whose parents choose to enroll them. <u>More than half</u> of the state's 4-year-olds are now enrolled.

1996 – <u>James Banks'</u> book, *Multicultural Education: Transformative Knowledge and Action*, makes an important contribution to the growing body of scholarship regarding multiculturalism in education.

1996 – The Oakland, California School District sparks <u>controversy</u> as it proposes that <u>Ebonics be recognized as the native language of African American children</u>.

1996 – President Bill Clinton signs the <u>Illegal Immigration Reform and Immigrant Responsibility Act of 1996</u> into law on September 30. It prohibits states from offering higher education benefit based on residency within a state (in-state tuition) to undocumented immigrants unless the benefit is available to any US citizen or national. This law conflicts, however, with practices and laws in several US states.

1997 – <u>New York</u> follows Georgia's lead and passes legislation that will phase in voluntary pre-kindergarten classes over a four-year period. However, preschool funding is a casualty of September 11, 2001 as New York struggles to recover. As of 2008, about 39% of the state's 4-year olds, mostly from low-income families, are enrolled.

1998 – California voters pass <u>Proposition 227</u>, requiring that all public school instruction be in English. This time the law withstands <u>legal challenges</u>.

1998 – The Higher Education Act is <u>amended and reauthorized</u> requiring institutions and states to produce "<u>report cards</u>" about teacher education (<u>See Title II</u>).

1998 – <u>Google</u> co-founders <u>Larry Page and Sergey Brin</u> set up a workplace for their <u>newly incorporated search engine</u> in a Menlo Park, California garage.

1999 – On April 20, two <u>Columbine High School students go on a killing spree</u> that leaves 15 dead and 23 wounded at the Littleton, Colorado school, making it the nations' deadliest school shooting incident. Though schools tighten safety procedures as a result of the Columbine massacre, <u>school shootings continue to occur at an alarming rate</u>.

2000 – Diane Ravitch's book, _Left Back: A Century of Failed School Reforms_, criticizes progressive educational policies and argues for a more traditional, academically-oriented education. Her views, which are reminiscent of the "back to the basics" movement of the late 1970s and 1980s, are representative of the current conservative trend in education and the nation at large.

2000 – In yet another case regarding school prayer (Santa Fe School District v. Doe), the US Supreme Court rules that the district's policy of allowing student-led prayer prior to football games violates the Establishment Clause of the First Amendment.

2001 – Nineteen al-Qaeda terrorists hijack four commercial jet airliners on the morning of September 11. They crash two into the twin towers of the World Trade Center and another into the Pentagon. The fourth plane crashes in a rural area of Pennsylvania as passengers try to retake it from the hijackers. A total of 2,976 victims as well as the 19 terrorists are killed. The attacks have a devastating effect on both the US and world stock markets, result in the passage of the Patriot Act, formation of the Department of Homeland Security, provide the impetus for two wars, and take a lasting toll on Americans' sense of safety and well-being.

2001 – The controversial No Child Left Behind Act (NCLB) is approved by Congress and signed into law by President George W. Bush on January 8, 2002. The law, which reauthorizes the ESEA of 1965 and replaces the Bilingual Education Act of 1968, mandates high-stakes student testing, holds schools accountable for student achievement levels, and provides penalties for schools that do not make adequate yearly progress toward meeting the goals of NCLB.

2002 – In the case of Zelman v. Simmons-Harris the US Supreme court rules that certain school voucher programs are constitutional and do not violate the Establishment Clause of the First Amendment.

2002 – The North American Reggio Emilia Alliance (NAREA) is formally launched as an organization. Its goals include promoting the rights of young children and providing information about the Reggio Emilia approach to early childhood education.

2003 – The Higher Education Act is again amended and reauthorized, expanding access to higher education for low and middle income students, providing additional funds for graduate studies, and increasing accountability.

2003 – The North American Council for Online Learning (NACOL), a non-profit organization dedicated to enhancing K-12 online education, is "launched as a formal corporate entity."

2004 – H.R. 1350, The Individuals with Disabilities Improvement Act (IDEA 2004), reauthorizes and modifies IDEA. Changes, which take effect on July 1, 2005, include modifications in the IEP process and procedural safeguards, increased authority for school personnel in special education placement decisions, and alignment of IDEA with the No Child Left Behind Act. The 2004 reauthorization also requires school districts to use the Response to Intervention (RTI) approach as a means for the early identification of students at risk for specific learning disabilities. RTI provides a three-tiered model for screening, monitoring, and providing increasing degrees of intervention using "research-based instruction" with the overall goal of reducing the need for special education services.

2005 – In the latest incarnation of the "Monkey Trial," the US District Court of Pennsylvania rules in the case of Kitzmiller v. Dover Area School District that teaching "intelligent design" as an alternative to evolution is a violation of the First Amendment.

2007 – On January 1, 2007, the American Association on Mental Retardation (AAMR) became the American Association on Intellectual and Developmental Disabilities (AAIDD), joining the trend toward use of the term intellectual disability in place of mental retardation.

2007 – Cho Seung-Hui, a 23-year-old student, <u>kills two students in a dorm and then 30 others in a classroom building at Virginia Tech University</u>. Fifteen others are wounded. His suicide brings the death toll to 33, making it the deadliest school shooting incident in US history.

2007 – In the cases of <u>Parents involved in Community Schools v. Seattle School District No 1</u> and <u>Meredith v. Jefferson County Board of Education</u>, the US Supreme Court ruled 5-4 that race cannot be a factor in assigning students to high schools, thus rejecting integration plans in Seattle and Louisville, and possibly affecting similar plans in school districts around the nation.

2007 – Both the House and Senate pass the Fiscal Year 2008 Labor-HHS- Education appropriation bill which includes reauthorization of the No Child Left Behind Act. However, the bill is <u>vetoed by President Bush</u> because it exceeds his budget request. Attempts to override the veto fall short.

2008 – Less than one year after the Virginia Tech massacre, former graduate student Stephen P. Kazmierczak <u>kills five and wounds 17 in a classroom at Northern Illinois University</u>. He later takes his own life.

2008 – <u>Barack Obama</u> defeats <u>John McCain</u> and is elected the 44th President of the United States. Substantial <u>changes in the No Child Left Behind Act</u> are eventually expected, but with two ongoing wars as well as the current preoccupation with our nation's economic problems, reauthorization of NCLB is unlikely to happen any time soon.

2009 – The <u>American Reinvestment and Recovery Act of 2009</u> provides more than 90 billion dollars for education, nearly half of which goes to local school districts to prevent layoffs and for school modernization and repair. It includes the <u>Race to the Top</u> initiative, a 4.35-billion-dollar program designed to induce reform in K-12 education. For more information on the impact of the Recovery Act on education, go to <u>ED.gov</u>.

2009 – The <u>Common Core State Standards Initiative</u>, "a state-led effort coordinated by the <u>National Governors Association Center for Best Practices (NGA Center)</u> and the <u>Council of Chief State School Officers</u>," is launched. It is expected that many, perhaps most, <u>states will adopt them</u>.

2009 – <u>Quest to Learn (Q2L)</u>, the first school to teach primarily through game-based learning, opens in September in New York City with a class of sixth graders. There are plans to add a grade each year until the school serves students in grades six through twelve.

2010 – With the US economy mired in a <u>recession</u> and employment remaining high, <u>states have massive budget deficits</u>. As many as <u>300,000 teachers face layoffs</u>.

2010 – <u>New Texas social studies curriculum standards</u>, described by some as "ultraconservative," spark controversy. Many fear they <u>will affect textbooks and classrooms in other states</u>.

2011 – <u>Sylvia Mendez</u>, whose parents were lead plaintiffs in the historic civil rights case, <u>Mendez vs. Westminster and the California Board of Education</u>, is awarded the <u>Presidential Medal of Freedom</u> on February 16th.

2011 – In spite of workers' protests and Democratic legislators leaving the state to delay the vote, the <u>Wisconsin legislature passes a bill</u> removing most collective-bargaining rights from many public employees, including teachers. Governor Scott Walker signs the bill into law on March 11. After legal challenges are exhausted, it is finally implemented in June. Similar proposals are <u>being considered in Ohio</u> and several other states.

2011 – <u>President Barack Obama announces</u> on September 23 that the US Department of Education is inviting each state educational agency to <u>request flexibility</u> regarding some requirements of the <u>No Child Left Behind Act</u>.

2011 – <u>Alabama becomes the first state "to require public schools to check the immigration status"</u> of students. Though the law does not require schools to prohibit the enrollment nor report the names of undocumented children, opponents nevertheless contend it is unconstitutional based on the <u>Plyer v. Doe ruling</u>.

2012 – In his January 24 <u>State of the Union Address</u>, President Barack Obama calls for requiring students to stay in school until they graduate from high school or reach age 18. <u>Twenty states and the District of Columbia currently require attendance until age 18</u>.

2012 – President Barack Obama announces on February 9 that the applications of <u>ten states seeking waivers</u> from some of the requirements of the <u>No Child Left Behind law</u> were approved. <u>New Mexico's application is approved</u> a few days later, bringing the number of states receiving waivers to 11. An <u>additional 26 states applied</u> for waivers in late February.

2012 – Speaking at an economic summit hosted by the Latino Coalition on May 23, Republican presidential candidate <u>Mitt Romney warns of a "National Education Emergency,"</u> blames teachers unions for blocking needed education reform, and calls for expanding school choice by offering vouchers to low-income students and those with disabilities.

2012 – On July 6, <u>Washington and Wisconsin become the two most recent states to be granted waivers</u> from some requirements of the federal No Child left Behind law, bringing the <u>total number of states granted waivers to 26</u>. Several more states have submitted waiver applications and are waiting for approval.

2012 – November 6, Barack Obama wins a second term as President of the United States in a close election.

2012 – On December 14, 20-year-old Adam Lanza fatally shot twenty children and six adult staff members in a mass murder at Sandy Hook Elementary School in the village of Sandy Hook in Newtown, CT.

2013 – March, Kendall Hunt Publishing of Dubuque, Iowa Published "Innovative Educational Leadership Through The Cycle of Change" edited by Daniel T. Cunnif, Wayne Padover, and Donna Elder.

Please consider this timeline to be a work in progress. Think of it as sort of a "semi-wiki." If you see an error or have a suggestion for an important event that should be added, send it to me at esass@csbsju.edu. I will review your idea, and if I think it has merit, I will add it to the timeline.

Special thanks to <u>Post University</u> graduate students for your excellent suggestions, many of which have been added to the timeline!

Permission is granted to anyone wishing to use this page or the related lesson plan for instructional purposes as long as you credit the author (me!) and the web page source. My name is <u>Edmund Sass, EdD.</u>, and I am a Professor of <u>Education</u> at the <u>College of Saint Benedict/Saint John's University</u>. Please understand, however, that the content of this page is my intellectual property and cannot be duplicated or displayed on another web site or in a publication without my permission.

Epilogue

The time of this publication occurs after the conclusion of the 2012 United States presidential election. Historians will offer detailed analysis of the anatomy of the election over time and yet several points relative to the nature of "Innovative Leadership Through a Cycle of Change" seem instructive by example.

Clearly, the election was a **cyclical event** and President Obama utilized the advantage of running unopposed in the Democratic Party to plan his reelection campaign years in advance of the election. In comparison, his opponent, Governor Romney received his party's nomination only months prior to the election and his level of **preparedness** was over-matched by all accounts. President Obama's campaign **utilized data to support decisions** which, as an example, indicated a significant change of demographic information relative to Hispanic, single women and young voters in a variety of states as compared to the 2008 election. Finally, the President's campaign made **targeted use of financial and human resources**. He selected specific battle-ground states and overwhelmed his opponent with the large number of local campaign offices and related local election activity. The President also made excellent use of former President Clinton's popularity, having him campaign on his behalf which brought about a very positive result.

The precepts for innovative educational leadership are similar to other fields of specialization as noted throughout this publication. As noted in the example cited above, the opportunities to view innovative leadership at work are omnipresent...we only need to be aware.

Index

E

Education
- application of psychological theories to, 107
- relationship of epistemology to, 105–106
- steps for improving quality of, 110
- use of technology in, 61

Educational leadership
- concepts of, 82
- cycle of change related to, 4
- innovative. *See* Innovative educationalleadership
- overcoming barriers, when working with students and parents, 84
- personal skill, 89
- relationship with student achievement, 118

Educational Leadership Policy Standards (ISLLC), 101

Effective leadership, research on
- contribution of
  - Barth, Roland, 59
  - Darling-Hammond, Linda, 58–59
  - Lortie, Dan, 60
  - Reeves, Douglas, 61–62
  - Schmoker, Mike, 57
  - Wiggins, Grant, 60–61
- for improving student academic performance, 57

Electronic portfolio, 73

E-mail (electronic mail), 71

E-Mentoring, 70

Emergent structures, of an organization, 39

English Language Learners (ELLs), 128

F

Facilitative leadership style, 19, 27–28, 32

Friedman, Michael, 180

G

Gagne, R., design for instructional events, 107–108

Grants, learning
- budget, 189
- case study, 190
- cover letter, 189
- evaluation, 189
- goals and objectives, 189
- grant abstract, 189
- grant writing team, 187–188
  - reader, 188
  - researcher, 188
  - school administrators, 188
  - writer, 188–189
- program description, 189
- statement of need, 189

"Great Man" theory, 79

Great Recession, 56

Great Society legislation of 1960s, 5

Group interaction, 140
- principles of, 41

H

Hands-on activities, 106

Hawthorne Effect, 25, 31

Heart, as a leadership skill, 92

Heuristic instructional strategies, 107

Hierarchical leadership, 18

Higher education administration, leadership skills for
- confidence, 93
- discipline, 92
- heart, 92
- passion, 91–92
- perseverance, 93
- public support, 90
- speed, 93
- strategies, 91
- strength, 94
- talent, 92
- trust, 93

Historical events and technology, that shaped America, 19

Homeschooling, 179, 182, 183, 221

I

Innovative educational leaders
- historical perspective relative to, 5–6
- implications for, to work with LEFs, 174–175
- implications of neurological research for, 9
- management cycle, 163–164
  - evaluating, 165
  - implementing, 165
  - outcomes, 165–166
  - planning, 164
  - reporting, 165
- as motivator for others, 8
- personal price, 6
- as problem-solver, 7
- process for identification of, 5
- professional talents and skills, 7
- qualities of, 6
- responsibility to manage personal state of mind, 7

Innovative educational leadership, 161
- for community development, 173–174
- innovation theory and, 5
- meaning of, 4
- role of, 6–7

Inquiry model, for decision-making, 5

Instantaneous leader, 27

Institutional Review Board (IRB), 73, 135, 165

Instructional design, 103, 109
- impact of learning theories on, 107–108

Instructional leadership, 57, 73, 81–82, 101, 108, 118, 128, 163

Internal Revenue Service Code, 172

Interstate School Leaders Licensure Consortium (ISSLC), 127

IRIS camera, 73, 135–137

IRIS Connect, 135, 136, 139–141, 143

O

Online leadership, 81–82
Open-ended assignments, 108
Organizational change, leadership strategies for
    conflict management, 42
    first-order, 38
    forces affecting, 39
        culture, 40, 46, 47, 48
        people, 40–41, 46, 47
        resources, 41, 46–47, 48
        structures, types of, 39–40, 46, 47, 48
    high stakes testing of, 37
    influence of, 42
    model for
        application of, 43, 46–48
        human side of, 43–44
        non-human side of, 44–46
    principles of, 48–49
    second-order, 38
    types of, 38–39
Organizational charts, 43, 91
Organizational communication, 40–41

P

P-12 education, 149, 153–154, 172
Parent-Teacher Associations (PTAs), 172–173
Parent-Teacher Organizations (PTOs), 172–173
Participative leadership, 26, 31, 46, 48
Partnership education, 67, 70, 74
Passion, for the profession, 91
"The Pathways Program," 68
Pavlov's findings on animal responses, 104
Pedagogical content knowledge, 120
People, affecting organizational change, 40–41,
    46, 47
Performance-based assessment, 60–61
Perseverance, as a leadership skills, 93
Personal leadership skill set, 91, 94
Peters, Tom, 25, 26
Phil Delta Kappa, 69, 80, 127
Piaget's theory of cognitive development, 105
Pirtle, Sarah, 70
Plan Do Check Act cycle (PDCA), 128
Podcasts, 72
PreK-12 school partnerships, 67–68, 74
Principal leadership, 118–119
Principal's role
    in improving student achievement, 108–109
    in setting positive school climate, 118–119
Problem-solving, 109, 121
    Kepner Tregoe approach for, 164, 166
Professional learning, 58–59
Professional Learning Communities (PLC),
    127–128
Programme for International Assessment
    (PISA), 202
Project-based learning, 60, 202
Public education, 5, 171
    charter schools, 181–182
    homeschooling, 182
    magnet schools, 179–180
    vouchers, 180
Public Schools Accountability Act (PSAA, 1999),
    56, 127

R

Race to the Top program (2009), 5, 149, 225
Reality therapy, 121
Reeves, Douglas, 55, 61–62
Remote observation and videotaping
    best practices for
        additional considerations, 138–139
        cognitive coaching, 139
        face-to-face observations, 137–138
        online discussions with peers, 138
        professional development, 140
        reflective practices, 139
        small group collaboration, 139
        social, affective, psychomotor, and
            cognitive domains, 139
    research methodology, 142–143
        adaptations to enhance school site
            control, 143
        Clouds, 144
        cost/benefit analysis, 143
        Faculty Community Network, 144
        Internet technologies, 143–144
        preliminary findings, 143
        repositories, 144
Request for Proposal (RFP), 188, 189
Resources
    affect on organizational change, 41, 46–47
    dependence theory, 41

S

Schmoker, Mike, 55, 57, 62
Scholastic Achievement Test, 61
School accountability
    case study, 128–129
    and emphasis on academics, 151–153
    high-level standards, development of, 150
    interfering with success in the Global Age,
        154
    knowledgeworkers, values of, 153
    standards and knowledgework, 150–151
    telling, notion of, 127–128
    and values to be fostered, 151
School-based management (SBM), 80–81
School climate, factors to measure, 119
School community, utilization of human re-
    sources, 172–173
School discipline system, 119
School districts and universities, partnerships
    between
    Adopt-A-School program, 69
    advantages in leadership preparation pro-
        grams, 73
    blogs, 72
    cost savings, 74
    electronic portfolio, 73
    e-mail, 71
    E-Mentoring, 70
    IRIS Cameras, 73
    Memoranda of Agreement or Understand-
        ing (MOAs or MOUs), 69–70
    Nu-FAST and beyond, 71–72
    podcast, 72
    technology in partnerships, 70–71
    theory and practice, linking, 70